Illuminati

Illuminati

Quinn Silver

Introduction: The Enigma of the Illuminati

For centuries, a shadowy myth has persisted, captivating imaginations and fueling countless conspiracy theories: the Illuminati. To some, this secret society controls the world's most powerful institutions, manipulating events to establish a New World Order (NWO) and bring about global governance. From political revolutions to financial collapses, from technological surveillance to cultural influence, the Illuminati has been invoked as the invisible hand guiding the course of human history. But is it real, or simply a modern legend born from fear and uncertainty?

The idea of a powerful secret society has its roots in ancient history, yet the Illuminati, as it is popularly understood, arose from an 18th-century group known as the Bavarian Illuminati. Founded in 1776 by Adam Weishaupt, this group aimed to promote Enlightenment ideals, rational thought, and opposition to religious and political oppression. However, the Bavarian Illuminati was short-lived, disbanded by government authorities in the late 18th century. Despite its dissolution, rumors of its influence persisted, growing over time and intertwining with other conspiracy theories.

Today, the word "Illuminati" evokes much more than a historical group. It has become a symbol of hidden power, a catch-all term for any conspiracy involving global elites, secret societies, and world domination. The myth has evolved to include references to the New World Order, a hypothetical authoritarian world government allegedly being established behind the scenes by an elite cabal. From world leaders to pop stars, from financial institutions to media empires, almost every influential figure or organization has, at some point, been accused of being part of this elusive network.

In the age of the internet, the reach and impact of Illuminati theories have expanded dramatically. Forums, social media platforms, and video-sharing sites have amplified the spread of these ideas, creating a global culture where distrust of institutions and authority is pervasive. Every world event—whether it be economic turmoil, political unrest, or a global health crisis—is scrutinized through the lens of conspiracy, with some convinced that the Illuminati is orchestrating these occurrences to tighten its control over humanity.

Yet, there is a stark contrast between the historical facts and the modern mythology of the Illuminati. What started as a small Enlightenment-era society has transformed into a sprawling, complex narrative that is largely fictional. This raises important questions: Why do so many people believe in the Illuminati? What psychological and societal forces make these theories so compelling? How have they persisted, even in the face of evidence to the contrary? And what are the real-world consequences of these beliefs?

This book seeks to explore these questions and more. It will journey through the origins of the Illuminati, tracing its evolution from a historical group to a modern conspiracy theory. We will examine the symbols, the alleged members, and the events often linked to the Illuminati, while also debunking the myths and investigating the psychology behind the allure of conspiracy theories. Along the way, we will analyze how these ideas have infiltrated politics, culture, and society, and the tangible effects they have on public trust and democratic institutions.

In a world increasingly defined by misinformation and division, understanding the origins and influence of conspiracy theories like the Illuminati is more important than ever. By the end of this book, you will not only have a deeper understanding of the Illuminati myth but also a greater appreciation for the complexities of human belief, power, and the need for critical thinking in an age of uncertainty.

This is the story of the Illuminati—not just as a secret society, but as a persistent legend, a symbol of hidden power that continues to shape how we see the world.

Chapter 1: The Origins of the Illuminati Myth

The Rise of Secret Societies in History

The fascination with secret societies stretches back through millennia, rooted in the human desire for power, knowledge, and protection. While the term "secret society" evokes modern images of shadowy elites meeting behind closed doors, the concept is far from new. In fact, secretive groups have been a part of human culture for centuries, often arising during periods of political or religious turmoil when alternative ideas and dissenting beliefs had to be concealed from authority.

One of the earliest examples of a secret society is the Pythagoreans, a group of ancient Greek philosophers founded by Pythagoras in the 6th century BCE. While today, Pythagoras is best known for his contributions to mathematics, particularly the Pythagorean Theorem, his followers were much more than just mathematicians. The Pythagoreans were a closed, highly secretive community that combined philosophy, mathematics, and spirituality. They believed that numbers held the key to understanding the universe and, thus, should be safeguarded and studied in a controlled, hidden environment. Their rituals were mysterious, and only initiates could access the group's deeper teachings. This veil of secrecy made them both intriguing and, to some, dangerous.

Similarly, the Freemasons, perhaps the most well-known secret society, trace their origins to medieval stonemasons' guilds in Europe. By the 16th and 17th centuries, the Freemasons had transformed into a more philosophical and fraternal organization, promoting ideas about individual liberty, equality, and brotherhood—principles that aligned with the growing intellectual movement of the Enlightenment. Their meetings, held in lodges and steeped in symbolic rituals, were hidden from the public eye, giving rise to suspicions about their true intentions. While the Freemasons openly claimed to be a force for good, the mystery surrounding their rituals and hierarchy naturally led to fears of their potential influence over political and social affairs.

Another secret society that gained attention in Europe was the Rosicrucians, a mystical organization that emerged in the early 17th century. The Rosicrucians claimed to possess esoteric knowledge rooted in ancient wisdom, blending elements of alchemy, Kabbalah, and Christian mysticism. Though much of what is known about the Rosicrucians comes from a few anonymous manifestos that appeared in Europe, the group quickly attracted both followers and skeptics. Like the Freemasons, the Rosicrucians thrived in the shadows, adding to the perception that they were part of a broader, hidden network influencing the course of history.

What these secret societies shared—beyond their secretive nature—was a sense of exclusivity. Membership was often by invitation only, and initiates were expected to adhere to strict codes of silence and loyalty. This secrecy, while perhaps a practical necessity for protecting their members and their teachings, also made them the subject of suspicion. The very fact that these groups operated behind closed doors fueled rumors that they were wielding far more power than they let on. As their influence spread, so did the paranoia about their true intentions.

The social and political climate of the Enlightenment further nurtured the rise of secret societies. During this period, Europe was undergoing profound shifts, with intellectuals questioning traditional authority structures—both religious and monarchical. New ideas about reason, liberty, and individual rights were spreading, often in direct opposition to the established order. In many cases, these ideas had to be discussed in private settings, away from the prying eyes of authorities that might see them as dangerous or subversive. The secret society provided the perfect forum for these revolutionary ideas to flourish, away from the reach of government and church censorship.

It is within this broader historical context that the Bavarian Illuminati emerged. Like the Freemasons, the Pythagoreans, and the Rosicrucians before them, the Illuminati sought to advance knowledge, challenge existing power structures, and protect their members from persecution. However, their ambitions, secrecy, and eventual suppression would make them the most notorious secret society of all time—one whose myth has endured long after the group itself disappeared.

In the coming sections, we will delve deeper into the specific circumstances that gave rise to the Bavarian Illuminati, how their activities mirrored and diverged from their predecessors, and how their ultimate disbandment would lead to the birth of one of history's most enduring conspiracy theories. But first, it is essential to understand the broader allure and dangers of secret societies—mysterious organizations that have, for centuries, attracted both idealists and conspiracists alike.

The Bavarian Illuminati's Founding

In the spring of 1776, amidst the intellectual fervor of the Enlightenment, a small group of forward-thinking individuals in Bavaria formed what would become one of history's most notorious secret societies: the Illuminati. Founded by Adam Weishaupt, a professor of canon law at the University of Ingolstadt, the Bavarian Illuminati was intended to be a vehicle for the spread of rational thought, humanism, and opposition to the oppressive power of both church and state. While it began with noble intentions, the society's secretive methods and eventual suppression fueled myths that have long outlasted its actual existence.

Weishaupt, raised in a deeply religious environment and educated by the Jesuits, became disillusioned with the constraints of organized religion and the intellectual limitations it imposed. The rigid Catholic orthodoxy that dominated Bavaria in the 18th century left little room for the critical thinking and scientific inquiry that Weishaupt had come to embrace. The Enlightenment had ignited a new wave of progressive thought across Europe, promoting reason, skepticism of authority, and the pursuit of knowledge. Weishaupt envisioned a group that could secretly spread these ideals and challenge the structures of power that he believed held society back.

On May 1, 1776, Weishaupt officially established the Order of the Illuminati, which he originally called the "Perfectibilists." The group's purpose was to advance Enlightenment principles, combat superstition, and promote the moral improvement of humanity. Weishaupt believed that by educating individuals in positions of influence, his group could eventually reshape society from within. The goal was nothing less than a societal transformation, achieved through gradual infiltration of the political and religious institutions that governed Europe.

To achieve these aims, Weishaupt designed the Illuminati to operate in secrecy. The order was modeled on existing secret societies, especially the Freemasons, whom Weishaupt admired for their structure and rituals. Like the Freemasons, the Illuminati adopted a hierarchical system, with members progressing through various levels or "grades" of initiation. This structure ensured that only the most trusted members would gain access to the group's inner workings and ultimate goals. Weishaupt hoped this secrecy would protect the Illuminati from outside scrutiny and allow them to operate beneath the radar of the church and state.

The Illuminati's recruitment strategy was deliberate and careful. Rather than attracting large numbers of people, Weishaupt sought to recruit intellectuals, government officials, and other influential figures—individuals who could help spread the order's ideals from within the institutions of power. At its height, the Illuminati reportedly had a membership of a few thousand across Europe, including prominent scholars, politicians, and aristocrats. Many of these recruits were already members of Masonic lodges, making it easier for Weishaupt to integrate them into the Illuminati.

Among the Illuminati's notable members was Baron Adolph von Knigge, a German nobleman and influential Freemason, who joined the order in 1780. Von Knigge's involvement was a significant turning point for the Illuminati, as his leadership and organizational skills helped formalize the order's structure and expand its membership. Under his guidance, the Illuminati began to grow more rapidly, attracting individuals who shared Weishaupt's vision of challenging established power structures and promoting Enlightenment values. Von Knigge also helped align the Illuminati more closely with the Freemasons, further blending the two organizations' rituals and symbols.

However, this rapid expansion brought challenges. The Illuminati's growing influence and secrecy started to attract the attention of the authorities, particularly the Catholic Church and the Bavarian government, which were deeply suspicious of any group promoting ideas that could undermine their power. Weishaupt's goal of infiltrating institutions was becoming a double-edged sword, as the more successful the Illuminati became, the more dangerous they appeared to the powers they sought to change.

Despite its small size and limited reach, the Illuminati's mission to reshape society through clandestine means was an audacious and, in the eyes of many, dangerous proposition. The very idea of an underground organization plotting to alter the political and religious fabric of Europe sparked both fascination and fear. To those sympathetic to the Enlightenment cause, the Illuminati represented hope for a future free from tyranny and ignorance. To their detractors, however, the group was seen as a threat to the established order, a radical force aiming to destabilize governments and sow chaos.

As the Illuminati's membership grew and its methods of operation became more elaborate, the organization increasingly attracted suspicion. Rumors began to swirl about the true extent of the group's influence, with whispers of Illuminati agents secretly pulling the strings behind the scenes of major political and religious events. While these fears were largely exaggerated at the time, they planted the seeds for the Illuminati's transformation from a relatively obscure intellectual society into the global symbol of conspiracy it would later become.

Weishaupt's vision was ambitious—too ambitious, it would turn out, for the turbulent political climate of 18th-century Europe. His ideals, while grounded in the principles of the Enlightenment, were seen as a direct challenge to the very institutions that held power. This, coupled with the group's secretive nature, would ultimately lead to its downfall, as the Illuminati's enemies would soon conspire to put an end to the order.

But as we will explore in the next section, the Illuminati's disbandment only fueled further speculation about their true power, setting the stage for the myths that would follow. The Illuminati was, for all intents and purposes, short-lived, but its legacy—both real and imagined—was only just beginning.

Opposition and the Disbanding of the Bavarian Illuminati

As the Bavarian Illuminati grew in both numbers and influence, so did the suspicion and hostility surrounding the group. To the ruling authorities in 18th-century Bavaria, the secretive nature of the Illuminati, combined with its progressive ideals, posed a significant threat to the established order. The society's open criticism of religious and political institutions, particularly the Catholic Church and the monarchy, sparked alarm among those who saw the Illuminati not as intellectual reformers, but as dangerous subversives intent on destabilizing society.

The Bavarian government, under the leadership of Duke Karl Theodor, became increasingly wary of secret societies, particularly the Freemasons and the Illuminati, which were seen as breeding grounds for revolutionary ideas. The Enlightenment had already stirred unrest across Europe, and the ruling elite feared that underground movements like the Illuminati were planting the seeds for rebellion. In an age where monarchs ruled by divine right, any challenge to the established hierarchy was considered not only seditious but also blasphemous. The notion that a clandestine group could be plotting to undermine religious authority and the power of the state was intolerable.

The Catholic Church, too, was deeply opposed to the Illuminati. The Church had long been the dominant institution in Bavaria, wielding enormous influence over political life and education. The

Illuminati's promotion of secularism, its opposition to superstition, and its rejection of the Church's dominance were viewed as existential threats. The idea of an organization deliberately working to weaken the Church's grip on society was enough to incite a vigorous response from religious authorities, who had the ear of the Bavarian rulers.

The turning point came in the early 1780s, when documents belonging to the Illuminati were discovered by Bavarian authorities. These documents, which outlined the group's goals, organizational structure, and methods of operation, confirmed the worst fears of the ruling class. While the Illuminati had been relatively discreet about its aims, the revelations about its secret agenda stoked fears of a hidden network of intellectual radicals bent on eroding the foundations of church and state. To many, this was not just a group of scholars and freethinkers—this was a conspiracy.

Duke Karl Theodor acted swiftly. In 1784, he issued an edict banning all secret societies, including the Freemasons and the Illuminati. This decree was part of a broader effort to suppress Enlightenment ideas that were viewed as threatening to the established order. However, the Illuminati, believing that their mission was too important to abandon, continued to meet in secret. When this defiance was discovered, the crackdown escalated. In 1785, a second edict was issued specifically targeting the Illuminati, ordering the dissolution of the group and the arrest of its members.

This was a death blow to the Bavarian Illuminati. Many of its leaders, including Adam Weishaupt, were forced into exile. Weishaupt fled Bavaria in 1784 and found refuge in nearby Gotha, where he spent the rest of his life writing philosophical works, but he never succeeded in reviving the Illuminati. Other prominent members were arrested, and the group's internal correspondence and records were seized by authorities. These documents, published and disseminated by the Bavarian government, were used to further tarnish the reputation of the Illuminati, portraying them as a dangerous and corrupt organization bent on overthrowing governments and undermining religion.

The Illuminati's downfall was swift, but its influence persisted in the shadows. Ironically, the very secrecy that had once protected the group became its undoing. The more clandestine and mysterious the Illuminati appeared, the more fertile the ground became for rumors and conspiracy theories. The government's suppression of the group fueled speculation that the Illuminati hadn't disappeared at all, but had instead gone deeper underground, continuing to operate in secret to achieve its goals of world domination.

Despite the order's formal dissolution, whispers of its continued existence began to circulate throughout Europe. Critics of the Enlightenment, particularly conservative clerics and monarchists, seized upon the Illuminati as the embodiment of all their fears. To them, the Enlightenment represented an existential threat to traditional authority, and the Illuminati became a convenient scapegoat for the social and political upheaval of the time. The group's name became synonymous with radicalism, revolution, and the overthrow of established power.

In the years that followed, the Illuminati was increasingly blamed for everything from political unrest to natural disasters. As revolutionary movements swept across Europe, most notably the French Revolution in 1789, the Illuminati were implicated in the chaos. Writers like Augustin Barruel and John Robison, two of the most influential early conspiracy theorists, argued that the Illuminati had been behind the French Revolution, using it as a stepping stone toward establishing a new world order devoid of monarchy and religious authority. According to these theorists, the Illuminati's influence had spread far beyond Bavaria, infiltrating governments across Europe with the goal of global domination.

In reality, the Bavarian Illuminati had been effectively disbanded by 1785, with no credible evidence that it survived beyond its suppression. But in the public imagination, the Illuminati had transformed into something far more enduring. The crackdown by the Bavarian authorities, intended to eliminate the threat, had instead planted the seeds of the Illuminati myth. The idea that a secret society could be working behind the scenes to manipulate world events became a cornerstone of conspiracy theories for centuries to come.

While the Illuminati as an organization ceased to exist, its myth only grew stronger in its absence. The shadowy nature of the group, combined with its lofty ambitions and mysterious downfall, created a perfect storm for the birth of a legend. The disbanding of the Illuminati was not the end of the story, but the beginning of a much larger narrative—one that would take on a life of its own and continue to captivate and terrify people for generations.

The Birth of the Illuminati Myth

With the Bavarian Illuminati officially disbanded in 1785, the group's influence in real terms quickly evaporated. Yet, ironically, its disbandment marked the beginning of something far more significant: the birth of the Illuminati myth. This myth would evolve into a powerful narrative, suggesting that the Illuminati had not only survived but had continued operating in secret, wielding tremendous influence over world events from the shadows. What began as a relatively short-lived intellectual group would grow into one of the most pervasive and enduring conspiracy theories in history.

The groundwork for the Illuminati myth was laid almost immediately after the society's dissolution. In the late 18th century, Europe was a continent in turmoil. The Enlightenment had unleashed a torrent of new ideas, challenging the legitimacy of monarchies and religious institutions. Revolution was in the air, most notably in France, where the French Revolution of 1789 overthrew centuries of monarchical rule and threatened to spread its radical ideals across Europe. Against this backdrop of uncertainty and upheaval, the Illuminati, with its secretive methods and ambitious aims, became the perfect scapegoat for conservative forces looking to explain the chaos that had gripped the continent.

The first major architect of the Illuminati myth was Augustin Barruel, a French Jesuit priest who published *Memoirs Illustrating the History of Jacobinism* in 1797. In this multi-volume work, Barruel argued that the French Revolution had been the result of a deliberate conspiracy orchestrated by secret societies, particularly the Illuminati. According to Barruel, the Illuminati had infiltrated key institutions in France, working behind the scenes to incite revolution and overthrow the monarchy. He claimed that the group's ultimate goal was the destruction of all religious and political authority, paving the way for a new secular world order dominated by the Illuminati's ideals.

Barruel's thesis was compelling for many, especially those who had witnessed the violence and radicalism of the French Revolution. In a time of such profound social upheaval, the idea that a hidden cabal had masterminded these events offered a clear, if sinister, explanation for the chaos. Barruel's work became highly influential among conservative thinkers, who saw the Enlightenment, and by extension the Illuminati, as existential threats to the established order. It wasn't long before the Illuminati were blamed not only for the French Revolution but for a broader plot to destabilize Europe and usher in an age of secularism, atheism, and republicanism.

Around the same time, John Robison, a Scottish physicist and Freemason, published *Proofs of a Conspiracy* in 1797. Robison's book echoed Barruel's claims, alleging that the Illuminati had infiltrated Freemasonry and was using it as a tool to spread its influence across Europe. Robison argued that the Illuminati's goal was to abolish all monarchies and organized religions, replacing them with a rationalist, humanist society governed by the principles of the Enlightenment. His work added further fuel to the growing belief that the Illuminati, far from being disbanded, had merely gone underground and continued to operate in secret.

Both Barruel and Robison's writings helped cement the idea that the Illuminati were not only still active but had become the driving force behind revolutionary movements and political upheavals across Europe. The fact that the Illuminati had disbanded over a decade earlier seemed irrelevant to these authors; what mattered was the symbolic power of the Illuminati as an embodiment of radical change. The group, or at least the idea of it, provided a convenient explanation for the rapid social transformations sweeping through Europe during the late 18th and early 19th centuries.

This narrative of an all-powerful, secret society orchestrating world events from behind the scenes resonated deeply with those who felt threatened by the changes taking place. For conservative monarchists, religious leaders, and anyone alarmed by the rise of secularism, the Illuminati represented a malevolent force seeking to upend centuries of tradition and stability. As the myth spread, it gained new layers, with claims that the Illuminati had infiltrated every corner of society—from governments to educational institutions to financial systems.

The success of the Illuminati myth was due in part to its adaptability. As the political landscape of Europe and the world shifted, the Illuminati could be invoked as a shadowy force behind almost any event that seemed to undermine traditional authority. In the early 19th century, the Napoleonic Wars, the rise of republicanism, and the growing power of secular intellectual movements were all, at various times, attributed to the hidden hand of the Illuminati. Each new crisis or revolution seemed to confirm the existence of a secret group pulling the strings.

As the 19th century progressed, the Illuminati myth crossed the Atlantic and found fertile ground in the United States. In the young American republic, which had itself been born out of revolution, fears of secret societies took on a new dimension. The Anti-Masonic movement of the 1820s and 1830s in the U.S. was fueled by the belief that the Freemasons, with their secretive rituals and elite membership, were a threat to democracy. Given the association between Freemasonry and the Illuminati in Europe, it wasn't long before conspiracy theorists began to claim that the Illuminati had infiltrated American institutions as well, working to subvert the republic from within.

By the mid-19th century, the Illuminati had become more than just a historical footnote; it had evolved into a symbol of the unknown, the feared, and the incomprehensible. Whenever a political or social movement threatened the status quo, the specter of the Illuminati could be invoked to explain it. Whether it was revolutionaries in Europe or reformers in America, the notion that a powerful, secretive group was manipulating events behind the scenes became an enduring feature of conspiracy thinking.

While the actual Bavarian Illuminati had long since faded into obscurity, the myth of the Illuminati was just getting started. It would grow in complexity and influence over the next two centuries, eventually becoming a central feature of modern conspiracy theories, from fears of global governance to claims of elite domination in the 21st century. What began as a small, intellectual society in Bavaria had now become a global legend, far more powerful in myth than it ever had been in reality.

The Evolution of the Illuminati in Modern Conspiracy Theories

As the 19th century progressed, the Illuminati myth gained traction, transcending its historical origins and evolving into a powerful symbol of hidden control. By the time the 20th century arrived, the Illuminati had become a cornerstone of modern conspiracy theories. What was once a small, intellectual society in Bavaria had transformed into a vast, shadowy network supposedly manipulating world events for its own nefarious purposes. The group's portrayal shifted from a reformist organization into a symbol of elite domination, a mysterious force responsible for steering global events from behind the scenes.

The 20th century witnessed major social, political, and technological transformations, and with each new upheaval, the Illuminati myth expanded, adapting to fit new fears and uncertainties. The rapid growth of industry, the emergence of global financial systems, the rise of totalitarian regimes, and the outbreak of two world wars fueled the notion that unseen hands were orchestrating these momentous changes. The Illuminati became the face of these invisible forces, used to explain the chaos and complexity of a rapidly changing world.

Perhaps the most significant development in the evolution of the Illuminati myth was its entanglement with the fear of global governance. In the wake of World War I and World War II, the idea of a "New World Order" emerged, often intertwined with the concept of the Illuminati. The term "New World Order" refers to the fear that a secret elite, often linked to the Illuminati, is working to establish a global government that will control all aspects of human life—economics, politics, media, and even thought itself. This belief took root during the tumultuous periods of war, as people sought explanations for the devastation and the sudden emergence of international bodies like the League of Nations and later, the United Nations.

As international cooperation increased, particularly through organizations such as the United Nations, NATO, and the World Bank, conspiracy theorists seized on these institutions as evidence of a covert plan for global domination. The Illuminati, long linked with the idea of world control, became a convenient figurehead for these fears. Any movement toward internationalism, whether in diplomacy or trade, could be framed as a step toward a one-world government secretly controlled by the Illuminati. The idea resonated particularly with nationalist and isolationist movements, who viewed these international institutions as threats to national sovereignty.

The Cold War era provided yet another opportunity for the Illuminati myth to evolve. As the rivalry between the United States and the Soviet Union intensified, fears of communist infiltration and secret societies spread like wildfire. In this atmosphere of paranoia, the Illuminati became a catch-all explanation for everything from economic instability to political assassinations. The assassination of President John F. Kennedy in 1963, for example, sparked numerous conspiracy theories, some of which implicated the Illuminati as orchestrators of the event in a bid to control the U.S. government.

It wasn't just political events that became fodder for Illuminati theories. The rise of mass media, particularly Hollywood, was soon linked to the idea of Illuminati influence. In the 1960s and 1970s, countercultural movements sought explanations for perceived corruption in politics, society, and the media. The Illuminati became synonymous with the hidden forces of power behind the entertainment industry, particularly in music and film. From rock stars to major movie studios, the entertainment world was accused of subtly promoting the Illuminati's agenda through symbolism and messaging embedded in popular culture.

By the late 20th century, these theories exploded in popularity, with books, documentaries, and radio shows spreading the idea that the Illuminati were using mass media to manipulate the public. This theory was bolstered by the rise of figures like David Icke, a British conspiracy theorist who claimed that world leaders, celebrities, and wealthy elites were part of a hidden cabal, with some even suggesting they were shape-shifting reptilian aliens—a far-fetched but widely followed offshoot of Illuminati conspiracies.

With the advent of the internet in the late 1990s, the Illuminati myth entered an entirely new era. The internet allowed conspiracy theories to spread more rapidly and broadly than ever before. Websites, forums, and later, social media platforms, became fertile ground for Illuminati speculation, and the reach of these ideas expanded exponentially. Symbols like the all-seeing eye, pyramids, and certain hand gestures were now being seen everywhere—from dollar bills to music videos—and were interpreted as evidence of the Illuminati's pervasive influence.

In the 21st century, the Illuminati conspiracy theory became deeply embedded in global pop culture. High-profile musicians, actors, and politicians were frequently accused of being members of the Illuminati. The music industry, in particular, became a target, with artists like Jay-Z, Beyoncé, and Kanye West repeatedly cited as supposed Illuminati agents due to their success, influence, and the use of certain symbols in their music and imagery. Concert performances, music videos, and even Super Bowl halftime shows were scrutinized for hidden messages that allegedly pointed to an Illuminati agenda.

At the same time, the idea of the Illuminati merged with broader fears about global elites. In political movements such as the anti-globalization protests of the early 2000s, the Occupy Wall Street movement, and more recently, the populist waves in the U.S. and Europe, the Illuminati was invoked as the unseen force behind financial institutions, governments, and multinational corporations. The concept of the 1%—the wealthy elite controlling the vast majority of the world's resources—was often tied back to Illuminati conspiracies. The secretive meetings of groups like the Bilderberg Group and the World Economic Forum, which bring together world leaders and business executives, further fueled the narrative that the Illuminati were pulling the strings behind closed doors.

In modern conspiracy culture, the Illuminati myth is often used as a shorthand for a wide array of fears about power, control, and manipulation. Whether it's concerns about global surveillance, financial collapse, or cultural brainwashing, the Illuminati serves as a catch-all explanation for how a shadowy, elite few supposedly control the lives of billions. These fears have been amplified by the rise of social media, where misinformation spreads rapidly, and communities dedicated to conspiracy theories thrive.

Today, the Illuminati conspiracy theory remains one of the most persistent and influential in the world. Despite a lack of evidence that the original Bavarian Illuminati survived beyond the 18th century, its myth continues to evolve, morphing to fit new contexts and new fears. From a historical footnote to a modern-day cultural phenomenon, the Illuminati myth is a testament to the enduring appeal of hidden knowledge, secret power, and the search for simple explanations in an increasingly complex world.

Chapter 2: Conspiracy Theories and the Illuminati'

The Rise of Conspiracy Thinking

The 19th and early 20th centuries marked a significant shift in the way people viewed the world, and along with this came a dramatic rise in conspiracy thinking. The seeds of suspicion had always existed—historically, secret societies, hidden alliances, and covert power struggles have captivated the human imagination. However, the modern age, with its rapid advancements in technology, mass communication, and the rise of nation-states, provided fertile ground for the development of large-scale conspiracy theories. At the heart of many of these theories was the notion that powerful, hidden forces—like the Illuminati—were manipulating world events from the shadows.

The 19th century was a time of enormous change. The Industrial Revolution was transforming economies and societies at a breathtaking pace. Steam power, railroads, and mechanized production reshaped the daily lives of millions, creating new classes of wealth and power but also displacing old social structures. Political revolutions swept across Europe and the Americas, with the French and American revolutions acting as blueprints for republican movements around the world. In the face of these profound transformations, many people, especially those who felt left behind or threatened by modernization, began to search for simple explanations for the upheaval.

The proliferation of newspapers, pamphlets, and later radio, brought information to the masses like never before. However, this explosion of information also meant an increase in disinformation and propaganda. In this environment, rumors and conspiracies flourished, often filling the gaps left by a lack of understanding of complex political and social changes. The spread of literacy and the rise of mass media allowed conspiracy theories to circulate more widely, giving them a much larger audience than ever before. The Illuminati myth, which had already begun to take shape in the late 18th century, was perfectly suited to this new age of paranoia and speculation.

Politicians and elites of the time were often viewed with suspicion, particularly in periods of economic or political crisis. The wealthy industrialists who emerged in the wake of the Industrial Revolution were seen by many as wielding disproportionate power over governments and economies. The idea that these elites were part of a secret society bent on world domination began to take root. The Illuminati, despite its dissolution decades earlier, became the go-to symbol of this hidden power. Many believed that the Illuminati, far from being a defunct group, had simply gone underground, continuing to pull the strings of world events from behind the scenes.

Religious and nationalist movements of the 19th century were particularly fertile ground for conspiracy theories. As secularism and liberal ideals spread through Europe and America, conservative forces—especially within the Church—sought to explain the erosion of traditional authority. The Illuminati, which had been portrayed by figures like Augustin Barruel as an anti-religious, anti-monarchist force, became an easy target for blame. In the eyes of many religious leaders, the Illuminati was part of a broader conspiracy aimed at dismantling both the Church and the traditional social order.

As the 19th century wore on, political revolutions, economic downturns, and international conflicts further stoked the fires of conspiracy thinking. Events like the European revolutions of 1848, the rise of socialist and anarchist movements, and the increasingly visible influence of secret societies like the Freemasons all contributed to the growing belief that shadowy forces were at work behind the scenes. The Illuminati, once a small intellectual society in Bavaria, now took on a far more menacing and far-reaching role in the popular imagination.

The rise of conspiracy thinking during this period wasn't confined to Europe. In the United States, the late 19th and early 20th centuries were marked by profound social and political changes. The rapid industrialization of the U.S. economy, the influx of immigrants, and the rise of labor movements created a climate of tension and fear. As in Europe, people sought explanations for the upheavals they were experiencing, and conspiracy theories flourished. The idea that secret societies like the Illuminati were manipulating events behind the scenes resonated with many Americans, who feared that their democratic institutions were being subverted by unseen forces.

This fear was compounded by the rise of powerful, transnational organizations. By the late 19th century, international banking families like the Rothschilds were becoming prominent, and their wealth and influence sparked suspicion. Many began to believe that these financial elites were part of a global conspiracy, working in concert with groups like the Illuminati to establish a new world order. This theory would later become one of the central tenets of modern Illuminati conspiracies, linking financial power to secret societal control.

In short, the 19th and early 20th centuries provided the perfect breeding ground for the rise of conspiracy thinking. Rapid industrialization, political revolutions, and the rise of mass communication combined to create an atmosphere of uncertainty and fear. The Illuminati, though largely forgotten in reality, was resurrected in the public imagination as a symbol of hidden power. In an increasingly complex and chaotic world, many found comfort in the idea that a secret society could explain the turbulence of the times, even if that explanation was rooted in fear and misinformation.

The Illuminati and Global Events

Throughout the 19th and early 20th centuries, as the world underwent dramatic social and political shifts, the Illuminati myth became deeply entangled with global events. Despite the Bavarian Illuminati's disbandment in 1785, the belief that this secret society was still active—working behind the scenes to manipulate world affairs—began to gain traction. The narrative of a hidden, all-powerful group orchestrating revolutions, wars, and financial crises proved irresistibly compelling to those seeking a simple explanation for the increasingly complex dynamics of global change.

In particular, the French Revolution of 1789 was one of the first events to be directly linked to the Illuminati in conspiracy theories. The Revolution, which saw the overthrow of the French monarchy and the rise of radical republicanism, shocked Europe's monarchies and aristocracies. Many conservative thinkers and religious leaders were desperate to explain how centuries of established order had been so violently dismantled. The writings of Augustin Barruel and John Robison, both of whom claimed that the Illuminati had infiltrated key institutions in France and incited the Revolution, provided a convenient scapegoat.

According to Barruel and Robison, the Illuminati's ultimate goal was the destruction of all monarchies and religious institutions in Europe, paving the way for a secular, humanist world order. This narrative, while historically inaccurate, gained traction among those who saw the Enlightenment and its emphasis on reason and individual rights as a direct threat to the Church and the aristocracy. The Illuminati, therefore, became the face of this feared secular revolution, with conspiracy theorists claiming that the group had not only orchestrated the French Revolution but was also responsible for a series of uprisings across Europe in the following decades.

The revolutions of 1848, sometimes called the "Springtime of Nations," further cemented the link between political upheaval and the Illuminati in the minds of conspiracy theorists. In 1848, a wave of revolutionary movements swept across Europe, leading to the overthrow of several monarchies and the establishment of short-lived republics. Once again, these sudden and widespread uprisings were attributed to a hidden force. For many conservatives and monarchists, it was inconceivable that such dramatic political change could emerge spontaneously from the people. The Illuminati, with its supposed network of secret members working to undermine traditional power structures, provided a convenient explanation for these revolutions.

As the 19th century progressed, the industrial revolution and the rise of capitalism introduced new dimensions to the Illuminati myth. The rapid expansion of global trade, the accumulation of vast wealth by industrialists and bankers, and the increasing power of financial institutions all contributed to a growing sense of unease among the working classes. Economic instability, frequent financial crises, and the widening gap between rich and poor led to widespread dissatisfaction, particularly in Europe and the United States. In this context, conspiracy theorists began to claim that the Illuminati had shifted its focus from political revolution to economic control.

The Rothschild family, one of the wealthiest and most influential banking dynasties of the 19th century, became a central figure in these emerging financial conspiracy theories. Accusations that the Rothschilds were secretly controlling global financial systems, often in collaboration with the Illuminati, began to circulate widely. The Rothschilds' immense wealth and involvement in international finance made them an easy target for these theories, which accused them of using their power to manipulate markets, provoke wars, and control governments. The idea that a secret cabal was working to establish a global economic order resonated with those who felt alienated by the rapid changes of the industrial age.

The outbreak of World War I in 1914 provided yet another opportunity for the Illuminati myth to evolve. As the first truly global conflict, World War I devastated Europe and set the stage for radical political and social change. In the aftermath of the war, with millions dead and entire empires collapsed, people sought explanations for the catastrophe. Conspiracy theories began to circulate that the war had been deliberately engineered by the Illuminati to destabilize Europe and accelerate the push toward a New World Order. This narrative was bolstered by the fact that the war had led to the creation of international organizations like the League of Nations, which many saw as the first step toward global governance.

The Russian Revolution of 1917, which led to the establishment of the world's first communist state, was also linked to Illuminati conspiracies. As communism spread, particularly in the years following World War I, fears of a global communist revolution took hold in both Europe and the United States. Conservative thinkers, particularly those opposed to socialism, viewed the spread of communism as evidence of a broader conspiracy aimed at overthrowing capitalism and Western democracy. In their view, the Illuminati was working hand-in-hand with communist leaders to dismantle existing power structures and replace them with a global regime based on secular, socialist principles.

This period also saw the rise of anti-Semitic conspiracy theories that tied the Illuminati to Jewish elites, particularly in the banking and financial sectors. The infamous *Protocols of the Elders of Zion*, a forged document that purported to outline a Jewish plan for global domination, became a central text in this conspiracy narrative. The Illuminati, in this version of the myth, was often portrayed as a Jewish-controlled organization working to undermine Christian civilization and establish a one-world government. This toxic blend of anti-Semitism and Illuminati conspiracy theories would later be embraced by fascist movements, including Nazi Germany.

By the early 20th century, the idea of the Illuminati manipulating world events had become deeply embedded in conspiracy thinking. The Illuminati myth had evolved far beyond its historical roots, absorbing new fears and anxieties as global events unfolded. Wars, revolutions, financial crises, and the rise of international organizations were all seen as evidence of a hidden hand steering the course of history. For many, the Illuminati represented the ultimate explanation for the turbulence of the modern world—an invisible, malevolent force controlling the fate of nations and peoples.

As the world hurtled toward yet another global conflict in the 1930s, the Illuminati conspiracy theory was poised to enter its next phase, blending with new political ideologies and global fears to shape the conspiratorial thinking of the 20th and 21st centuries.

The Illuminati and Freemasonry

As the 19th century progressed, another secret society became inextricably linked to the growing legend of the Illuminati: the Freemasons. Freemasonry, a fraternal organization with its roots in medieval stone masonry guilds, had evolved into a widespread and influential network by the 18th century. Its rituals, symbols, and emphasis on Enlightenment values of reason, fraternity, and progress made it both admired and feared. By the early 1800s, conspiracy theorists began to claim that the Illuminati had infiltrated Freemasonry, using it as a vehicle to advance their alleged plot for global domination. This association between the two secret societies became a cornerstone of the Illuminati myth, casting a long shadow over Freemasonry's reputation for centuries to come.

Freemasonry was already a subject of suspicion long before it became linked to the Illuminati. Its secretive nature, complex rituals, and exclusive membership drew the ire of both religious and political authorities. In Catholic Europe, the Church was particularly hostile toward Freemasonry, viewing it as a rival system of thought that promoted secularism and undermined religious authority. In countries where monarchies held significant power, Freemasonry's emphasis on republican ideals and the rights of the individual was seen as a threat to the established order.

The connection between the Illuminati and Freemasonry was cemented by conspiracy theorists such as Augustin Barruel, who in his influential work *Memoirs Illustrating the History of Jacobinism* (1797) claimed that the Illuminati had infiltrated Masonic lodges and used them to spread their radical ideas. Barruel argued that the Illuminati's goal of overthrowing monarchies and the Church aligned with the principles of Freemasonry, creating a powerful alliance between the two groups. He warned that the Illuminati had used Masonic networks to influence the French Revolution, and by extension, sought to control the political and intellectual movements sweeping across Europe.

This narrative gained further credibility when John Robison, a Scottish physicist and Freemason, published *Proofs of a Conspiracy* in 1798, in which he echoed Barruel's claims of Illuminati infiltration. Robison's insider status as a Freemason added weight to his accusations, and his work was widely read in both Europe and the United States. He argued that the Illuminati had co-opted Masonic lodges to create a vast, secret network of influence across Europe. According to Robison, this network was responsible for inciting political revolutions, undermining religious institutions, and spreading dangerous Enlightenment ideas. The Illuminati's ultimate aim, Robison suggested, was to create a godless, egalitarian society ruled by reason, with no place for traditional authority or religious belief.

The impact of these works was profound, particularly in the United States, where anti-Masonic sentiment took on a life of its own. In the early 19th century, the United States experienced a wave of anti-Masonic fervor, fueled by fears that Freemasonry had become a tool of the Illuminati. This culminated in the creation of the Anti-Masonic Party in 1828, the first third-party political movement in the country's history. The Anti-Masonic Party was formed in response to the mysterious disappearance of William Morgan, a former Mason who had threatened to expose the secrets of the Freemasons. Many believed that Morgan had been murdered by Freemasons to protect their secrets, and this scandal stoked public outrage.

The Anti-Masonic Party capitalized on these fears, promoting the idea that Freemasonry—and by extension, the Illuminati—was a corrupt, elitist organization intent on undermining American democracy. The party's platform centered on opposition to secret societies and called for greater transparency in government. While the Anti-Masonic Party ultimately faded from the political landscape, its brief success reflected the deep mistrust of secret organizations that had taken hold in American society, a sentiment that would persist throughout the 19th and 20th centuries.

In Europe, the supposed link between the Illuminati and Freemasonry became a rallying cry for conservative forces seeking to resist the spread of liberal, republican ideals. In countries like France, Italy, and Germany, where Freemasonry was associated with progressive intellectuals, revolutionaries, and anti-clerical movements, it was easy to portray the organization as part of a larger conspiracy to overthrow traditional authority. The Catholic Church, in particular, remained a staunch opponent of Freemasonry, viewing it as a mortal threat to its influence. Papal decrees condemning Freemasonry, such as Pope Leo XIII's encyclical *Humanum Genus* in 1884, warned of the dangers posed by secret societies that sought to erode the moral and social fabric of Christian civilization.

Despite the Illuminati's historical disbandment, the myth of its infiltration of Freemasonry continued to thrive, taking on new forms as the centuries progressed. In the minds of many conspiracy theorists, Freemasonry and the Illuminati became indistinguishable, two heads of the same hydra. The use of esoteric symbols by both groups—such as the all-seeing eye, the pyramid, and the compass and square—only reinforced the belief that they were connected. For conspiracy theorists, these symbols, which were visible in architecture, on currency, and in art, were interpreted as evidence of the Illuminati's continued influence over global events.

As political and social movements evolved, the Illuminati-Freemasonry connection adapted to fit new fears and anxieties. In the 19th century, it was the fear of republicanism and secularism. In the 20th century, with the rise of fascism, communism, and globalization, the Illuminati conspiracy became linked to the broader fear of a New World Order. Freemasonry, with its international reach and secretive rituals, remained at the heart of this conspiracy narrative. From the halls of power to the shadows of revolution,

Freemasonry was portrayed as the Illuminati's instrument, guiding the world toward a hidden agenda of global control.

This convergence of Freemasonry and the Illuminati in conspiracy theory culture would have a lasting impact. It blurred the lines between historical reality and myth, making it nearly impossible to separate the two in the public imagination. Even today, in the age of the internet, the idea of a Masonic-Illuminati alliance persists in various forms, influencing how people interpret world events. From accusations of Masonic influence in politics to claims of Illuminati symbols hidden in pop culture, the legacy of this conspiracy theory continues to resonate across generations. The Illuminati, as a shadowy puppet master, and Freemasonry, as its tool of influence, remain potent symbols of hidden power in the collective imagination of the modern world.

The Cold War and New World Order Theories

The Cold War era marked a significant evolution in the Illuminati myth, as fears of global conspiracy and secret control found new life in the tensions between the East and West. The ideological clash between the United States and the Soviet Union, the looming threat of nuclear war, and the complex web of espionage and proxy conflicts created a fertile ground for conspiracy theories. The Illuminati, which had long been portrayed as a hidden force influencing world events, now became central to the belief that a "New World Order" was being orchestrated behind the scenes by a shadowy global elite. For many conspiracy theorists, the Cold War wasn't just a geopolitical struggle—it was part of a grander design by the Illuminati to establish a one-world government.

The concept of the New World Order—an all-encompassing, centralized global government—began to take shape in the mid-20th century, coinciding with the establishment of international organizations like the United Nations (UN) and NATO. To many, these institutions represented hope for global cooperation and peace in the aftermath of two world wars. But to conspiracy theorists, they were the first steps toward an authoritarian world government led by a secret elite. The Illuminati, long thought to have faded into obscurity, was revived in the public imagination as the driving force behind these global entities.

One of the key factors fueling New World Order theories during the Cold War was the fear of communism. In the United States, particularly during the Red Scare of the 1950s, there was widespread anxiety that communism wasn't just a political ideology, but part of a larger conspiracy to destroy Western values and replace them with a totalitarian regime. Conspiracy theorists argued that communism was merely a tool being used by the Illuminati to destabilize the world and pave the way for their global domination. This theory merged the fear of external communist threats with internal suspicions about subversive elements within Western governments and institutions.

The work of conservative authors and commentators during this period played a significant role in promoting the idea that communism and globalism were intertwined with the Illuminati's goals. Books like *None Dare Call It Conspiracy* by Gary Allen and *The Naked Capitalist* by W. Cleon Skousen, published in the 1970s, popularized the notion that a small group of powerful elites—bankers, industrialists, and politicians—were working together to create a socialist one-world government. These elites were often depicted as members of secret societies like the Illuminati, using communism as a way to erode national sovereignty and individual freedoms.

At the same time, the United Nations became a focal point for New World Order conspiracy theories. Established in 1945 to promote international cooperation and prevent future conflicts, the

UN was seen by conspiracy theorists as a vehicle for global governance. The organization's focus on human rights, economic development, and international law was framed as a threat to national sovereignty and an attempt to centralize power in the hands of a global elite. The Illuminati, it was claimed, had infiltrated the UN and other international institutions to advance their agenda of world domination. Every action taken by the UN—from peacekeeping missions to environmental regulations—was viewed through this conspiratorial lens, reinforcing the belief that the organization was a front for the Illuminati.

As the Cold War progressed, New World Order theories continued to evolve, incorporating new geopolitical developments into the Illuminati narrative. The rise of multinational corporations, the spread of capitalism, and the increasing influence of organizations like the World Bank and the International Monetary Fund (IMF) were all seen as evidence that a secret global elite was consolidating power. Conspiracy theorists argued that these institutions were part of a carefully orchestrated plan to control the world's economies and resources. Whether through communism or capitalism, the ultimate goal was the same: to create a system in which a few powerful individuals could govern the world.

One of the most enduring symbols of this conspiracy is the idea that the Illuminati has secretly influenced not only global organizations but also major political figures. The belief that U.S. presidents, Soviet leaders, and European heads of state were either members of the Illuminati or under their control gained traction during the Cold War. For example, President John F. Kennedy's assassination in 1963 became a focal point for Illuminati theories, with some claiming that he was killed because he threatened the secret order's plans. The symbolism of his murder, occurring during one of the tensest periods of the Cold War, reinforced the notion that unseen forces were manipulating world events.

The Cold War also saw the rise of anti-Semitic variations of the Illuminati conspiracy, with claims that a Jewish cabal, often linked to banking dynasties like the Rothschilds, was using communism to establish global control. These theories built on older, deeply ingrained anti-Semitic myths that tied Jewish people to secret world domination plots. The Illuminati, in this version of the conspiracy, was not just a secret society but part of a larger Zionist plan to control world governments and economies.

As tensions between the U.S. and Soviet Union reached their peak, the idea of a New World Order remained at the heart of many conspiracy theories. The constant threat of nuclear war, the arms race, and the presence of secretive intelligence agencies like the CIA and KGB further fueled the belief that world events were being orchestrated by unseen hands. Every major geopolitical development—from the Cuban Missile Crisis to the construction of the Berlin Wall—was viewed as part of the Illuminati's master plan.

By the end of the Cold War, with the fall of the Soviet Union in 1991, the world was left in a state of uncertainty. The rapid shift from a bipolar world dominated by two superpowers to a new global order of interconnected economies and rising international organizations intensified fears of the Illuminati's influence. Conspiracy theorists saw the end of the Cold War not as a victory for freedom, but as the next phase in the Illuminati's plan to establish a unified global government.

In the post-Cold War world, the New World Order theory would continue to evolve, but the Cold War had set the stage. The fear of communism, the rise of multinational organizations, and the ever-present threat of nuclear annihilation had all been woven into the fabric of the Illuminati conspiracy. As the 21st century began, these fears would only intensify, as new global challenges emerged and conspiracy theories adapted to a rapidly changing world.

Modern Conspiracy Culture and the Internet Age

The end of the Cold War did little to diminish the belief in the Illuminati's influence. Instead, the myth adapted and grew, finding new life in the rapidly evolving world of the 21st century. As globalization expanded and technology advanced at an unprecedented pace, the Illuminati conspiracy became more pervasive, fed by the growing mistrust of governments, corporations, and institutions. The rise of the internet, social media, and alternative media channels allowed conspiracy theories to flourish, giving the Illuminati myth a global platform and an audience more vast than ever before.

In the internet age, the Illuminati conspiracy became a cultural phenomenon, touching almost every aspect of public life, from politics to entertainment. One of the key factors driving this resurgence was the increasing visibility of global elites and the perception that a few powerful individuals and corporations were controlling the world's political and economic systems. High-profile organizations like the World Economic Forum, the Bilderberg Group, and the Council on Foreign Relations became frequent targets for conspiracy theorists, who claimed that these meetings of influential leaders were secret gatherings of Illuminati members plotting to establish a New World Order.

For many, the financial crisis of 2008 was a turning point. The collapse of major financial institutions, the subsequent bailouts, and the growing economic inequality that followed were seen as proof that a shadowy cabal of bankers and corporate elites—often linked to the Illuminati—was manipulating the global economy. The widespread anger and distrust that arose from the crisis fueled populist movements on both the political left and right, many of which embraced Illuminati conspiracy theories. In the eyes of these movements, the financial elites were not only corrupt but were working toward a hidden agenda to control the world's wealth and resources.

The entertainment industry also became a central focus for modern Illuminati conspiracy theories. Musicians, actors, and public figures were frequently accused of being Illuminati members, using their fame and influence to promote the group's agenda. Celebrities like Beyoncé, Jay-Z, Kanye West, Rihanna, and others were often depicted as pawns of the Illuminati, with their music videos, stage performances, and public personas filled with alleged Illuminati symbols like the all-seeing eye, pyramids, and occult imagery. These theories were fueled by the global reach of pop culture, where seemingly innocuous artistic choices were interpreted as signs of a vast conspiracy. The entertainment industry, in this narrative, became a tool for mind control, subtly shaping public opinion in favor of the Illuminati's plans.

Social media platforms, particularly YouTube, Twitter, and Facebook, became breeding grounds for these theories. Videos analyzing music videos, dissecting public speeches, and highlighting alleged Illuminati symbols proliferated, reaching millions of viewers. With the advent of algorithm-driven content, conspiracy videos often gained significant traction, allowing the Illuminati myth to spread faster and further than ever before. Hashtags, memes, and viral videos transformed the Illuminati into a pop culture reference, making it almost impossible to distinguish between genuine believers and those treating the idea as an internet joke.

At the same time, the rapid rise of technology, particularly in the realms of artificial intelligence, surveillance, and biotechnology, sparked new fears that were quickly absorbed into the Illuminati narrative. Conspiracy theorists claimed that the Illuminati was behind the development of these technologies, using them to monitor, control, and eventually enslave humanity. Concerns over privacy, government surveillance programs like the NSA's PRISM, and the increasing integration of AI into daily life were interpreted as steps toward a dystopian future where the Illuminati would have total control over human behavior and thought.

In particular, the spread of microchip technology and discussions about implantable devices ignited fears that the Illuminati was working to create a "cashless society" in which every individual could be tracked and controlled through digital means. This idea was often tied to biblical prophecies about the "Mark of the Beast" from the Book of Revelation, reinforcing the belief that the Illuminati was not just a political or financial entity but part of a larger, spiritual war against humanity. These theories were further amplified during global crises, such as the COVID-19 pandemic, when fears of government overreach, mandatory vaccines, and digital health passports were interpreted as signs of the impending New World Order.

Political movements, particularly in the United States, also began to integrate Illuminati conspiracy theories into their platforms. The rise of populist figures like Donald Trump and the emergence of movements such as QAnon tapped into the long-standing belief that a secret elite was controlling world events. QAnon, in particular, blended the Illuminati myth with newer conspiracies about a global cabal of elites involved in child trafficking, satanic rituals, and other nefarious activities. Although QAnon's specific focus was different, its foundational belief—that a hidden group of powerful individuals was controlling the world—drew heavily on the centuries-old Illuminati narrative.

The Illuminati myth also found fertile ground in debates about globalization, immigration, and the erosion of national sovereignty. For those who opposed global institutions like the European Union, the World Health Organization, and the United Nations, these organizations were viewed as stepping stones toward a one-world government controlled by the Illuminati. The spread of trade agreements, international regulations, and open-border policies were seen as attempts to dissolve national identities and consolidate power in the hands of a global elite.

The 21st century also saw a shift in how the Illuminati myth intersected with politics. In the age of political polarization, conspiracy theories became tools for discrediting political opponents. Both the political left and right accused each other of being influenced by the Illuminati, with accusations that progressive policies like climate change initiatives, universal healthcare, and social justice movements were part of a larger plot to undermine individual freedoms and create a centralized world government. On the other side, right-wing populist movements were often portrayed as tools of authoritarian regimes working toward the same goal. In both cases, the Illuminati narrative served to demonize political opponents and create an "us versus them" mentality.

As conspiracy theories became more mainstream, the Illuminati myth continued to adapt, absorbing new fears and anxieties. What began as a belief in a secret society manipulating world events in the shadows had evolved into a sprawling, multi-faceted conspiracy narrative that touched every aspect of modern life. From global politics and financial systems to pop culture and technology, the Illuminati myth had woven itself into the fabric of the internet age, shaping how millions of people viewed the world around them.

Even in the face of overwhelming evidence debunking the Illuminati's existence, the power of the myth remained undiminished. In an era of increasing complexity, where technology and global interconnectedness often feel beyond individual control, the Illuminati conspiracy offers a simple, if dark, explanation for the chaos and uncertainty of modern life. For many, the idea of a hidden hand pulling the strings is more comforting than the reality of a world shaped by chance, complexity, and human error. The Illuminati, whether real or imagined, remains a symbol of ultimate power in the popular imagination—an enduring specter that continues to shape our understanding of authority, influence, and the unknown forces guiding the course of history.

Chapter 3: Symbols and Signifiers

Origins of Illuminati Symbolism

The symbols associated with the Illuminati did not appear out of thin air. Like most secret societies throughout history, the Illuminati adopted existing symbols that carried deep philosophical, spiritual, and cultural meanings, transforming them into visual representations of their core ideals. To understand why certain symbols became linked to the Illuminati, we first need to examine the historical and intellectual context in which these symbols emerged.

The Bavarian Illuminati, founded in 1776 by Adam Weishaupt, was a product of the Enlightenment—a period defined by the pursuit of knowledge, reason, and the challenge to traditional authority, particularly the Church and monarchies. Weishaupt, a professor of canon law and a strong proponent of Enlightenment values, envisioned the Illuminati as a secret society that would promote rational thought, scientific inquiry, and the eventual overthrow of oppressive structures in society. To communicate these lofty goals while maintaining the society's secrecy, Weishaupt and his followers turned to symbolic language.

One of the key symbols adopted by the Illuminati was the owl, often referred to as the "Owl of Minerva." In classical mythology, the owl was associated with Athena, the Greek goddess of wisdom, and Minerva, her Roman counterpart. The owl symbolized knowledge, insight, and the ability to see what others could not—qualities the Illuminati prized. The group believed they possessed a higher understanding of the world, one that was hidden from the masses, just as the owl could see through the darkness. The owl became a metaphor for the Illuminati's pursuit of intellectual enlightenment and their mission to shine a light on the ignorance they believed was fostered by religious and political authority.

Another important symbol for the Illuminati was the pyramid, an ancient architectural form loaded with meaning. Pyramids had long been associated with both the physical and spiritual realms, representing humanity's connection to the divine. In the context of the Illuminati, the pyramid took on an additional layer of meaning: it symbolized the structured path to enlightenment. The pyramid's wide base represented the masses, who lived in ignorance and darkness, while the apex symbolized the few who had attained true knowledge and power. To the Illuminati, their members were positioned near the top of this symbolic pyramid, having achieved a higher understanding that most people were incapable of reaching.

This idea of gradual enlightenment was central to the Illuminati's mission. The pyramid reflected the belief that, through education and reason, humanity could progress step by step toward a more just and rational society. Each level of the pyramid represented a stage in that journey, with only the most enlightened reaching the summit. This symbolic hierarchy resonated with the Illuminati's secretive, tiered membership structure, where initiates progressed through various ranks, each level granting them greater access to the society's inner teachings.

The use of symbols also allowed the Illuminati to communicate without words. In an age of censorship and suspicion, where overt opposition to the Church or monarchy could result in persecution, symbolic imagery provided a way to convey ideas subtly. The Illuminati were not the only group to recognize this. Other secret societies of the time, most notably the Freemasons, employed similar symbolic languages. In fact, the Illuminati borrowed heavily from Freemasonry, adopting many of its rituals, symbols, and organizational structures. This cross-pollination between secret societies helped solidify the symbolic lexicon that would later be associated with the Illuminati in conspiracy theories.

At the heart of Illuminati symbolism was the idea of hidden knowledge—truths that were kept from the general population but accessible to those who sought them out. This theme of secrecy, which ran through their use of symbols, reflected the group's belief that the world was controlled by forces unseen. They sought to uncover and harness this hidden knowledge for the betterment of society, but they also understood the danger of revealing too much too soon. To protect themselves and their ideas, the Illuminati operated in the shadows, leaving behind only symbols for those perceptive enough to interpret them.

These symbols, particularly the owl and the pyramid, laid the foundation for the visual language that would later be associated with the Illuminati. Though the Bavarian Illuminati itself was short-lived, its symbols endured, taking on new and sometimes darker meanings as they became intertwined with conspiracy theories. Today, these symbols are often seen as evidence of a secret agenda for world domination, but in their original context, they represented the Illuminati's more idealistic mission to enlighten humanity and challenge oppressive power structures. The evolution of these symbols from representations of knowledge and progress to markers of conspiracy and control is a reflection of how the Illuminati myth has grown and adapted over time.

In their early days, the symbols of the Illuminati were tools for revolution—ways to inspire their members and communicate their values. However, as we'll explore in the following points, these same symbols would later be co-opted, misunderstood, and used to fuel the narrative that the Illuminati was a sinister force working behind the scenes to control the world. The symbols that once represented enlightenment became, in the minds of conspiracy theorists, signs of a hidden cabal manipulating global events. This transformation of meaning is key to understanding the enduring power of Illuminati symbols in modern culture.

The All-Seeing Eye and Pyramid

Of all the symbols associated with the Illuminati, none have captured the public imagination quite like the all-seeing eye and the pyramid. These two images have become synonymous with the idea of a hidden elite controlling world events, often viewed as concrete evidence of the Illuminati's influence on global affairs. Yet, their origins and the reasons they were adopted by conspiracy theorists are more complex than the theories would suggest. These symbols have deep historical and cultural roots, long predating the Illuminati, and their association with secret societies has evolved over centuries.

The all-seeing eye, often depicted within a triangle and radiating light, is perhaps the most iconic of all Illuminati symbols. Known formally as the "Eye of Providence," it represents the eye of God watching over humanity, a symbol of divine omniscience and protection. Its roots can be traced back to ancient Egypt, where it appeared as the Eye of Horus, a symbol of power, protection, and royal authority. In Egyptian mythology, Horus, the falcon-headed god of the sky, lost his left eye in a battle with his uncle Set. The eye was later restored, becoming a symbol of healing, renewal, and divine watchfulness. The concept of a divine eye transcending earthly concerns resonated across cultures and time, finding its way into Christian iconography during the Renaissance.

In Christian art, the all-seeing eye was used to symbolize the ever-present gaze of God. It was often placed within a triangle to represent the Holy Trinity, emphasizing God's omnipotence, omnipresence, and omniscience. This symbol was not originally associated with any secret societies, nor was it connected to the Illuminati during its early years. However, the symbol's depiction of divine insight and invisible control made it a natural fit for the narratives that later surrounded the Illuminati myth. By the 18th and 19th centuries, as conspiracy theories about shadowy elites began to flourish, the all-seeing eye was reinterpreted as a symbol of an all-powerful, hidden force watching and controlling human affairs—not God, but an earthly cabal.

The pyramid, often shown beneath the all-seeing eye, has its own rich symbolism. Most famously associated with the ancient Egyptian pyramids, it represents strength, stability, and a connection between the earthly and the divine. The pyramid's geometric precision and monumental scale have long fascinated historians, mystics, and conspiracy theorists alike. For the Illuminati, as well as other secret societies, the pyramid came to symbolize the hierarchical nature of knowledge and power. At its base are the uninformed masses, and at its apex are the enlightened few—the elite, possessing the knowledge and understanding to guide society.

The combination of the pyramid and the all-seeing eye first gained widespread attention in a surprising place: the Great Seal of the United States. The reverse side of the seal, which appears on the back of the U.S. dollar bill, features a 13-step pyramid topped with an eye in a triangle, surrounded by the Latin phrase "Annuit Coeptis," meaning "He [God] has favored our undertakings." Beneath the pyramid is another Latin phrase, "Novus Ordo Seclorum," meaning

"New Order of the Ages." These phrases, along with the imagery, were intended to symbolize the birth of a new nation under divine guidance. However, in the eyes of conspiracy theorists, this became evidence of a hidden Illuminati agenda embedded in the very fabric of American government.

The appearance of the all-seeing eye and pyramid on the dollar bill gave rise to one of the most enduring myths about the Illuminati: that the founders of the United States were secretly part of the order and that America itself was designed as a vehicle for the Illuminati's vision of a New World Order. This theory is often bolstered by the fact that several of the founding fathers, including George Washington, Benjamin Franklin, and Thomas Jefferson, were Freemasons, a fraternal organization frequently linked to the Illuminati. Freemasonry shares many of the same symbols, including the pyramid and the all-seeing eye, though the two groups are historically distinct.

While the symbols on the dollar bill were meant to reflect Enlightenment ideals and the divine blessing of the American experiment, conspiracy theorists latched onto them as proof of the Illuminati's control. The Latin phrase "Novus Ordo Seclorum" was particularly fertile ground for speculation. Taken out of context, it was reinterpreted to mean "New World Order," a term that would later become central to modern conspiracy theories about global governance and the Illuminati's alleged agenda to dominate the world. The idea that these symbols were hidden in plain sight, right on the nation's currency, fueled the belief that the Illuminati's influence was both real and widespread.

As the Illuminati myth grew in popularity, the all-seeing eye and the pyramid became universal symbols of conspiracy. They were no longer confined to their original historical or religious meanings. Instead, they evolved into markers of hidden power and control, often cited as evidence that the Illuminati—or other secretive groups—were manipulating world events from behind the scenes. These symbols were found not just in government, but in corporations, entertainment, and global institutions, leading believers to see them everywhere.

In the modern age, the internet has further amplified the association of the all-seeing eye and pyramid with the Illuminati. Social media, blogs, and online videos often feature breakdowns of how these symbols appear in music videos, corporate logos, architecture, and art. The belief that these images are being deliberately placed in public view as part of a broader agenda has become a central tenet of Illuminati conspiracy theories. For many, the very ubiquity of these symbols in popular culture is seen as undeniable proof of their significance.

The original meanings of the all-seeing eye and pyramid have been largely overshadowed by these modern interpretations. What were once symbols of divine protection and human aspiration have been reinterpreted as emblems of control, surveillance, and conspiracy. This shift in meaning reflects a broader change in how society views power and authority. In a world where institutions are increasingly mistrusted, and global events seem beyond individual control, symbols like the all-seeing eye and pyramid have become convenient shorthand for a hidden, malevolent force shaping the course of history. In this way, they have transcended their origins and become powerful, if misunderstood, icons in the ongoing narrative of the Illuminati myth.

Hidden Messages in Pop Culture

In the last few decades, the symbols of the Illuminati have made a striking transition from obscure references in historical texts to omnipresent icons in modern pop culture. These symbols—particularly the all-seeing eye and pyramid—have become embedded in music videos, films, and other forms of media, sparking widespread speculation about hidden messages and secret agendas. From chart-topping musicians to blockbuster movies, Illuminati symbols have seemingly permeated every corner of the entertainment world, leading many to believe that pop culture is a primary tool for spreading the influence of this secretive society.

One of the most prominent areas where Illuminati symbols are said to appear is in the music industry, particularly in the work of globally recognized artists. Musicians like Beyoncé, Jay-Z, Kanye West, Rihanna, and Lady Gaga have all been accused of incorporating Illuminati symbolism into their music videos, performances, and album art. For example, Beyoncé's use of the pyramid gesture—where she forms a triangle with her hands—during performances has been interpreted by conspiracy theorists as an overt display of allegiance to the Illuminati. Similarly, Jay-Z, who uses the "Roc Sign" (a diamond-shaped hand gesture) as a symbol of his record label Roc-A-Fella Records, has had his actions interpreted as another nod to the Illuminati, with the diamond being a stand-in for the pyramid.

Music videos often provide fertile ground for these theories. The intricate and often surreal imagery used in these videos can be viewed through the lens of Illuminati symbolism by those predisposed to believe in the conspiracy. Rihanna's "Umbrella," for instance, features her dancing in a triangle-shaped cage and being doused in liquid that has been interpreted as symbolizing mind control. Lady Gaga's performances and videos, which frequently contain elaborate and provocative imagery, are also dissected for Illuminati symbols, particularly her use of the all-seeing eye motif, which she has emphasized by covering one eye in photos or videos.

These interpretations are fueled by the belief that the entertainment industry is controlled by a hidden elite—often said to be the

Illuminati—who use their power to manipulate the masses. According to this theory, celebrities are not just performers, but pawns in a larger agenda to desensitize or indoctrinate the public. The repetition of symbols like the all-seeing eye and pyramid in pop culture is seen as a way to normalize these images and subtly condition people to accept the control of the Illuminati. This belief often dovetails with ideas about mind control, where celebrities are thought to be "programmed" by the Illuminati to influence the public through their music and public personas.

In this context, the concept of "selling out" takes on a new, more sinister meaning. For conspiracy theorists, when an artist becomes globally successful or signs with a major record label, it is seen as evidence that they have joined the Illuminati. Their fame and fortune are not the result of talent or hard work, but of allegiance to this secretive group. The notion of "selling your soul" for fame has long been a trope in entertainment, but within the Illuminati narrative, this phrase is taken literally. Artists who achieve mainstream success are seen as having made a Faustian bargain, trading their individuality and freedom for wealth and influence under the watchful eye of the Illuminati.

The spread of these theories has been accelerated by the rise of social media and the internet, where fans and conspiracy theorists alike can share images, videos, and breakdowns of supposed Illuminati messages in pop culture. Platforms like YouTube are filled with videos dissecting music videos frame by frame, pointing out hidden pyramids, eyes, and other symbols that are said to be evidence of Illuminati influence. Twitter, Instagram, and TikTok have also become hotbeds for these discussions, with users sharing clips and memes that fuel the speculation. What might once have been dismissed as coincidence or artistic expression is now scrutinized and reinterpreted through the lens of the Illuminati conspiracy.

This phenomenon is not limited to the music industry. Hollywood films, television shows, and even corporate logos are often subject to the same kind of analysis. For instance, movies like *Eyes Wide Shut*, directed by Stanley Kubrick, are frequently cited as containing veiled references to secret societies and Illuminati rituals. In Kubrick's film, which revolves around an elite society engaging in secret ceremonies, conspiracy theorists see a depiction of the very real power structures they believe exist behind the scenes. Kubrick himself has been speculated to have had insider knowledge of the Illuminati, a theory that gained traction after his sudden death shortly after the film's release.

Corporate logos, too, are often analyzed for Illuminati symbolism. Companies like CBS, whose logo prominently features a stylized eye, and AOL, which uses a pyramid-like triangle in its branding, are said to be displaying their affiliation with the Illuminati openly. The fact that these symbols are so widespread in the business world is seen by some as further evidence that the Illuminati controls not only governments but also major corporations, which in turn control media, entertainment, and finance.

However, it is important to recognize that much of this symbolism in pop culture is either coincidental or deliberately ironic. In many cases, artists and filmmakers are well aware of the conspiracy theories surrounding the Illuminati and use these symbols either to play into the narrative for publicity or to subvert it. By including the all-seeing eye or pyramid in their work, they are often making a tongue-in-cheek reference to the very conspiracy theories that claim they are part of a global elite. In a media landscape driven by attention and controversy, playing into the mystery of the Illuminati can be an effective way to spark discussion and keep audiences engaged.

The result is a feedback loop where the more these symbols appear, the more they are scrutinized, and the more the Illuminati myth is perpetuated. Whether these symbols are used as a genuine artistic choice, a marketing tactic, or simply as a result of their ubiquity in culture, they continue to fuel the narrative that the Illuminati is real and that its members are using pop culture to spread their influence. This interplay between art, conspiracy, and media ensures that the Illuminati myth remains a potent and pervasive force in modern culture, constantly evolving and adapting to new forms of expression.

Corporate Logos and Brand Imagery

In the world of conspiracy theories, corporate logos are not just designs meant to represent companies; they are seen as powerful symbols that communicate the hidden influence of the Illuminati. Over the years, countless brands have been accused of embedding Illuminati symbols into their logos, subtly broadcasting their allegiance to the secret society. Whether it's through the use of pyramids, eyes, or other geometric shapes associated with the Illuminati, these logos are perceived as clues pointing to a global conspiracy that controls not just governments but the corporate world as well. This belief is a core part of modern conspiracy theories surrounding the Illuminati, where multinational corporations are often depicted as the true power brokers behind the scenes.

One of the most frequently cited examples is the CBS logo, which features a stylized eye. Conspiracy theorists argue that this all-seeing eye is an explicit reference to the Illuminati's symbol of omnipresent control. While the CBS eye was originally designed to reflect the nature of television—an eye on the world—it has become, in the conspiracy realm, a sign that the media company is part of the Illuminati's apparatus for influencing and controlling public perception. This interpretation aligns with broader conspiracy theories that claim the media is a tool used by the Illuminati to shape public opinion, promote their agenda, and keep the masses distracted from their secret plans for world domination.

Another frequent target of Illuminati speculation is the AOL logo. The original AOL logo featured a pyramid with a stylized eye at its top, which conspiracy theorists argue is a blatant reference to the Illuminati's pyramid and all-seeing eye symbol. This use of such a recognizable symbol fueled the idea that AOL, one of the early giants of the internet, was part of the Illuminati's larger scheme to control digital communication and, by extension, the flow of information. In this view, the internet—often seen as a tool for freedom and democratization—is instead portrayed as a vehicle for the Illuminati to monitor and influence global populations through surveillance and data control.

The symbolism conspiracy theorists see in corporate logos isn't limited to traditional media companies. Brands from a wide range of industries are accused of embedding Illuminati symbols in their designs. For example, the logo of Delta Air Lines, which features a triangle shape, is often interpreted as a nod to the Illuminati's pyramid symbol. Similarly, the logo for financial institution Fidelity Investments includes a pyramid-like design, leading some to believe that the Illuminati has deep ties to the financial sector, using companies like Fidelity to manipulate the global economy and maintain control over wealth and resources.

Even automotive brands are not immune to this scrutiny. The Volkswagen logo, with its interlocking "V" and "W," is sometimes interpreted as containing hidden geometric symbols that point to Illuminati influence. While the design may seem innocuous at first glance, conspiracy theorists argue that the use of certain shapes and angles is intentional, designed to subtly communicate the company's participation in a larger conspiracy. This interpretation extends to many other brands, where seemingly ordinary design elements are reimagined as coded messages to those "in the know."

These claims are often linked to a broader narrative that sees multinational corporations as extensions of the Illuminati's power. In this worldview, corporations are not just businesses; they are tools of control used to manipulate everything from public behavior to economic systems. The repetitive appearance of certain symbols across multiple industries is viewed as proof that these companies are connected, all part of a secret web of influence that spans the globe. Whether it's the food we eat, the technology we use, or the products we buy, conspiracy theorists argue that the Illuminati is behind it all, using corporate power to push forward its agenda of a New World Order.

It's important to recognize that many of the symbols in corporate logos are rooted in traditional design principles rather than any hidden agenda. For instance, the triangle is a common geometric shape in logo design because of its balance, strength, and simplicity. The same is true of the eye, which is a universally understood symbol of vision, awareness, and clarity. Designers often choose these elements because they are visually effective, not because they carry secret meanings. However, the very simplicity of these symbols makes them easy targets for reinterpretation by conspiracy theorists.

The belief in Illuminati influence over corporations also speaks to broader anxieties about power and control in the modern world. As corporations grow larger and more influential, they often appear distant and unaccountable, leading to suspicions about their true motives. The idea that a small group of elites controls global corporations—and by extension, global economies and societies—resonates with people who feel powerless in the face of such vast institutions. In this context, the Illuminati serves as a convenient scapegoat, a symbol of the unseen forces that seem to dictate the course of world events.

Another element that fuels these theories is the idea of "predictive programming," a concept that suggests that the Illuminati uses media and corporate branding to subtly prepare the public for future events. According to this theory, logos and symbols are used to condition people to accept certain ideas or developments, such as the rise of a global government or the introduction of new forms of social control. By embedding these symbols in everyday life—through corporate logos, advertisements, and entertainment—the Illuminati is said to be gradually shaping the public's perception, making its ultimate goals easier to achieve.

While it's easy to dismiss these theories as paranoid delusions, their persistence reveals something important about how people understand power in the modern world. The belief in Illuminati symbolism in corporate logos is not just about the symbols themselves; it reflects a deep mistrust of corporations and the global systems they are part of. Whether or not these symbols actually carry any hidden meaning, their presence in everyday life acts as a reminder of the vast, often invisible, forces that shape our world. In a time of increasing economic inequality, political instability, and corporate influence, it's no surprise that people turn to conspiracy theories to make sense of it all.

In the end, the idea that corporate logos are part of a grand Illuminati conspiracy is a reflection of broader societal concerns about control, power, and transparency. It taps into the fear that the world is being run by unseen elites who use corporations as their tools for domination. While the symbols themselves may be benign, the narratives built around them speak to the very real anxieties people have about the growing power of corporations and the lack of accountability in global systems of governance.

Modern Technology and Digital Surveillance

In the 21st century, the Illuminati conspiracy theory has evolved alongside advancements in technology, with modern gadgets, digital platforms, and global surveillance systems becoming central to the belief in a shadowy elite controlling the world. The rapid rise of the internet, smartphones, and social media has not only transformed the way people communicate and consume information but has also provided new fodder for conspiracy theorists who see these innovations as tools of control. For those who believe in the Illuminati, modern technology is not just about convenience and connectivity—it is about surveillance, manipulation, and the consolidation of power by an unseen few.

One of the most pervasive fears within this context is the idea that digital surveillance, often carried out under the guise of national security or corporate efficiency, is actually a key instrument of the Illuminati's plan for world domination. From this perspective, the vast networks of surveillance cameras, online tracking, and data collection systems are not designed solely to monitor criminals or improve services, but to keep tabs on ordinary citizens, amassing unprecedented amounts of personal data. This data, conspiracy theorists argue, is then used by the Illuminati to maintain control, manipulate behavior, and predict future actions. The ability to track people's movements, purchases, and even thoughts (through online searches and social media posts) gives this supposed global elite unparalleled insight into the population.

Central to this fear is the widespread use of smartphones and smart devices, which have become integral parts of everyday life. Many conspiracy theorists believe that these devices, with their microphones, cameras, and GPS capabilities, are the perfect surveillance tools. They argue that the very devices we rely on for communication and convenience are also used to monitor and record our activities, often without our consent. This concern is heightened by the fact that major tech companies, which produce and control these devices, are seen as potential collaborators in the Illuminati's agenda. Companies like Apple, Google, Facebook, and Amazon have access to vast amounts of user data, and conspiracy theorists claim that this data is either being sold or shared with secretive government agencies controlled by the Illuminati.

The fear of digital surveillance also extends to the concept of a cashless society, another popular talking point in Illuminati conspiracies. As digital payment systems such as credit cards, mobile payments, and cryptocurrency gain traction, the idea of eliminating physical currency has become a significant concern for those who believe in the Illuminati. A cashless society, they argue, would allow the global elite to track every transaction, eliminating any form of anonymous exchange and giving them even more control over people's financial lives. The transition to digital currency is seen as part of the broader plan for a New World Order, where every aspect of life—economic, social, and political—is under constant surveillance and control.

One particularly influential figure in these theories is the tech mogul. Individuals like Bill Gates and Elon Musk are frequently accused of being agents of the Illuminati, using their wealth, influence, and technological innovations to further the agenda of global domination. Gates, for instance, has been the target of numerous conspiracy theories, particularly in relation to vaccines and global health initiatives. Some believe that his philanthropic efforts, particularly through the Bill & Melinda Gates Foundation, are part of a larger scheme to depopulate the planet or implant microchips in the population under the guise of public health. These microchips, theorists argue, would allow the Illuminati to track and control individuals on an unprecedented scale.

Elon Musk, with his ambitious projects in space exploration and artificial intelligence, is another frequent target. His work with companies like Tesla, SpaceX, and Neuralink is seen by some conspiracy theorists as evidence that he is part of a grand plan to control humanity's future. Musk's interest in artificial intelligence, in particular, has sparked fears that AI could be used as a tool of oppression in the hands of the Illuminati, leading to a dystopian future where human lives are governed by machines and algorithms controlled by the global elite. In this scenario, AI is not just a technological innovation but a weapon to suppress freedom and autonomy, cementing the Illuminati's grip on the world.

The development of 5G technology has also become a focal point for conspiracy theories linking modern technology to the Illuminati. While 5G is simply the next generation of wireless communication, designed to provide faster internet speeds and more reliable connections, it has been the subject of intense speculation and fear. Some believe that 5G towers are being used to control minds, weaken immune systems, or even spread diseases like COVID-19, all as part of the Illuminati's larger plan to control and reduce the global population. The fact that 5G has been rapidly deployed across the world has only intensified these fears, with some claiming that the speed of its rollout is evidence of a coordinated effort by the Illuminati to establish global control through technology.

Even social media platforms, which many people use to connect with friends, share information, and express themselves, are seen as tools of manipulation by the Illuminati. Platforms like Facebook, Instagram, and Twitter collect vast amounts of personal data, which is then used to tailor content and advertisements. Conspiracy theorists argue that this data is not just being used for commercial purposes, but also to influence political opinions, shape public perception, and manipulate behavior on a massive scale. Algorithms that determine what content users see are viewed as a means of controlling the flow of information, subtly guiding people's thoughts and actions without their knowledge. This, in turn, is seen as a way for the Illuminati to maintain control over the population, using social media to push their agenda while keeping dissent in check.

The rise of facial recognition technology, particularly in places like airports, shopping malls, and public squares, has further contributed to the belief that we are living in a surveillance state controlled by the Illuminati. These systems, which can identify individuals based on their facial features, are often presented as tools for security and convenience. However, conspiracy theorists believe that they are being used to track and monitor people's movements, creating a society where anonymity is impossible, and privacy is a thing of the past. This belief is rooted in the fear that the Illuminati is working toward creating a totalitarian state where everyone is watched, controlled, and manipulated through technology.

In this digital age, the Illuminati myth has expanded to incorporate the ever-growing presence of technology in our lives. From smartphones and social media to AI and surveillance systems, modern tools are viewed not as neutral innovations but as part of a grand design to control the masses. For those who believe in the Illuminati, the increasing digitization of society is not about progress or convenience—it is about the loss of freedom and the rise of a new form of control, one that operates invisibly through the very devices and platforms we use every day. In this narrative, the Illuminati has moved from the shadows of history into the bright glare of the digital age, using technology to achieve their ultimate goal of global domination.

Chapter 4: The Illuminati and Religion

Historical **Conflict Between the Illuminati and the Church**

The roots of the Illuminati's supposed conflict with organized religion, particularly the Catholic Church, stretch back to the Enlightenment era. The Illuminati, founded in 1776 by Adam Weishaupt, was born in an intellectual climate where reason, science, and secularism were gaining ground against centuries of religious authority. Weishaupt, a professor of canon law at the University of Ingolstadt in Bavaria, initially created the group as a secret society aimed at promoting the ideals of the Enlightenment: rationality, freedom of thought, and opposition to the dogma and superstition that he believed were imposed by both religious and political powers.

The Church, however, viewed these new ideologies with deep suspicion and hostility. The Illuminati's emphasis on questioning religious authority and advocating for secular governance directly threatened the Church's centuries-old influence over European society. At a time when the Church held immense power, not only as a spiritual authority but also as a political one, the rise of a group that promoted the separation of church and state and challenged religious orthodoxy was seen as dangerous and subversive.

The tension between the Illuminati and the Church was part of a broader cultural clash between traditional religious values and the emerging ideas of the Enlightenment. Across Europe, many intellectuals, philosophers, and scientists were pushing for a world where knowledge was based on empirical evidence and reason, rather than faith and religious doctrine. The Church, on the other hand, saw these developments as a direct assault on its authority and a pathway toward moral decay. The Illuminati's clandestine nature, coupled with its progressive ideas, made it an easy target for those who feared the erosion of religious influence in society.

One of the key goals of the Illuminati was to undermine the absolute power of monarchies and the Church, both of which they saw as oppressive institutions that kept people in ignorance and submission. Members of the Illuminati believed that through education, rational debate, and secret alliances, they could promote reforms that would lead to a more just and equitable society. This vision, however, was diametrically opposed to the interests of the Church, which had long been aligned with monarchical power and relied on the support of rulers to maintain its own position of privilege and control.

In response to the growing influence of groups like the Illuminati, the Church condemned them as dangerous heretics and atheists. This was not just a theological disagreement; it was a battle over the future direction of European civilization. The Church, which had dominated Western thought for centuries, was now facing an existential challenge from movements that promoted reason over revelation and individual liberty over hierarchical control. The Illuminati, though small in numbers, became a symbol of this broader threat.

The Illuminati's emphasis on secrecy further fueled suspicion and paranoia within religious circles. Unlike other Enlightenment groups that openly advocated for change, the Illuminati operated in the shadows, using covert methods to spread their influence. This secrecy gave rise to numerous conspiracy theories, many of which were propagated by the Church itself. Religious leaders warned that the Illuminati sought to overthrow Christian values and replace them with secularism and atheism. This perception was not entirely unfounded, as the Illuminati did, in fact, seek to diminish the role of the Church in public life. However, the scale of their influence was vastly exaggerated in these accounts, which often portrayed the Illuminati as a vast, all-powerful network capable of orchestrating revolutions and societal collapse.

These early conspiracy theories about the Illuminati's anti-religious agenda were not limited to the Catholic Church. Protestant leaders, too, viewed the Illuminati with suspicion, fearing that the group's ideals would undermine their own religious authority. In both Catholic and Protestant countries, governments and religious institutions took steps to suppress the Illuminati. In Bavaria, for example, the Illuminati was officially banned by the government in 1784, following pressure from the Catholic Church. Weishaupt was forced into exile, and the group's influence quickly waned. Yet, despite its brief existence, the legend of the Illuminati endured, largely due to the Church's efforts to cast it as a nefarious force plotting against Christian civilization.

The Church's portrayal of the Illuminati as a dangerous anti-religious force persisted well into the 19th and 20th centuries, long after the group had ceased to exist in any meaningful form. The Illuminati became a convenient scapegoat for a variety of social changes that were seen as threatening to traditional religious values. From the French Revolution, which overthrew the monarchy and diminished the power of the Catholic Church in France, to the rise of secularism and scientific progress, the Illuminati was often blamed for the decline of religious influence in the modern world.

In reality, the historical Illuminati was far more modest in its goals and achievements than the grand conspiracies that would later surround it. While it sought to promote Enlightenment ideals and reduce the power of the Church, it was neither as influential nor as organized as its detractors claimed. Nonetheless, the idea of a secret society working to undermine religion took hold in the public imagination, and the Illuminati became a symbol of the broader conflict between reason and faith, secularism and religious authority.

This historical conflict between the Illuminati and the Church laid the foundation for many of the modern conspiracy theories that link the Illuminati to efforts to destroy or weaken religious institutions. Even today, echoes of this centuries-old struggle can be heard in discussions about the role of religion in public life, the separation of church and state, and the influence of secularism in global politics. What began as a real, though limited, conflict between an Enlightenment-era secret society and the Catholic Church has evolved into a powerful and enduring myth that continues to shape the way people understand the relationship between religion and power in the modern world.

The Illuminati in Christian Conspiracy Theories

In modern times, the Illuminati has become a focal point for many Christian conspiracy theorists who believe that the organization is working to undermine the moral and spiritual foundations of society. For these theorists, the Illuminati represents more than just a historical secret society—it is a symbol of an ongoing struggle between good and evil, with the Illuminati serving as agents of darkness. In particular, many evangelical Christian groups have embraced the idea that the Illuminati is part of a satanic agenda aimed at corrupting the world and preparing the way for the rise of the Antichrist.

The notion that the Illuminati is an existential threat to Christianity first gained significant traction in the late 20th century, as evangelical preachers and authors began to weave the Illuminati into their end-times narratives. These narratives often draw heavily from the Bible, particularly the Book of Revelation, which speaks of a coming period of tribulation, the rise of a global dictatorship under the Antichrist, and the eventual second coming of Christ. The Illuminati, in this framework, is portrayed as a secretive organization working behind the scenes to erode Christian values, weaken religious institutions, and usher in a godless New World Order.

One of the most influential figures in spreading the belief that the Illuminati is part of a satanic conspiracy was Christian author and preacher John Todd. In the 1970s, Todd claimed to be a former member of the Illuminati who had converted to Christianity and sought to expose the group's plans for global domination. He spoke of the Illuminati as a powerful, satanic organization that controlled governments, media, and entertainment, working to corrupt the masses and prepare the world for the Antichrist. Though his claims were later debunked and dismissed as fabrication, Todd's stories captured the imaginations of many evangelicals, helping to cement the idea of a vast Illuminati conspiracy in Christian circles.

Todd's allegations were further popularized by other Christian authors, such as Texe Marrs, whose books in the 1980s and 1990s portrayed the Illuminati as a central figure in the New World Order conspiracy. Marrs claimed that the Illuminati was working with global elites, including political leaders, business magnates, and celebrities, to bring about a one-world government that would suppress Christianity and pave the way for the Antichrist's rule. Marrs also linked the Illuminati to the occult, suggesting that they were not only atheistic but actively engaged in satanic rituals and black magic.

The fear of the Illuminati's influence has been further amplified by evangelical leaders in the age of mass media, particularly through television and radio programs. Prominent televangelists such as Pat Robertson have warned their audiences about the dangers of secret societies like the Illuminati, often framing current events as evidence of the group's plans. In Robertson's 1991 book *The New World Order*, he argued that the Illuminati was part of a larger conspiracy involving Freemasonry, globalist politicians, and financial elites, all working together to establish a world government that would ultimately persecute Christians.

For many evangelical Christians, these conspiracy theories resonate deeply because they align with a worldview that sees contemporary cultural and political changes as part of a larger spiritual battle. The decline of traditional religious values, the rise of secularism, and the increasing prominence of global institutions such as the United Nations are interpreted not just as political or social shifts, but as evidence that the Illuminati's plans are coming to fruition. The idea that a hidden cabal is working to undermine Christianity fits neatly into a broader narrative of spiritual warfare, in which believers are called to resist the forces of evil and prepare for the return of Christ.

This belief is further reinforced by the presence of Illuminati symbolism in popular culture, which conspiracy theorists interpret as evidence of the group's influence. Symbols like the all-seeing eye, pyramids, and pentagrams are often spotted in music videos, films, and even corporate logos, leading some Christians to believe that the entertainment industry is being used to subtly indoctrinate the masses into Illuminati beliefs. For example, pop stars such as Beyoncé, Jay-Z, and Lady Gaga have been accused of being Illuminati members due to the use of these symbols in their work. In the eyes of conspiracy theorists, these celebrities are not just entertainers—they are agents of the Illuminati, spreading messages of moral decay, materialism, and occultism to undermine Christian values.

In addition to cultural influence, the Illuminati is often linked to political events that are seen as hostile to Christianity. The push for secular governance, the legalization of same-sex marriage, the spread of abortion rights, and the growing acceptance of alternative spiritual practices are all interpreted by some evangelicals as part of the Illuminati's agenda to weaken Christian influence in society. This perspective leads to a deep mistrust of global institutions such as the European Union, the World Health Organization, and the United Nations, which are often portrayed as instruments of the Illuminati's plan for world domination.

The fear of an Illuminati-driven New World Order is not confined to fringe elements of the Christian community; it has also influenced mainstream conservative politics, particularly in the United States. The belief that global elites are conspiring to undermine national sovereignty, promote secularism, and erode religious freedoms has fueled opposition to policies such as international trade agreements, immigration reform, and efforts to combat climate change, all of which are seen as steps toward a one-world government. Political figures who advocate for these policies are sometimes accused of being either unwitting tools or active participants in the Illuminati's scheme.

For many Christians who subscribe to these conspiracy theories, the Illuminati represents the ultimate embodiment of the spiritual forces arrayed against them. The group is seen as the hidden hand behind the moral and cultural changes that they believe are eroding the foundations of Western civilization. Whether through media, politics, or education, the Illuminati is viewed as working to dismantle

Christian influence and prepare the world for the Antichrist's rule. This fear has persisted and evolved over the decades, adapting to new cultural and political developments, but always maintaining the central belief that the Illuminati is a key player in a cosmic battle between good and evil.

Thus, the Illuminati has come to occupy a unique place in the Christian imagination, serving as a convenient explanation for the complex and often unsettling changes occurring in the world. While the historical Illuminati was a relatively short-lived and obscure organization, its legacy as a symbol of conspiracy, secrecy, and anti-Christian sentiment continues to thrive in evangelical circles, shaping how millions of believers view the world and their place in it.

The Illuminati and Satanism

One of the most persistent and chilling aspects of modern Illuminati conspiracy theories is the claim that the group is not only anti religion but actively involved in Satanism. For decades, conspiracy theorists have linked the Illuminati to occult practices, black magic, and devil worship, alleging that the group is part of a larger satanic conspiracy aiming to undermine moral values, corrupt society, and pave the way for global enslavement under a demonic force. While these claims are often based on little more than speculation, symbolism, and paranoia, they have gained widespread popularity, particularly in religious circles where the Illuminati is viewed as an enemy of Christianity.

The association between the Illuminati and Satanism can be traced back to the early days of the Illuminati mythos, but it really took root in the 20th century as fears of occultism and satanic influence grew in mainstream culture. During the 1980s and 1990s, the United States experienced a period known as the "Satanic Panic," when concerns about ritual abuse, satanic cults, and devil worship reached fever pitch. In this environment of moral panic, the Illuminati became a convenient scapegoat, with many believing that the organization was behind a network of satanic practices infiltrating politics, entertainment, and even everyday life.

At the core of these beliefs is the idea that the Illuminati engages in secret rituals that involve the invocation of demonic powers. Conspiracy theorists claim that these rituals are not only designed to secure wealth and power for the group's elite members but also to further the cause of Satan on Earth by spreading chaos, immorality, and spiritual corruption. Central to these claims is the use of occult symbolism, which conspiracy theorists argue can be found hidden in plain sight in popular culture, architecture, and the actions of public figures.

For example, the image of Baphomet—a goat-headed figure that represents the blending of opposites, often used in occult and esoteric traditions—has become synonymous with Illuminati imagery. Originally associated with the Knights Templar and later adopted by occultists such as Aleister Crowley and the Church of Satan, Baphomet is frequently cited as evidence of the Illuminati's ties to satanic worship. Conspiracy theorists claim that this figure, along with other occult symbols like inverted pentagrams and the "all-seeing eye," is a clear sign of the Illuminati's dark, supernatural affiliations.

These theorists believe that the Illuminati uses these symbols not only in its rituals but also in popular culture to subtly indoctrinate the public. In particular, music videos, films, and performances by high-profile entertainers are often singled out as evidence of Illuminati influence. The music industry, in particular, has become a breeding ground for Illuminati-related speculation. Artists such as Jay-Z, Beyoncé, Kanye West, and Lady Gaga have all been accused of promoting Illuminati ideals through the use of occult symbolism in their work. Their hand gestures, clothing, and imagery are often scrutinized by conspiracy theorists who interpret them as hidden messages endorsing satanic practices.

Take, for instance, the widespread belief that the "all-seeing eye" symbol, which appears on the U.S. dollar bill and is often associated with Freemasonry, is a representation of the Illuminati's control and surveillance over humanity. When celebrities are seen making a gesture that covers one eye or features the eye in their artwork, theorists point to it as proof that these individuals are part of the Illuminati's plan to normalize occult imagery and condition the public to accept satanic influence.

Similarly, the use of pyramids and pentagrams in music videos or stage performances is viewed as further evidence that the Illuminati is working through the entertainment industry to corrupt young minds and lead them away from traditional moral and religious values. According to this narrative, the glamorization of wealth, power, and fame is part of a larger scheme to distract people from spiritual truths and lure them into a materialistic, morally bankrupt lifestyle—a key goal of the alleged Illuminati.

Another major component of the Illuminati-Satanism theory involves accusations of ritualistic human sacrifice. Conspiracy theorists claim that the Illuminati participates in secret ceremonies where human lives are sacrificed in exchange for power, wealth, and influence. This aspect of the conspiracy theory taps into long-standing fears about satanic cults and ritual abuse, fears that have been stoked by various high-profile but largely debunked cases throughout history. The idea that powerful elites are engaged in hidden, diabolical acts adds an extra layer of horror and intrigue to the Illuminati myth, making it all the more compelling for believers.

These narratives often blend together real historical facts, religious texts, and pure fantasy, creating a complex and often contradictory web of beliefs. For instance, conspiracy theorists often point to biblical passages about false prophets and the rise of the Antichrist to support their claims that the Illuminati is working toward a satanic New World Order. This mixing of religious prophecy and modern conspiracy has created a powerful framework that explains contemporary events through the lens of a cosmic battle between good and evil, with the Illuminati serving as the human agents of Satan's plan.

Moreover, the belief that many world leaders, politicians, and billionaires are secretly involved in Illuminati practices is a persistent theme. Figures such as George Soros, the Rothschild family, and members of the British royal family are frequently accused of being part of the Illuminati's satanic agenda. This claim ties into broader fears about the concentration of power in the hands of a global elite and the belief that this elite is manipulating world events to serve their own nefarious purposes. For conspiracy theorists, the Illuminati is the ultimate hidden hand behind the corruption and moral decline they see in the modern world.

While these allegations are rooted in deeply held religious and cultural anxieties, they are not based on any verifiable evidence. The historical Illuminati, as it existed in the 18th century, was a relatively small and short-lived group that promoted Enlightenment ideals of reason and secularism. There is no credible proof linking the group to Satanism or occult practices. However, the enduring power of the Illuminati myth in popular culture and conspiracy theory circles has ensured that the organization continues to be a symbol of hidden, malevolent forces at work in the world.

In the end, the portrayal of the Illuminati as a satanic force reflects broader fears about the erosion of traditional values, the rise of secularism, and the concentration of power among global elites. Whether through the spread of occult imagery, accusations of human sacrifice, or claims of ritualistic magic, the Illuminati's alleged involvement in Satanism serves as a compelling narrative for those who believe that the world is being led astray by forces of darkness. For these individuals, the battle against the Illuminati is not just a political or cultural struggle—it is a spiritual war for the soul of humanity.

The Illuminati and the Decline of Traditional Religious Authority

The Illuminati, as a symbol of subversion and secret influence, has often been blamed for the perceived decline of traditional religious authority in the modern world. While secularism, scientific advancement, and social progress have undeniably played significant roles in reshaping the cultural landscape, many conspiracy theorists point to the Illuminati as the hidden force driving this transformation. The idea that an elite, secretive group is working to weaken religious institutions and promote secularism feeds into a broader narrative of spiritual decline, where the Illuminati is seen as the orchestrator of a deliberate erosion of faith.

This belief is particularly prevalent among conservative religious communities, where the decline in church attendance, the rise of moral relativism, and the growing acceptance of secular ideologies are often viewed as signs of a broader spiritual crisis. In this context, the Illuminati serves as a convenient explanation for why these changes are happening so rapidly and pervasively. Rather than seeing these shifts as a natural outcome of modernity, proponents of this theory argue that the Illuminati is actively working to dismantle religious influence in society, creating a world where faith plays a diminished role in public and private life.

One of the key elements of this narrative is the idea that the Illuminati promotes secularism as a means of control. By weakening the influence of religion—an institution that has historically provided moral guidance and social cohesion—the Illuminati allegedly seeks to create a more fragmented, morally ambiguous society where individuals are more easily manipulated. According to this theory, religion provides a moral compass that stands in opposition to the Illuminati's goals of global dominance and the creation of a New World Order. Without the grounding influence of faith, people are thought to become more susceptible to materialism, consumerism, and hedonism—all values that, according to conspiracy theorists, the Illuminati seeks to promote.

One common theme in this line of thinking is the belief that the Illuminati uses education and media to subtly undermine religious authority. Public schools, universities, and media outlets are often accused of promoting secular values, encouraging critical thinking, and questioning religious dogma in ways that are seen as hostile to faith. These institutions, according to conspiracy theorists, are part of a larger Illuminati-controlled system designed to indoctrinate young people into a worldview that prioritizes reason and science over faith and spiritual truth. By promoting a secular, humanistic approach to knowledge and morality, the Illuminati is seen as chipping away at the foundations of religious authority.

The perceived attack on traditional values goes hand in hand with the broader cultural shifts of the 20th and 21st centuries, particularly those associated with the sexual revolution, gender equality, and the LGBTQ+ rights movement. Conspiracy theorists often interpret these changes as evidence of the Illuminati's influence, arguing that the breakdown of traditional family structures and the increasing acceptance of non-traditional lifestyles are part of a deliberate effort to weaken religious moral teachings. For instance, the legal recognition of same-sex marriage, the availability of birth control, and the broader acceptance of divorce are seen not as societal progress, but as steps toward moral decay orchestrated by the Illuminati to undermine religious principles.

Additionally, many religious conspiracy theorists argue that the rise of alternative spiritual practices—such as New Age beliefs, yoga, meditation, and other forms of non-Christian spirituality—are part of the Illuminati's plan to dilute traditional religious teachings. These practices, often associated with personal empowerment and spiritual exploration, are viewed by some as deceptive tools used to lure people away from Christianity and into a more relativistic, individualistic worldview. In this framework, the Illuminati is seen as promoting spiritual confusion, encouraging people to seek truth within themselves rather than through established religious institutions.

This narrative also ties into the broader fear of a one-world religion, a concept often discussed in evangelical Christian circles as a precursor to the rise of the Antichrist. The Illuminati, in this view, is thought to be working toward the creation of a global, unified religion that blends aspects of different faiths and spiritual practices but is ultimately devoid of true moral authority. This one-world religion is seen as a tool for controlling the masses, erasing the distinctions between faiths, and paving the way for the Antichrist to assume power in a godless, spiritually bankrupt world.

The notion that the Illuminati is behind the decline of traditional religious authority is further reinforced by the perception that many of the world's most powerful individuals and organizations are hostile to religion. Political leaders who advocate for secular governance, celebrities who promote non-religious lifestyles, and corporations that embrace progressive social causes are often accused of being part of the Illuminati's agenda to marginalize religious voices. Even the Vatican has not been immune to such accusations, with some conspiracy theorists suggesting that the Catholic Church itself has been infiltrated by the Illuminati, particularly in light of its internal scandals and shifting positions on social issues.

In this worldview, the decline of religious influence is not merely a reflection of societal change but a deliberate, orchestrated effort by the Illuminati to weaken the spiritual fabric of the world. The secularization of public life, the questioning of traditional religious teachings, and the rise of moral relativism are seen as part of a larger plot to create a more controllable, spiritually unmoored society. For believers in this conspiracy, the Illuminati's ultimate goal is to create a world where religion no longer provides a counterbalance to their power, allowing them to fully implement their New World Order without opposition from religious institutions.

What makes this theory particularly potent is its ability to resonate with real-world anxieties about the role of religion in modern life. As more people, particularly in the West, move away from organized religion and embrace secular or alternative spiritual practices, there is a growing sense among religious conservatives that their values are under siege. The Illuminati, as a symbol of hidden, malevolent forces working behind the scenes, provides a compelling explanation for why these changes are happening and why traditional religious authority seems to be losing its grip.

Ultimately, the belief that the Illuminati is responsible for the decline of traditional religious authority reflects broader fears about the changing role of faith in an increasingly secular world. While there is no evidence to suggest that the Illuminati, or any secret group, is behind these changes, the power of this narrative lies in its ability to provide a simple, cohesive explanation for complex social transformations. In a world where the influence of religion is waning and secularism is on the rise, the idea of a shadowy organization working to undermine faith offers both a sense of urgency and a call to action for those who still hold religious beliefs dear.

The Role of the Illuminati in Religious Prophecy

One of the most compelling and persistent aspects of the Illuminati myth is its connection to religious prophecy, particularly in the context of end-times scenarios. Many conspiracy theorists and religious groups view the Illuminati not only as a subversive, worldly organization but as an essential player in a divine or cosmic narrative, a precursor to the apocalyptic events foretold in religious texts. In this view, the Illuminati serves as the earthly manifestation of forces that are working against God's will, paving the way for the rise of the Antichrist and the eventual establishment of a one-world government and one-world religion—key elements of many Christian interpretations of the end times.

Central to this belief is the idea that the Illuminati is orchestrating global events to fulfill these prophecies, manipulating world leaders, governments, and institutions to align with a greater satanic agenda. According to this perspective, the Illuminati's goal is not just political or economic dominance, but the complete spiritual subjugation of humanity, leading to the final confrontation between good and evil as described in the Bible, particularly in the Book of Revelation.

For many evangelical Christians and other religious groups that hold apocalyptic views, the Illuminati's alleged actions are seen as evidence that we are living in the "last days." They argue that the organization's supposed efforts to promote secularism, moral relativism, and globalism are all part of a larger plan to destabilize the world's traditional religious and moral structures, creating the chaos necessary for the Antichrist to rise to power. This interpretation views the Illuminati as a key agent of Satan, working in concert with demonic forces to prepare the world for this ultimate showdown.

One of the primary ways in which the Illuminati is believed to be fulfilling prophecy is through its promotion of global governance. Many conspiracy theorists argue that the group's influence is behind the push for international organizations like the United Nations, the European Union, and other transnational bodies that erode national sovereignty. In their view, the establishment of a one-world government is a crucial step in the Antichrist's rise to power, as it centralizes authority and control in a way that allows for the complete domination of humanity. For those who subscribe to this theory, every step toward globalization—whether it's economic cooperation, political alliances, or the creation of global institutions—is seen as evidence of the Illuminati's progress toward their ultimate goal.

The concept of a one-world religion is also deeply intertwined with this prophetic narrative. According to conspiracy theorists, the Illuminati is working to create a global, syncretic faith that blends elements of different religions while rejecting traditional moral teachings, particularly those of Christianity. This one-world religion is often described as being rooted in New Age spirituality, occult practices, or even outright Satanism. For these theorists, the growing popularity of non-traditional spiritual practices, the increasing dialogue between world religions, and the perceived decline of Christian influence in the West are all signs that the Illuminati's plan is coming to fruition.

This belief is further reinforced by interpretations of certain symbolic events as prophetic markers. For instance, the construction of iconic buildings, political gatherings of world leaders, or major global initiatives are often seen as orchestrated by the Illuminati to align with religious prophecy. Events like the signing of global treaties, the formation of economic unions, and even the appearance of particular symbols in architecture or popular culture are interpreted as part of a deliberate, prophetic timeline.

One example often cited by conspiracy theorists is the creation of the State of Israel in 1948, an event that many see as fulfilling biblical prophecy. According to this view, the Illuminati played a hidden role in orchestrating Israel's establishment as part of a larger plan to bring about the final battle of Armageddon, which many believe will take place in the Middle East. The rise of tensions in that region, particularly between Israel and its neighbors, is frequently pointed to as evidence that the Illuminati is pushing the world toward this prophesied conflict.

In addition to Christian interpretations of prophecy, the Illuminati myth also intersects with other religious traditions. For example, some Muslim conspiracy theorists incorporate the Illuminati into their eschatological beliefs, viewing the group as a tool of the Dajjal (the Islamic equivalent of the Antichrist). Similarly, within Jewish apocalyptic thought, the Illuminati is sometimes linked to the forces of evil that will oppose the coming of the Messiah. In all of these interpretations, the Illuminati is not just a worldly organization with political ambitions, but a cosmic force playing a central role in a divine struggle.

One of the most famous symbols associated with both the Illuminati and religious prophecy is the "all-seeing eye," often depicted within a pyramid and associated with the concept of omnipresent control. For conspiracy theorists, this symbol is not only a mark of the Illuminati's influence but also a representation of their role in the fulfillment of prophecy. The eye, which can be found on the U.S. dollar bill and in numerous works of art, is often seen as a sign of the coming New World Order. Its placement in various forms of media and government insignia is interpreted as evidence that the Illuminati is signaling their control over world events and their intention to bring about the prophesied global order.

Despite the lack of concrete evidence to support these claims, the narrative of the Illuminati as a player in religious prophecy has a powerful hold on the imaginations of many believers. This is in part because it provides a clear, coherent explanation for the uncertainties and anxieties of the modern world. In a time of rapid change, social upheaval, and growing secularism, the idea that these developments are not random but part of a larger, divinely ordained plan offers a sense of understanding and, for many, a call to action.

For those who believe in this narrative, the battle against the Illuminati is not just a political or cultural fight—it is a spiritual one. The Illuminati is seen as the earthly manifestation of Satan's influence, working to deceive humanity and lead it astray. Fighting against this group, therefore, becomes a way of standing up for religious truth and preparing for the coming of Christ or the arrival of a messianic figure. This belief fuels activism among certain religious communities, who view their opposition to globalism, secularism, and moral relativism as part of their duty to resist the forces of evil at work in the world.

Ultimately, the idea that the Illuminati is fulfilling religious prophecy adds a profound spiritual dimension to the conspiracy. It transforms the group from a mere collection of elites seeking power into a key player in the cosmic struggle between good and evil. This belief not only ties the Illuminati myth to deeply rooted religious traditions but also provides a framework through which believers can interpret and respond to the changes they see happening around them.

Chapter 5: The New World Order: Fact or Fiction?

The Origins of the New World Order (NWO) Concept

The term "New World Order" (NWO) conjures images of secretive cabals, shadowy elites, and a global plot to establish one-world governance. But long before it became the stuff of conspiracy theories, the idea of a world order was rooted in political and philosophical thought, grounded in the chaos of international conflicts and the hope for lasting peace. To understand how the concept of the NWO evolved into a modern conspiracy theory, we must first trace its origins back to its intellectual and political beginnings.

The idea of a new global order emerged from the ashes of devastating wars, particularly the Napoleonic Wars in the early 19th century and the two World Wars of the 20th century. Each of these cataclysmic events shattered old systems of governance and created power vacuums that made world leaders question how to prevent further global destruction. In this context, the notion of a unified world order wasn't born out of malevolent schemes but rather from the desire to maintain international peace and stability.

One of the earliest proponents of global governance was Immanuel Kant, the 18th-century German philosopher. In his 1795 essay "Perpetual Peace," Kant laid out the idea that lasting peace could only be achieved through a federation of free states, governed by a collective set of rules that would prevent future conflicts. His vision was rooted in rationalism and the Enlightenment ideal that human progress could be achieved through reason, cooperation, and universal moral principles. Kant's work planted the seeds for the idea that some form of international cooperation or governance could be necessary to prevent wars, a theme that would later resurface in the modern New World Order debate.

Fast forward to the 20th century, and the catastrophic devastation of World War I gave rise to concrete steps toward global governance. In 1919, U.S. President Woodrow Wilson proposed the formation of the League of Nations, an international organization designed to resolve disputes between countries and prevent future conflicts. Wilson's idea, while noble, was viewed by some as the first step toward a world government—a notion that would later fuel conspiracy theories. The League of Nations ultimately failed to prevent World War II, but the idea of a global governing body took root and resurfaced in the postwar period with the creation of the United Nations in 1945.

It wasn't until the late 20th century, however, that the term "New World Order" gained prominence in the public consciousness, especially during times of global transition. One key moment came in 1991, when U.S. President George H.W. Bush used the phrase during a speech to describe the geopolitical changes occurring after the end of the Cold War. With the Soviet Union's collapse, Bush envisioned a world where the major powers would cooperate through international institutions like the United Nations to ensure peace and security, rather than rely on military dominance and ideological competition. He stated, "We have before us the opportunity to forge for ourselves and for future generations a new world order—a world where the rule of law, not the law of the jungle, governs the conduct of nations."

To many, Bush's words reflected optimism for a peaceful, cooperative global order. But for others, the phrase struck a nerve. It sounded, to conspiracy theorists, like confirmation of their long-held belief that a powerful elite was plotting to control the world. In fact, Bush's speech reignited older suspicions about globalist movements and sparked a wave of conspiracy theories that persist to this day.

The roots of the New World Order conspiracy theory can also be traced back to the writings of influential thinkers like H.G. Wells. In his 1940 book *The New World Order*, Wells, an advocate of world socialism, proposed a global government that would ensure peace and address economic inequality. While Wells' ideas were far from nefarious, his vision of centralized global authority played into fears of concentrated power, particularly among those skeptical of government control. For many, Wells' work epitomized the elitist drive toward a one-world government, even though his intentions were more utopian than sinister.

Another early influence on the NWO concept was the Illuminati, a secret society founded in Bavaria in 1776 with the aim of promoting Enlightenment ideals such as reason, secularism, and the separation of church and state. Although the Illuminati was officially disbanded after only a few decades, its reputation as a shadowy organization with hidden influence endured. Throughout the 19th and early 20th centuries, various writers and conspiracy theorists wove the Illuminati into their narratives of a global elite working behind the scenes to control governments and economies. These stories gave rise to the modern image of the Illuminati as the central force behind the NWO, often in alliance with other secretive groups like the Freemasons.

Over time, as global institutions such as the United Nations, World Bank, and International Monetary Fund (IMF) gained power and influence, the fear of a centralized world authority grew. For those skeptical of globalization and the influence of elite power structures, these organizations became symbols of a broader agenda to consolidate control at a global level, which they viewed as the unfolding of a New World Order.

In summary, the idea of a New World Order began as a noble, if idealistic, attempt to create a more peaceful and cooperative world through international governance. From Kant's philosophical musings to Wilson's League of Nations and Bush's post-Cold War optimism, the concept was rooted in efforts to prevent war and promote stability. However, as power increasingly became concentrated in global institutions, and as conspiracy theorists seized upon the language of global governance, the NWO evolved from a political vision into a symbol of hidden, malevolent control—a transformation that continues to shape its role in modern conspiracy culture.

The New World Order in Modern Conspiracy Theories

The concept of the New World Order (NWO) has been a fixture in conspiracy theory circles for decades, evolving from a political idea into a potent symbol of shadowy, elite control over global events. While the term itself may have originated in the diplomatic and philosophical discourses of world governance, it has taken on a darker, more sinister meaning within conspiracy theory narratives. Today, the NWO is synonymous with a global plot orchestrated by powerful elites to impose a one-world government, strip away individual freedoms, and establish total control over humanity. But how did this transformation take place, and why has the NWO become such a central pillar of modern conspiracy culture?

One of the key drivers of the NWO conspiracy theory is the fear of globalism—the idea that international organizations and agreements are eroding national sovereignty and pushing the world toward a single, centralized power structure. For many conspiracy theorists, the NWO is not just about political cooperation on a global scale; it is about the deliberate dismantling of national borders, traditions, and individual freedoms in favor of a totalitarian regime controlled by a small, secretive group of elites. This fear is often couched in the language of patriotism, with conspiracy theorists viewing their opposition to the NWO as a defense of national identity and personal liberty.

The John Birch Society, an influential conservative organization founded in 1958, played a pivotal role in popularizing the NWO as a conspiracy theory. The society was deeply suspicious of international organizations like the United Nations and the World Bank, which it saw as threats to American sovereignty. In their eyes, these institutions were tools of a hidden elite intent on creating a socialist one-world government. The John Birch Society's anti-globalist rhetoric gained traction during the Cold War, a period marked by heightened fears of communism and authoritarianism. The society's members believed that the NWO was part of a communist plot to subvert Western democracy, and they warned that global institutions were laying the groundwork for totalitarian control.

Throughout the latter half of the 20th century, the New World Order conspiracy theory continued to evolve and gain new adherents. The collapse of the Soviet Union in 1991, and the subsequent geopolitical shift, provided fertile ground for NWO conspiracies to flourish. When President George H.W. Bush used the term "New World Order" in his speeches about the post-Cold War world, conspiracy theorists latched onto it as confirmation of their worst fears. Bush's vision of a more cooperative and interconnected world, governed by international law and organizations, was interpreted as evidence that the elites were moving toward the creation of a one-world government. This interpretation was reinforced by the growing influence of global financial institutions like the International Monetary Fund (IMF) and the World Trade Organization (WTO), which were seen as key players in the alleged NWO agenda.

As the internet became more accessible in the 1990s and 2000s, it provided a platform for conspiracy theorists to spread their ideas to a wider audience. The rise of alternative media outlets, message boards, and later, social media, created a fertile environment for the NWO conspiracy to thrive. Online communities formed around these theories, allowing like-minded individuals to share information, analyze world events through the lens of the NWO, and recruit new believers. The internet democratized conspiracy theories, making it easier for individuals to produce and disseminate content that aligned with their beliefs, often without the need for traditional gatekeepers like publishers or media networks.

One of the most influential figures in the modern NWO conspiracy movement is Alex Jones, a radio host and conspiracy theorist who has built a massive following through his website *Infowars* and various media channels. Jones has consistently warned his audience about the impending rise of the New World Order, framing global events—ranging from economic crises to natural disasters—as evidence of a coordinated plot by elites to gain control over humanity. His incendiary rhetoric, combined with his use of fear-mongering tactics, has drawn millions of listeners who view him as a whistleblower exposing the hidden truths behind world events. Jones frequently links the NWO conspiracy to other popular conspiracy theories, such as those involving the Illuminati, Freemasonry, and secret government programs like MKUltra.

In addition to alternative media figures like Jones, popular culture has also played a role in shaping and perpetuating the NWO conspiracy. Movies, television shows, and books often feature plotlines involving secret government cabals, global conspiracies, and dystopian futures ruled by authoritarian regimes. Films like *The Matrix* and *V for Vendetta* tap into the fears of a world controlled by unseen forces, resonating with audiences who already suspect that the New World Order is not just fiction, but an unfolding reality. These cultural touchstones provide a familiar narrative framework for conspiracy theorists to interpret real-world events, reinforcing their belief that the NWO is lurking just beneath the surface.

A significant factor contributing to the persistence of the New World Order conspiracy theory is its flexibility. The NWO can be adapted to fit almost any political, social, or economic crisis. Whether it's the 9/11 attacks, the 2008 financial crisis, or the COVID-19 pandemic, conspiracy theorists are quick to link these events to the NWO. In their view, these crises are either manufactured or exploited by global elites to advance their agenda of centralizing power and control. For instance, during the COVID-19 pandemic, conspiracy theorists claimed that the virus was either a hoax or a bioweapon created to justify lockdowns, vaccine mandates, and other measures designed to limit personal freedoms—measures they saw as steps toward the implementation of the New World Order.

This ability to absorb new events and crises into the NWO framework ensures that the theory remains relevant, regardless of the political or social landscape. It also allows believers to interpret complex world events through a single, unifying narrative. Rather than viewing global problems as the result of multiple factors—such as economics, politics, and cultural shifts—the NWO conspiracy offers a simpler explanation: everything is being orchestrated by a hidden elite for their own gain. This narrative provides a sense of clarity and control in a world that often seems chaotic and unpredictable.

In conclusion, the New World Order conspiracy theory has grown from a niche belief to a central pillar of modern conspiracy culture. Fueled by fears of globalization, the erosion of national sovereignty, and the influence of global elites, the NWO has become a powerful narrative that shapes the way millions of people view world events. As the internet and alternative media continue to amplify these theories, the NWO remains a potent and adaptable idea, capable of incorporating new crises and reinforcing the belief that global elites are working behind the scenes to create a one-world government.

Globalization and the Fear of Elite Control

At the heart of the New World Order (NWO) conspiracy theory lies a deep-seated fear of globalization and elite control. While globalization—the increasing interconnectedness of nations through trade, communication, and technology—has brought undeniable economic growth and cultural exchange, it has also sparked anxiety about the loss of national sovereignty and the consolidation of power in the hands of a few. This fear is a cornerstone of NWO conspiracies, which claim that a powerful global elite is using economic and political systems to manipulate and dominate the world.

Globalization, in its simplest form, refers to the growing interdependence of countries, facilitated by international trade agreements, multinational corporations, and global institutions like the United Nations, the World Trade Organization (WTO), and the International Monetary Fund (IMF). These entities are seen by many as mechanisms for cooperation, designed to manage global economic stability, resolve conflicts, and promote human rights. However, conspiracy theorists view them through a far darker lens. To those who believe in the NWO, these global organizations are not benign forces of international diplomacy but are rather tools of control, de-

signed to weaken individual nations and subjugate populations under a unified, authoritarian regime.

The crux of this fear centers on the idea that globalization allows
an elite few—typically wealthy business magnates, powerful politicians, and influential financiers—to control the fate of nations. In
this view, globalization is not about mutual benefit or international
cooperation but is rather a carefully orchestrated scheme by the ruling elite to consolidate power. Conspiracy theorists often cite organizations like the Bilderberg Group, the Trilateral Commission,
and the World Economic Forum as proof that an international cabal
of elites is working together to shape global policy and ensure their
dominance over the world's political and economic systems.

The Bilderberg Group, in particular, has become a frequent target in NWO conspiracies. Founded in 1954, the Bilderberg Group is
an annual private conference attended by political leaders, business
executives, academics, and media figures from Europe and North
America. The group's meetings are held behind closed doors, with
participants discussing a wide range of global issues, from economic
policy to international security. While the Bilderberg Group insists
that its meetings are simply informal, off-the-record discussions
meant to foster dialogue between Europe and North America, conspiracy theorists view it as a shadowy organization where the world's
most powerful figures secretly plot the future of the planet. The
group's secrecy has fueled speculation that its members are orchestrating the New World Order, with the ultimate goal of creating a
one-world government controlled by elites.

Similar fears are directed toward the Trilateral Commission, a
nongovernmental organization founded in 1973 by David Rockefeller to encourage cooperation among North America, Europe, and
Japan. Like the Bilderberg Group, the Trilateral Commission is accused of being a front for global elites, using its influence to shape

international policies and weaken the power of individual nations. Conspiracy theorists often claim that the commission is part of a larger strategy to merge nations into regional blocks, which would eventually be subsumed into a global governing structure. The European Union, for instance, is frequently cited as an example of this alleged regional consolidation, with the United Nations ultimately serving as the world's governing body in the New World Order framework.

One of the major fears surrounding globalization is the perceived loss of national sovereignty. For many, particularly those who hold nationalist or populist views, global institutions like the United Nations, the IMF, and the World Bank are seen as threats to a country's autonomy. The notion that international bodies could impose laws, regulations, or economic policies on sovereign nations is a powerful narrative within the NWO conspiracy theory. This fear has been particularly strong in the United States, where concerns about UN-imposed restrictions on gun ownership, environmental regulations, or even military action have circulated for decades. Conspiracy theorists claim that these global organizations are gradually eroding the power of national governments, preparing the way for a single world government that will impose its will on every nation.

Economic institutions, such as the IMF and World Bank, are also seen as critical components of the alleged NWO agenda. These organizations, which provide financial assistance to countries in need, are viewed by conspiracy theorists as tools of control. They argue that by offering loans and economic aid to struggling nations, the IMF and World Bank are able to impose harsh conditions—such as austerity measures, privatization, and deregulation—that weaken the recipient countries' economic independence. In this narrative, the ultimate goal is to create a global economic system that benefits the elites while keeping the masses in perpetual debt and dependency. These financial structures, according to conspiracy theorists, are designed to ensure that the world's wealth remains concentrated in the hands of a small group of globalists who control the financial institutions.

The role of multinational corporations in the New World Order conspiracy is another critical aspect of the fear of globalization. Large corporations, particularly tech giants, pharmaceutical companies, and financial institutions, are seen as central to the alleged NWO plan. Conspiracy theorists argue that these corporations, in collusion with governments and global organizations, are working to suppress individual freedoms and manipulate markets for their own gain. The rise of companies like Google, Facebook, and Amazon, with their vast data collection practices, has only deepened suspicions that these corporations are not just economic entities but instruments of social control. By gathering and analyzing data on billions of people, these corporations are seen as aiding the NWO's efforts to monitor, influence, and ultimately control the global population.

The fear of elite control through globalization is also fueled by real-world concerns about wealth inequality and corporate influence on politics. The gap between the rich and the poor has been widening for decades, with a small percentage of the global population controlling a disproportionate share of wealth and resources. This economic disparity is often cited by conspiracy theorists as evidence of the NWO in action, with the elite few tightening their grip on the world's resources while the majority are left behind. The influence of corporate money in politics—particularly in the United States, where political campaigns are often heavily funded by wealthy donors and corporations—further amplifies the belief that a small group of elites is pulling the strings behind the scenes.

In conclusion, the fear of globalization and elite control is a central element of the New World Order conspiracy theory. For those who believe in the NWO, globalization is not a path toward international cooperation but a deliberate strategy by powerful elites to consolidate control over the world's political and economic systems. From the influence of multinational corporations and global financial institutions to the perceived erosion of national sovereignty, the NWO conspiracy taps into deep anxieties about the loss of autonomy and the concentration of power in the hands of a few. While globalization has undoubtedly transformed the world, for conspiracy theorists, it is evidence of an impending global dictatorship orchestrated by a secretive elite.

Political Manipulation and the New World Order

A central tenet of the New World Order (NWO) conspiracy theory is the idea that global elites are using political manipulation to reshape world events in their favor. Proponents of this theory argue that influential leaders, organizations, and even entire governments are under the control of hidden forces working to establish a centralized world government. The narrative posits that this manipulation occurs not through overt means but rather through covert strategies, orchestrating conflicts, economic crises, and social upheavals to destabilize societies and justify the need for global governance.

For many believers in the NWO, political manipulation is visible in major world events, from wars to economic downturns to environmental crises. The theory asserts that these events are not random but are part of a broader agenda to create chaos, fear, and instability. According to this view, by destabilizing nations and creating global problems, the elites can position themselves as the solution, offering a one-world government as the only means of restoring order and security.

One of the most enduring elements of the NWO conspiracy is the belief that wars and military interventions are engineered by elites for profit and control. In this view, conflicts are not driven by legitimate geopolitical concerns or ideological differences but are instead planned by global elites to advance their agenda. The military-industrial complex—a term popularized by U.S. President Dwight D. Eisenhower in his 1961 farewell address—plays a central role in this theory. Conspiracy theorists argue that powerful corporations and financial interests benefit from wars, as they fuel the arms industry, increase government debt, and destabilize regions, making them ripe for global governance intervention.

The Gulf War in the early 1990s, for instance, is often cited as an example of this manipulation. When President George H.W. Bush referred to a "new world order" in speeches leading up to and during the conflict, conspiracy theorists interpreted his words as confirmation of their worst fears. They argued that the war was not merely about liberating Kuwait or containing Saddam Hussein's aggression but was part of a larger strategy to reshape the Middle East and expand global control. Similar claims have been made about subsequent U.S. military interventions, particularly in Iraq and Afghanistan, where conspiracy theorists suggest that the wars were orchestrated to secure oil, resources, or geopolitical power for the elites.

Economic manipulation is another key component of the NWO conspiracy theory. Many believe that financial crises, such as the 2008 global recession, are not accidental but are engineered to serve the interests of the global elite. According to this theory, financial institutions, central banks, and multinational corporations collude to create boom-and-bust cycles, destabilizing economies and causing widespread unemployment, poverty, and hardship. In times of economic crisis, governments are often forced to take extreme measures, such as bailouts, austerity programs, or even nationalization of industries—policies that conspiracy theorists argue are designed to centralize power and wealth.

The 2008 financial crisis, which resulted in the collapse of major financial institutions and led to a global recession, has been a focal point for NWO conspiracy theorists. They claim that the crisis was deliberately triggered by financial elites to bring about a restructuring of the global economy. The bailout of major banks, for instance, is seen as evidence that these institutions wield disproportionate influence over governments, controlling not only economic policies but also the fates of entire nations. The subsequent rise in unemployment, home foreclosures, and debt across the globe is viewed as part of the elites' strategy to weaken national economies and push for a global financial system that they control.

Conspiracy theorists also point to international organizations like the World Bank and the International Monetary Fund (IMF) as tools of economic manipulation. These institutions, which provide financial assistance to developing nations in the form of loans, are often accused of imposing harsh economic conditions in return for their aid. Critics argue that the austerity measures, structural adjustments, and privatization programs mandated by the IMF and World Bank lead to greater poverty, social unrest, and a loss of sovereignty. In the eyes of NWO theorists, these financial institutions are working to bring weaker nations into a global economic system that serves the interests of the elite, at the expense of ordinary citizens.

Political manipulation is also seen in efforts to influence global policy through climate change initiatives and environmental regulation. While climate change is widely accepted by the scientific community as a serious threat, conspiracy theorists argue that environmental concerns are being exaggerated or even fabricated to justify global governance. In this narrative, climate change is framed as a crisis engineered by elites to impose strict environmental regulations, carbon taxes, and energy controls, which in turn would centralize power in international organizations like the United Nations.

They claim that by creating a sense of impending ecological disaster, the elites can manipulate public opinion and convince people that global cooperation—and thus a one-world government—is the only solution.

The Paris Agreement, an international treaty on climate change adopted in 2015, is frequently cited by NWO conspiracy theorists as evidence of this manipulation. They argue that the agreement's goals—such as reducing greenhouse gas emissions and transitioning to renewable energy—are not about protecting the environment but about controlling the global economy and limiting the freedoms of nations and individuals. In their view, the real agenda behind climate action is to impose regulations that benefit multinational corporations and global financial institutions, while diminishing the power of national governments and small businesses.

In addition to manipulating policy through crises, NWO theorists believe that global elites use political organizations and secret societies to infiltrate governments and influence decision-making. Groups like the Bilderberg Group, the Trilateral Commission, and the Council on Foreign Relations are seen as behind-the-scenes power brokers that direct the policies of nations, particularly the United States. Conspiracy theorists argue that members of these organizations are embedded in key political positions and work in concert to shape foreign and domestic policies in ways that advance the NWO agenda. These secret meetings, attended by politicians, business leaders, and academics, are viewed not as benign discussions of world issues but as orchestrated gatherings where the fate of nations is decided without public knowledge or consent.

In conclusion, political manipulation plays a pivotal role in the New World Order conspiracy theory. Through orchestrated conflicts, economic crises, environmental policies, and secret organizations, global elites are believed to be working behind the scenes to destabilize nations and consolidate power. By creating fear and chaos, they seek to position themselves as the solution, ultimately leading to the imposition of a one-world government. Though the specifics of these conspiracies vary, they all share a common belief: that the political events shaping our world are not random, but part of a larger, hidden plan to control the future of humanity.

The Role of Technology in the New World Order

One of the most prominent and rapidly evolving elements of the New World Order (NWO) conspiracy theory is the role that technology plays in global control. As technological advancements accelerate, conspiracy theorists increasingly point to digital surveillance, artificial intelligence (AI), and centralized data systems as key tools in the alleged effort by elites to control populations. According to this view, the technological innovations that promise convenience, security, and connection are, in reality, part of a vast infrastructure designed to monitor and manipulate the lives of ordinary citizens.

Central to this belief is the idea that the global elite, including governments, multinational corporations, and intelligence agencies, are working in concert to create a "surveillance state." This concept refers to the pervasive use of technology to collect and analyze data on individuals, tracking their movements, communications, and even thoughts. From internet browsing habits to location data from smartphones, every digital interaction is seen as a potential means for elites to gather information, predict behavior, and ultimately exert control.

One of the most cited examples of this surveillance infrastructure is the rise of big tech companies like Google, Facebook, and Amazon, which have become synonymous with data collection. These companies gather immense amounts of personal information from their users, including search histories, social media activity, purchases, and even biometric data through facial recognition and voice assistants. While tech firms argue that this data collection improves user experience, conspiracy theorists claim it is part of a broader agenda to monitor individuals and influence their decisions. The fear is that this data can be weaponized—used by governments or corporations to control behavior, influence elections, or suppress dissent.

The revelations by former NSA contractor Edward Snowden in 2013, which exposed the U.S. government's mass surveillance programs, have added fuel to these fears. Snowden's leaks revealed that the National Security Agency (NSA) was collecting phone records, emails, and other forms of digital communication from millions of people around the world. This level of surveillance confirmed, for many believers in the NWO, that governments are deeply embedded in a global surveillance network. The extent of these operations, which were carried out with the cooperation of major tech companies, reinforced the idea that a secret alliance between state actors and private corporations is building a digital panopticon, where no individual is beyond the reach of surveillance.

In the view of NWO theorists, this surveillance is not limited to monitoring but also extends to the manipulation of thoughts and actions. The rise of AI and algorithms is seen as a tool for controlling the narrative, particularly through social media platforms. Platforms like Facebook and Twitter use algorithms to curate what content users see, which conspiracy theorists argue can be manipulated to shape public opinion, suppress dissenting views, and promote propaganda favorable to the global elites. AI systems that analyze vast amounts of data to predict behavior are seen as part of a broader strategy to control populations, with the end goal being a society where individuals have little to no autonomy over their thoughts or decisions.

Another technology often cited in NWO conspiracies is microchip implants and biometric identification systems. Some theorists believe that the global elite's ultimate plan is to create a cashless society, where all transactions are conducted electronically and every individual is identified by a microchip or biometric marker. This fear is frequently linked to concerns about digital currencies and central bank digital currencies (CBDCs). Proponents of the NWO theory argue that by eliminating physical currency and moving to a fully digital system, governments and corporations would have unprecedented control over people's finances, monitoring every transaction and potentially limiting access to funds for those who resist their agenda.

The idea of microchipping gained significant attention with the rise of technologies like radio-frequency identification (RFID) chips, which are already used in everything from pets to passports. Conspiracy theorists suggest that similar technologies will one day be implanted in humans, allowing elites to track individuals, control their finances, and even monitor their health. While RFID chips are currently used for relatively benign purposes, such as identification and logistics, theorists argue that these chips could be adapted for more nefarious purposes in the future, tying into fears of a dystopian future where individuals have no privacy or freedom from surveillance.

Biometric identification, which includes technologies such as facial recognition, fingerprint scanners, and iris scanning, is another concern. While these technologies are promoted as ways to improve security and streamline processes, such as airport check-ins or unlocking smartphones, conspiracy theorists argue that they are part of a broader agenda to build a global identification system. The ultimate fear is that these systems will be used to track and control individuals on a global scale, with a one-world government having the power to grant or restrict access to services based on compliance with its agenda.

A major focal point for conspiracy theorists is the introduction of 5G technology. The rapid rollout of 5G networks has sparked widespread concern, particularly among NWO believers, who argue that 5G is not just about faster internet speeds but about creating a network capable of real-time surveillance and control. The theory posits that 5G towers are part of an infrastructure that will allow elites to monitor every aspect of individuals' lives, from their physical location to their online activity. In some of the more extreme versions of the conspiracy, 5G is linked to mind control, with the claim that the technology can be used to influence human thoughts and behavior through electromagnetic waves.

Another significant concern within the NWO framework is the growing use of drones, robots, and autonomous technology for surveillance and control. Drones equipped with cameras and facial recognition software are already used for security purposes by governments and corporations. Conspiracy theorists, however, argue that these technologies could be used to monitor protests, track dissidents, and enforce laws in a future global police state. Similarly, the rise of robotic and autonomous systems in law enforcement and the military is seen as a sign that elites are preparing for a future where human soldiers and police are replaced by machines, which will be programmed to follow the orders of the global elite without question.

One of the more recent developments feeding into the NWO conspiracy is the use of digital health passports and contact tracing during the COVID-19 pandemic. Conspiracy theorists claim that these systems, which were implemented to track the spread of the virus and ensure compliance with health measures, are precursors to more invasive tracking systems. They argue that digital health passports, which store personal health information such as vaccination status, could be expanded to include other personal data, becoming a tool for monitoring movement and behavior on a global scale.

In conclusion, technology plays a crucial role in the New World Order conspiracy theory, acting as both a tool of surveillance and a mechanism for control. From the rise of AI and big data to fears about microchips, digital currencies, and 5G, believers in the NWO see technology as the key to the elites' plan to create a global dictatorship. While many of these technologies are designed to improve convenience, security, and efficiency, in the eyes of conspiracy theorists, they represent the foundation of a dystopian future where every action, thought, and decision is monitored, manipulated, and controlled by a hidden global elite.

Chapter 6: Illuminati in Popular Culture

The Birth of the Illuminati in Modern Pop Culture

The transition of the Illuminati from a historical secret society into a dominant figure in modern pop culture is a fascinating journey. While the Bavarian Illuminati officially dissolved in the late 18th century, its legacy survived through various conspiracy theories. However, it was not until the 20th century that the Illuminati truly began to embed itself into the cultural imagination. This shift was influenced by a growing interest in secret societies, political conspiracies, and the idea that unseen forces were shaping world events. In particular, the Illuminati myth found fertile ground in literature, which became a launching pad for its entrance into broader pop culture.

One of the early works that helped bring the concept of the Illuminati to a wider audience was Robert Shea and Robert Anton Wilson's *The Illuminatus! Trilogy* (1975). This satirical science fiction series blended real historical events with wild conspiracy theories, including the idea that the Illuminati was secretly controlling the world. Though the trilogy was intended to be humorous and exaggerated, its exploration of the Illuminati as a powerful, omnipresent force struck a chord with readers. The book series became a cult favorite, sparking curiosity and discussion about secret societies, and laying the groundwork for the idea that the Illuminati was not only real but also influential in shaping global events.

Another pivotal moment came with Dan Brown's novel *Angels & Demons* (2000), which took the Illuminati from the fringes of conspiracy theory culture and thrust it into the mainstream. Brown's book, a fast-paced thriller set against the backdrop of Vatican City, centered on the Illuminati's supposed revenge plot against the Catholic Church. While *Angels & Demons* was fictional, its intricate blending of historical facts, art, science, and religious symbolism captivated millions of readers. The Illuminati's portrayal as a shadowy organization seeking to influence the future of mankind resonated with a public that was increasingly skeptical of political and religious institutions. The novel's success, along with its film adaptation in 2009, turned the Illuminati from a fringe belief into a mainstream cultural symbol, fueling a modern fascination with the idea of secret elites controlling world events.

These works, and others like them, contributed to the development of a modern-day mythology surrounding the Illuminati. In many ways, the transition from a historical group of Enlightenment thinkers to a nefarious force pulling the strings of global power reflected broader societal anxieties. In the 20th and early 21st centuries, rapid technological advancements, political upheaval, and global economic shifts left many people feeling that unseen forces were at work behind the scenes. The Illuminati, as portrayed in these works of fiction, became a perfect symbol for those anxieties—a stand-in for the fear that the world was being controlled by an elite few whose motives were hidden from the public eye.

The rise of the internet in the late 20th century provided yet another platform for the Illuminati myth to spread. As online communities formed, conspiracy theories about secret societies gained new life. Forums and early websites allowed people to exchange ideas, debate, and explore the idea that the Illuminati was still active and influential. What had once been the realm of literature and occasional speculation in political or religious circles became a burgeoning online phenomenon, as people started to create their own theories and link current events to the actions of the Illuminati.

By the 1990s and early 2000s, the Illuminati had become a cultural touchstone, appearing not just in books and films but also in television shows, music videos, and video games. Shows like *The X-Files* tapped into the public's growing fascination with hidden powers and secret plots, often referencing secret organizations like the Illuminati as potential forces behind the strange events portrayed. The Illuminati began to show up in unlikely places, from casual mentions in late-night television monologues to serious discussions in political and academic circles about the influence of elites and the growing power of global organizations.

One of the key reasons the Illuminati myth took such a strong hold in pop culture was its adaptability. It could be whatever the storyteller needed it to be—an ancient brotherhood of enlightened thinkers, a modern-day cabal of wealthy elites, or even a puppet master pulling the strings of governments and corporations. Its flexibility allowed it to fit into nearly any narrative, from historical thrillers to contemporary conspiracy theories about the military-industrial complex or global finance.

In sum, the birth of the Illuminati in modern pop culture was the result of several converging forces: a long-standing fascination with secret societies, growing distrust of political and economic systems, and the power of literature, film, and media to shape collective imagination. What began as a fringe belief in an obscure group of 18th-century intellectuals transformed into a ubiquitous cultural symbol, one that still resonates in popular culture today. The Illuminati myth tapped into deep-seated fears and uncertainties, providing a narrative that explained the complexities of modern life through the lens of conspiracy, secrecy, and control. This fusion of historical fact, fiction, and modern anxieties created a fertile ground for the Illuminati to flourish as a powerful, adaptable figure in pop culture.

The Illuminati and Music Industry Allegations

In the early 21st century, a new frontier for Illuminati conspiracy theories emerged: the music industry. Suddenly, some of the world's most famous artists—ranging from hip-hop icons to pop superstars—became embroiled in rumors and accusations that they were part of the secretive, all-powerful Illuminati. These theories spread rapidly across social media, with fans, critics, and conspiracy theorists alike scrutinizing music videos, album covers, lyrics, and even hand gestures for signs of Illuminati influence. The music industry, with its high-profile celebrities and vast cultural reach, became fertile ground for these claims, turning the Illuminati from a niche historical topic into a mainstream phenomenon.

One of the central reasons the Illuminati became tied to the music industry was the alleged use of occult and Illuminati symbols in music videos and performances. Symbols like the all-seeing eye, pyramids, and the number 666 were frequently cited as evidence that certain artists were either members of the Illuminati or somehow connected to it. For instance, the "all-seeing eye," often depicted inside a pyramid, was said to be a hallmark of the Illuminati. This symbol's origins, which date back to ancient Egypt and were later adopted into the design of the U.S. dollar bill, became a centerpiece for conspiracy theorists who believed it signaled the artist's allegiance to the secret society.

Jay-Z, one of the most successful and influential figures in hip-hop, became a focal point for these conspiracy theories. His use of the "Roc-A-Fella diamond" hand gesture, which involves forming a triangle with both hands, was frequently interpreted as a subtle nod to the Illuminati's pyramid symbol. While Jay-Z has long insisted that the gesture represents his Roc-A-Fella Records label, conspiracy theorists saw something more sinister. His immense wealth, influence in the music industry, and connections to other powerful figures were all cited as "evidence" that he was part of a global elite pulling the strings behind the scenes.

Beyoncé, Jay-Z's wife and another global superstar, also found herself at the center of Illuminati allegations. Conspiracy theorists pointed to her music videos, particularly those for songs like "Run the World (Girls)" and "Formation," which featured imagery that was interpreted as Illuminati symbols. The fact that Beyoncé is often referred to as "Queen Bey" and hailed as pop music royalty only fueled these claims. For many conspiracy theorists, her massive success and dominance in the entertainment world could not be the result of mere talent and hard work—it had to be the product of some secret pact with the Illuminati. Her 2016 Super Bowl performance, which featured military-style costumes and precision choreography, was picked apart online, with some arguing it was full of occult symbols and hidden messages.

Kanye West, another towering figure in the music industry, also became embroiled in Illuminati conspiracy theories. His dramatic persona, outspokenness, and frequent references to power and influence in his music provided ample fodder for theorists. His 2010 song "Power" was seen by some as a declaration of his ties to the Illuminati, with its lyrics discussing fame, control, and influence. The music video for "Power" featured Kanye standing beneath a glowing halo, surrounded by mythical and religious imagery, which many took as confirmation that he was portraying himself as an Illuminati figure. In interviews, Kanye has addressed the Illuminati rumors, often dismissing them as absurd, but they continue to follow him, particularly after his more controversial public statements and actions.

Rihanna, another artist frequently linked to the Illuminati, faced similar scrutiny. Her music videos, especially for songs like "Umbrella" and "Diamonds," were picked apart for supposed Illuminati symbolism. In the "Umbrella" video, some conspiracy theorists claimed that Rihanna was depicted in a ritualistic pose, suggesting a connection to occult practices. Her frequent use of triangles and eyes in visual content was cited as further evidence of her involvement. Despite Rihanna's repeated dismissals of these rumors, the narrative persisted, fueled in part by her public image as a confident, powerful woman who rose quickly to superstardom.

These Illuminati accusations in the music industry weren't confined to just a few artists—they became a widespread phenomenon. Virtually any successful musician, particularly those who achieved rapid fame, became a target for these theories. Lady Gaga, Madonna, Justin Bieber, and even newer artists like Billie Eilish and Lil Nas X have been linked to the Illuminati by conspiracy theorists, who often cite their bold imagery, use of provocative symbols, and commercial success as proof. The internet, particularly platforms like YouTube, became a breeding ground for elaborate breakdowns of music videos, with self-proclaimed "researchers" dissecting every frame for signs of Illuminati influence.

Interestingly, many artists have played into these theories, either as a way to mock the absurdity of the claims or to use them for publicity. Jay-Z and Kanye West, for example, have both referenced the Illuminati rumors in their lyrics, poking fun at the idea that they are part of a secret society. Beyoncé's 2013 song "Formation" directly addressed some of the rumors, with lyrics that seemed to challenge those who believe she's involved in something nefarious. Other artists have embraced the imagery associated with the Illuminati—using triangles, pyramids, and the all-seeing eye in their performances and videos as a way to generate buzz and keep fans talking.

What's clear is that the Illuminati conspiracy has become an inextricable part of how we view certain celebrities. For some fans, these theories add an extra layer of intrigue and mystery to their favorite artists. For others, they represent genuine belief that powerful forces are manipulating global culture. Regardless, the connection between the Illuminati and the music industry continues to captivate the public imagination, with each new artist or music video serving as a potential sign of hidden influence.

In the end, whether as a marketing strategy or a symbol of genuine belief in unseen power, the Illuminati's connection to the music industry has cemented itself in popular culture. For those who believe the conspiracy, it's a sign that even the music we listen to is being used to subtly manipulate and control the masses. For artists and fans alike, however, it's just another aspect of the spectacle and drama that defines the modern music industry. Either way, the Illuminati remains a central figure in the ongoing narrative of fame, power, and influence in the world of music.

The Illuminati in Film and Television

The portrayal of the Illuminati in film and television has been one of the most enduring ways the conspiracy has infiltrated popular culture. Over the past few decades, the idea of a secret society controlling world events has become a common trope in both genres, often depicted as a shadowy, all-powerful organization with mysterious rituals and vast influence. Whether in blockbuster movies or long-running TV series, the Illuminati is consistently presented as an unseen force, pulling the strings behind major global events. This portrayal has helped cement the idea in the public's mind, blending fiction with the lingering suspicions that some unseen elite may indeed be guiding the course of history.

One of the most notable examples of the Illuminati's influence in film is *Angels & Demons* (2009), the film adaptation of Dan Brown's novel. In the movie, the Illuminati is depicted as a centuries-old enemy of the Catholic Church, bent on seeking revenge and destabilizing its influence. The film follows Harvard symbologist Robert Langdon as he uncovers clues that suggest the Illuminati is behind a series of murders and threats against the Vatican. Through its dramatic storyline, the film presents the Illuminati as a sophisticated organization with deep roots in both history and modern power structures, capable of orchestrating grand-scale schemes that threaten the very fabric of society. This cinematic portrayal further fueled public fascination with the Illuminati, blending historical fact with fiction in a way that made the conspiracy theory feel plausible to many viewers.

Another major contribution to the Illuminati's presence in film came from *National Treasure* (2004) and its sequel *National Treasure: Book of Secrets* (2007). While the films focus more broadly on secret societies and hidden knowledge, there are several references that nod toward the Illuminati, particularly through the use of symbols like the all-seeing eye and pyramids. The films explore themes of secret historical organizations guarding untold power and influence, and the central characters are often seen uncovering clues that suggest these groups have played a pivotal role in shaping the course of history. Though the Illuminati isn't explicitly named, the idea of powerful, secretive elites manipulating historical events aligns closely with the myth. These movies, intended as adventure stories, helped to further propagate the idea that the Illuminati could be real, deeply ingrained in historical mysteries and hidden truths.

Beyond film, television shows have also played a significant role in perpetuating Illuminati myths. One of the most influential TV shows to engage with conspiracy theories, including those related to secret societies, was *The X-Files* (1993–2018). The show's portrayal of hidden government conspiracies, alien cover-ups, and secretive groups pulling the strings of power captivated audiences for years. Although the show did not focus solely on the Illuminati, it often implied that shadowy organizations, similar in structure and influence, were behind the global manipulation of events. In *The X-Files*, the Illuminati-like groups were portrayed as almost omnipotent, using their wealth and connections to keep the truth hidden from the public. The show's eerie, mysterious tone, combined with the public's growing distrust of government institutions, made it the perfect medium for exploring themes of secret power, contributing to the Illuminati's rise in popular culture.

In more recent years, the Illuminati has also found its way into a variety of mainstream television shows, including *American Horror Story: Cult* (2017). In this season of the show, secret societies and their influence on political and social movements are a central theme. Although the storyline doesn't focus specifically on the Illuminati, it does explore the psychological impact of believing in unseen powers controlling the world. The season's portrayal of political cults and the ways in which fear can be manipulated by those in power resonated with contemporary concerns about hidden elites and government corruption, adding yet another layer to the ongoing fascination with conspiracies like the Illuminati.

The animated TV series *Gravity Falls* (2012–2016), while a children's show, also played with Illuminati imagery in a more lighthearted, satirical way. The show's main villain, Bill Cipher, is depicted as a one-eyed triangular being, resembling the all-seeing eye often associated with the Illuminati. Though intended as a joke, the use of these symbols in a widely popular children's series shows how deeply embedded the Illuminati's imagery has become in entertainment. Even in a show that is primarily comedic, the use of Illuminati-like symbols further normalizes the presence of these conspiracy theories in everyday culture, making them part of the fabric of how we view hidden powers.

What makes the Illuminati such an appealing trope for filmmakers and TV creators is its inherent mystery and the built-in audience fascination with the unknown. The idea of a secret organization pulling the strings of global power taps into a universal fear that the world is not as it seems—that unseen forces are shaping the future in ways that ordinary people cannot control or even comprehend. These fears are amplified in times of political or economic instability, and the portrayal of the Illuminati as the villain in many of these narratives provides a convenient explanation for complex problems. Instead of confronting the randomness and uncertainty of global events, films and TV shows offer the Illuminati as the mastermind behind it all, turning chaos into a controlled, if malevolent, order.

However, these portrayals also serve to blur the line between fact and fiction. Audiences are often left wondering how much of what they see is purely entertainment, and how much might be rooted in reality. By consistently portraying the Illuminati as a secretive organization with vast control, films and TV shows contribute to the persistence of conspiracy theories in the public imagination. For some viewers, these depictions become more than just entertainment—they serve as confirmation of their belief that a shadowy elite is orchestrating world events from behind the scenes.

In sum, the Illuminati's presence in film and television has been instrumental in cementing the conspiracy theory as a permanent fixture in popular culture. By portraying the Illuminati as a powerful, all-knowing force capable of influencing everything from politics to the media, these portrayals feed into deep-seated anxieties about power, control, and the unseen forces that shape our world. Whether intended as satire, entertainment, or social commentary, the consistent use of Illuminati themes in film and television has ensured that this once-obscure secret society remains a potent symbol of mystery and fear in the modern age.

The Role of Social Media in Spreading Illuminati Theories

In the age of social media, the spread of Illuminati conspiracy theories has taken on a new dimension. Platforms like YouTube, Twitter, Instagram, and Facebook have become breeding grounds for the rapid dissemination of these ideas, allowing them to reach a wider and more diverse audience than ever before. What once may have been relegated to obscure websites or late-night radio shows has now become mainstream content, readily available at the tap of a screen. Through memes, viral videos, and dedicated conspiracy forums, the Illuminati has been reborn as an omnipresent force in online culture, where fact and fiction often blur in a sea of speculation.

One of the key drivers behind the Illuminati's resurgence on social media has been YouTube. Since its inception, the platform has allowed users to create and share videos on any topic, and conspiracy theories quickly found a home there. Some of the most popular Illuminati-related videos are presented as exposés, claiming to reveal the secret symbols, codes, and messages allegedly hidden in plain sight. For instance, music videos, award show performances, and celebrity interviews are scrutinized frame-by-frame for evidence of Illuminati involvement. These videos often claim to "decode" the imagery and hand gestures used by public figures, tying them to ancient occult practices and Illuminati symbolism. Videos that show Beyoncé flashing an apparent triangle hand sign or Katy Perry dressed as an Egyptian goddess in her "Dark Horse" music video have garnered millions of views, with many users commenting that these visuals confirm the artists' allegiance to the Illuminati.

The beauty of social media, for conspiracy theorists, is its ability to rapidly spread content. A well-crafted Illuminati theory on YouTube can be watched, shared, and discussed by millions of people worldwide within hours. Algorithms on platforms like YouTube or TikTok even help boost such content, as sensational and controversial material often gets high engagement rates, prompting the platforms to promote it to more users. In many cases, individuals come across these videos by accident, as part of a recommendation chain, and become intrigued by the idea of hidden truths and secret societies. The visual format of YouTube makes these theories feel compelling and accessible, giving users the illusion that they are uncovering something secret and powerful. Through dramatic voiceovers, mysterious music, and carefully curated imagery, these videos provide a sense of urgency and discovery that hooks viewers in.

Beyond YouTube, Instagram and Twitter have also played a significant role in spreading Illuminati theories, particularly through the use of memes. Illuminati memes, which often include a triangular symbol or the all-seeing eye overlaid onto a celebrity's face, have become viral sensations. The "Illuminati confirmed" meme, for example, is used humorously in everyday contexts, mocking how any minor coincidence or odd behavior could be construed as evidence of the Illuminati's influence. Yet, as with many things online, the line between humor and belief can be thin. For every person sharing the meme as a joke, there are others who view it as part of a larger confirmation of the conspiracy. The simplicity of the meme format—a few images and a catchy caption—makes it easy to consume and share, further embedding Illuminati symbols and ideas into the broader online lexicon.

Twitter, with its rapid-fire nature and global reach, has become another hub for Illuminati-related content. Whenever a major event occurs, from political shifts to celebrity news, Twitter is flooded with tweets speculating on Illuminati involvement. Hashtags like #IlluminatiConfirmed or #WakeUpSheeple trend frequently after major events, with users debating whether the Illuminati was behind a particular occurrence. Celebrity deaths, in particular, often spark intense online discussions, with users pointing to the Illuminati as the true cause behind the demise of high-profile figures like Michael Jackson, Prince, or Kobe Bryant. These claims, however outlandish, spread quickly across the platform, with hundreds or thousands of retweets ensuring that the theory gains traction and visibility. For many people, this constant exposure reinforces the belief that the Illuminati is indeed at work behind the scenes, pulling the strings on major events.

Social media influencers and content creators have also played a significant role in amplifying Illuminati conspiracy theories. Many YouTubers or Instagram accounts, often focused on niche or alternative topics, post detailed breakdowns of the supposed hidden messages and symbolism associated with the Illuminati. These influencers, whether they truly believe the theories or simply see it as content that draws attention, help validate the idea for their followers. As their content gets shared, liked, and commented on, it builds a feedback loop that makes the Illuminati seem like a widely accepted, if controversial, topic. The more views and engagement these creators get, the more incentivized they are to continue posting about the Illuminati, perpetuating the cycle.

What's more, social media has fostered a sense of community among conspiracy theorists. Forums and comment sections on sites like Reddit or Facebook groups allow like-minded individuals to connect and discuss their theories, building a shared narrative about the Illuminati's role in global affairs. These spaces often serve as echo chambers, where believers can reinforce one another's views without the interference of opposing arguments. In these communities, skepticism about the Illuminati is often dismissed as naivety or evidence of being "brainwashed" by mainstream media. Theories grow more elaborate as users add new "evidence" or reinterpret existing events, fueling the belief that the Illuminati controls everything from global finance to pop culture.

Interestingly, the spread of Illuminati theories on social media is also fueled by the very institutions that conspiracy theorists distrust. As platforms like Facebook and YouTube have attempted to crack down on the spread of misinformation and conspiracy theories, some users view this as confirmation that these platforms are complicit in covering up the truth. The removal of videos or accounts that promote Illuminati theories is often interpreted as evidence that the powers behind these platforms—seen as tools of the elite—are trying to silence those who know the truth. In this way, social media's attempts to curb the spread of conspiracy theories have sometimes had the unintended consequence of further validating those theories in the eyes of believers.

Ultimately, social media has not only sustained but also amplified Illuminati conspiracy theories, making them a ubiquitous part of internet culture. Whether through YouTube exposés, Instagram memes, or Twitter discussions, the Illuminati has become a permanent fixture in the online world, constantly evolving and adapting to new platforms and trends. In the digital age, the line between entertainment, satire, and genuine belief has blurred, with the Illuminati myth living on in the memes, videos, and hashtags that circulate daily. For many, it remains a convenient way to explain the complexities and uncertainties of the modern world—an enduring symbol of secret power and hidden influence in the age of information.

Celebrities, Music, and the Rise of the Illuminati in Hip-Hop Culture

One of the most pervasive and intriguing ways the Illuminati has infiltrated popular culture is through its association with celebrities, particularly in the music industry. Over the years, countless singers, rappers, and actors have been accused of being involved in the Illuminati, with many conspiracy theorists claiming that these figures have "sold their souls" in exchange for fame and fortune. This narrative, which has become especially popular in hip-hop culture, is not only deeply fascinating to fans and critics alike but also a reflection of the broader anxieties surrounding power, success, and influence in the entertainment industry.

The roots of the Illuminati's presence in the music world can be traced back to the symbolism found in certain music videos, lyrics, and performances. Artists such as Beyoncé, Jay-Z, Kanye West, and Rihanna have all been frequently linked to the Illuminati due to their use of imagery like pyramids, all-seeing eyes, and occult symbols. One of the most famous examples is Beyoncé and Jay-Z's use of the triangle hand gesture, often interpreted as a representation of the Illuminati's pyramid symbol. Although the gesture was originally part of Jay-Z's "Roc-A-Fella" record label branding, conspiracy theorists have latched onto it as evidence of the couple's ties to the secret society.

Beyoncé's Super Bowl halftime performances and her *Lemonade* album are often dissected by theorists for alleged Illuminati references. From her use of African spiritual imagery to the choreography and visuals in her music videos, theorists argue that Beyoncé is sending coded messages to those "in the know" about her involvement with the Illuminati. These accusations intensified after the release of her song "Formation," which featured a range of powerful political and symbolic imagery, from references to Hurricane Katrina to scenes invoking historical themes of Black liberation. Despite the fact that much of her art is a celebration of Black culture and history, conspiracy theorists claim it hides a darker, more secretive message—one that ties her to a global elite pulling the strings behind the scenes.

Jay-Z, one of the most successful and influential rappers of all time, has also been at the center of Illuminati rumors for years. His frequent use of the all-seeing eye symbol and his adoption of phrases like "God MC" have been interpreted by some as indications of his supposed Illuminati allegiance. In the eyes of conspiracy theorists, his rapid ascent to power and wealth in both the music and business worlds is not the result of hard work and talent, but rather the consequence of a Faustian bargain with the Illuminati. These accusations became so widespread that Jay-Z directly addressed them in his 2011 song "Heaven," where he dismisses the conspiracy theories as absurd, yet ironically acknowledges how pervasive they've become.

Kanye West, another titan of the hip-hop industry, has also been embroiled in Illuminati rumors throughout his career. Known for his provocative public persona and controversial statements, West's eccentric behavior has led many to speculate about his involvement with the Illuminati. His frequent use of religious and spiritual imagery, such as in his *Yeezus* tour, which featured elaborate set pieces reminiscent of Christian and pagan symbolism, only fueled the conspiracy flames. Songs like "Power" and his infamous interruptions at award shows are often dissected as part of a larger narrative that positions Kanye as a puppet of the Illuminati, with his erratic actions seen as part of a wider, hidden agenda.

Rihanna, too, has found herself caught in the Illuminati web. Her music videos, particularly "Umbrella" and "Disturbia," have been scrutinized for their use of dark, occult-like visuals that conspiracy theorists claim are signs of Illuminati initiation. The imagery of Rihanna standing inside a triangle in the "Umbrella" video, coupled with her sultry, supernatural performances, have led some to believe that she, like many of her peers, is part of a secret society controlling the entertainment industry. Despite Rihanna publicly denying these allegations, the rumors persist, in part due to her continued use of provocative and symbolic imagery that conspiracy theorists link to Illuminati rituals.

The association between the Illuminati and the music industry, particularly in the hip-hop community, can be viewed as a reflection of the broader anxieties surrounding fame, wealth, and control. Hip-hop, as a genre, has always been about the rise from obscurity to prominence, often focusing on the pursuit of power, influence, and respect. The success of artists like Jay-Z, Kanye West, and Beyoncé is sometimes seen as suspicious, as if their accomplishments are too extraordinary to be attributed to talent and hard work alone. The Illuminati narrative provides a convenient explanation: their rise to the top, according to conspiracy theorists, could only be facilitated by an alliance with an all-powerful secret society.

Furthermore, the intersection of race, power, and conspiracy in these discussions cannot be ignored. The fact that many of the artists most frequently accused of being part of the Illuminati are Black suggests underlying racial and societal tensions. For some, it may be easier to believe that powerful Black artists are part of a secret society rather than acknowledging their success as a result of merit and cultural influence. The Illuminati narrative, in this sense, serves as a way to undermine and delegitimize the accomplishments of these artists, casting suspicion on their success and the broader social impact they've made.

Social media has played a crucial role in amplifying these celebrity Illuminati theories. Platforms like YouTube and Instagram are flooded with videos and posts dissecting every move these artists make, with conspiracy theorists pointing to hand gestures, lyrics, and even clothing as proof of their involvement with the Illuminati. Fan-made documentaries and exposés, claiming to reveal the hidden truth behind celebrity success, have gained millions of views, further entrenching the belief in a connection between the music industry and a shadowy global elite.

Ultimately, the link between celebrities and the Illuminati is a powerful example of how conspiracy theories evolve in the modern age. The allure of secret knowledge and the desire to make sense of the meteoric rise of cultural icons have transformed the Illuminati from an obscure historical footnote into a pervasive myth about power and control. While artists like Beyoncé, Jay-Z, and Kanye West continue to dominate global culture with their music, conspiracy theorists remain convinced that their success is not purely the result of talent, but rather evidence of their involvement in a grand, hidden agenda. This narrative has become so deeply embedded in popular culture that even when denied or debunked, the myth of the Illuminati persists, continuing to fascinate and captivate the imaginations of millions worldwide.

Chapter 7: Illuminati and the Financial Elite

The Origins of Illuminati-Finance Connections

The connection between the Illuminati and the world of finance is one of the oldest and most persistent conspiracy theories in modern history. While the original Bavarian Illuminati disbanded by the late 18th century, rumors about secret societies manipulating world events never quite disappeared. Instead, these theories evolved and grew, particularly in relation to banking and financial power. At the heart of this evolution lies the accusation that certain wealthy families and financial institutions are not only rich and influential but are also part of a secretive Illuminati elite that seeks to control global economic systems.

One of the earliest examples of this narrative centers around the Rothschild family. The Rothschilds were a prominent European banking dynasty that rose to prominence in the late 18th and 19th centuries. Their ability to establish a network of banking operations across Europe made them incredibly wealthy and influential. However, with that wealth came suspicion. Conspiracy theorists began to speculate that the Rothschilds' financial success was not due to shrewd business acumen, but rather because of their alleged connections to the Illuminati. These theories often suggested that the

Rothschild family, working in secret, was orchestrating major political and economic events to increase their power and wealth, all under the directive of a shadowy global elite.

The origins of this theory are deeply rooted in anti-Semitic sentiments, which have long associated Jewish families and individuals with the control of money and financial institutions. The Rothschilds, being Jewish and highly successful, became the primary target of such conspiracies. By the late 19th century, they were frequently accused of pulling the strings behind international conflicts, revolutions, and economic collapses—all for their personal gain and, allegedly, to further the goals of the Illuminati. Although these theories were based on little more than rumor and prejudice, they continued to spread, particularly as the family's wealth and influence grew.

As the 20th century approached, the idea of a secretive financial elite gained traction in various circles, with conspiracy theorists expanding the cast of characters said to be involved. It was no longer just the Rothschilds but also other banking dynasties like the Rockefellers, Morgans, and Warburgs who were allegedly tied to the Illuminati. The Rothschilds, in particular, remained a focal point, but their inclusion in these conspiracy theories laid the groundwork for a much larger mythos that would envelop nearly every major banking family and institution.

During this time, another theory emerged: that the Illuminati were not just controlling financial systems through families but through the creation of international financial institutions. The founding of the Federal Reserve in the United States in 1913, for instance, became a lightning rod for conspiracy theorists. Many believed that the Federal Reserve was not an independent central bank designed to stabilize the economy, but rather a tool created by the Illuminati to control America's money supply. The complex nature of the Federal Reserve, with its blend of public and private influences, only fueled these suspicions. Conspiracy theorists argued that the Federal Reserve was designed to benefit a select few—namely, the Illuminati elite—at the expense of the American public.

The Bretton Woods Conference in 1944, which led to the establishment of the World Bank and the International Monetary Fund (IMF), provided further fuel for those who believed in a global financial conspiracy. For many, these institutions were seen not as tools for global financial stability, but as mechanisms through which the Illuminati could manipulate and control the world economy. The very idea that a few powerful institutions could shape the economic policies of entire nations played into the fears that the world's wealth was concentrated in the hands of a secretive, untouchable elite.

The fear of concentrated financial power has continued to grow, with modern conspiracy theories building upon the groundwork laid in the 19th and 20th centuries. The Illuminati's alleged control over global finance is seen not just in individual families, like the Rothschilds, but in the structures of global capitalism itself. To believers in these theories, the Illuminati's ultimate goal is to control every facet of the financial world, from central banking to corporate monopolies, with the endgame being the creation of a New World Order—a world where the few control the many through the manipulation of money and resources.

It's important to note that the persistence of these theories says as much about public distrust of financial elites as it does about the allure of secret societies. The idea that an invisible hand—operating behind closed doors—controls the world's economy taps into a deep sense of anxiety and powerlessness. Throughout history, moments of financial crisis, inequality, or economic downturn have often led people to search for a convenient scapegoat. The Illuminati, in this sense, has become the ultimate explanation for the complex and often unfathomable workings of global finance. For many, it's easier to believe that a shadowy group is pulling the strings than to accept the randomness, volatility, and inequality that often define the world's economic systems.

Thus, the connection between the Illuminati and the financial elite remains a powerful narrative in conspiracy circles. It blends real historical events, like the rise of powerful banking families, with fantastical elements of secret societies, occult practices, and global domination. Even in the absence of solid evidence, these theories continue to thrive because they offer a way to make sense of the world's economic injustices. Whether through accusations against specific families or institutions, the myth of the Illuminati and its control over global finance remains an enduring part of conspiracy culture, feeding the belief that behind every economic boom or bust lies the hidden hand of a powerful, unseen elite.

Global Financial Institutions and Alleged Illuminati Control

The idea that the Illuminati controls global financial institutions is a pervasive theme in modern conspiracy theories. These institutions, such as the International Monetary Fund (IMF), the World Bank, and central banks like the U.S. Federal Reserve, are often viewed not as mechanisms for economic stability but as tools of manipulation by an elite group aiming to establish a New World Order. To conspiracy theorists, these organizations serve as the infrastructure through which the Illuminati exerts its influence over governments, economies, and ultimately, the lives of ordinary people.

The Federal Reserve, in particular, is one of the most common targets of these accusations. Established in 1913 to provide a stable monetary system in the United States, the Fed was intended to be a safeguard against economic crises. However, to conspiracy theorists, the Federal Reserve is seen as the opposite—a secretive organization controlled by private bankers, designed to manipulate the U.S. economy for the benefit of a hidden elite. The fact that the Federal Reserve operates somewhat independently of the government, combined with its ability to influence interest rates and money supply, only fuels suspicions. For those who believe in an Illuminati-led world order, the Federal Reserve is not just a central bank but the Illuminati's central lever of control over the U.S. economy.

This theory extends far beyond just American borders. Global institutions like the IMF and the World Bank, established in the aftermath of World War II to foster international economic cooperation and reconstruction, are also seen by conspiracy theorists as tools of the Illuminati. These institutions provide financial aid and loans to struggling nations, but with that assistance comes a set of conditions, often related to economic reform. Critics argue that these conditions can lead to what is termed "neocolonialism," where developing nations become dependent on loans and financial systems controlled by the global elite. For conspiracy theorists, these conditions are more than just economic policy—they are seen as part of a larger strategy to entrench Illuminati control over sovereign nations.

The IMF, in particular, has faced accusations of being a vehicle for the Illuminati's agenda. Its role in providing financial aid to countries in economic distress, often with strict austerity measures attached, is viewed with suspicion. The IMF's interventions in countries like Greece, Argentina, and African nations have sparked protests and accusations of financial imperialism. Conspiracy theorists latch onto these criticisms, arguing that the IMF's true purpose is to destabilize national economies, forcing them into dependence on the global financial system controlled by the Illuminati. They see these financial institutions not as impartial lenders but as part of a calculated effort to consolidate global economic power into the hands of a few elite families or organizations, all working behind the scenes.

Similarly, the World Bank is accused of operating as a front for the Illuminati. Established to provide financial and technical assistance to developing countries, the World Bank is often accused of perpetuating debt traps. Conspiracy theorists argue that the World Bank's projects, while ostensibly aimed at alleviating poverty, are in fact mechanisms to ensure developing nations remain economically dependent. This dependency is seen as a way for the Illuminati to exert control over national governments and resources, ensuring that no country can truly act independently on the world stage. From this perspective, the global aid provided by the World Bank is not humanitarian but strategic, allowing the Illuminati to entrench its power in every corner of the globe.

The idea that global financial institutions are controlled by the Illuminati is also intertwined with theories about a centralized global currency. Some conspiracy theorists believe that the IMF, World Bank, and Federal Reserve are all working toward the creation of a single global currency, which would be the final step in establishing the New World Order. This idea stems from the fact that global trade and finance are increasingly interconnected, and many international organizations, including the IMF, have suggested reforms to the global monetary system. For conspiracy theorists, these reforms are not simply about stabilizing international markets—they are part of a larger plot to eliminate national sovereignty and install a worldwide government controlled by the Illuminati.

One of the most influential proponents of these theories was the American author and political commentator Eustace Mullins, whose book *The Secrets of the Federal Reserve* claims that the Federal Reserve is part of a global conspiracy led by powerful banking families. Mullins argued that the creation of the Fed was orchestrated by private bankers who wanted to enslave nations through debt and interest payments. Although many of Mullins' claims have been debunked, his ideas remain popular in conspiracy circles and have shaped much of the modern narrative surrounding the Illuminati and global finance.

The Bilderberg Group, an annual private conference of world leaders, politicians, business executives, and academics, is often cited as further proof of the Illuminati's control over global finance. Conspiracy theorists argue that the Bilderberg meetings are a secret gathering where the world's elite make decisions that affect global economics and politics. Although the group's meetings are closed to the public, fueling accusations of secrecy and hidden agendas, no credible evidence has ever linked Bilderberg participants to Illuminati activities. However, the idea that global financial decisions are being made behind closed doors by an elite few plays perfectly into the Illuminati narrative.

Ultimately, these theories reflect a deep-seated mistrust of financial institutions and the global economic system. For many people, the complexities of modern finance—ranging from interest rates to international trade agreements—are difficult to understand and, as a result, are seen as inherently suspicious. The Illuminati, as a symbol of hidden power, offers a simple explanation for why financial inequality persists, why some nations seem perpetually in debt, and why certain families or corporations hold so much influence. In the minds of conspiracy theorists, the reason is clear: the Illuminati controls the global financial system, and through that control, they manipulate economies, governments, and societies for their own benefit.

In reality, global financial institutions are products of the world's complex political and economic history. They were created to address specific issues, such as economic instability, post-war reconstruction, and global development. While these institutions are not without flaws and have faced legitimate criticisms, the idea that they are controlled by a secret Illuminati cabal is unfounded. Still, the belief that a small group of elites wields undue influence over the world's finances continues to resonate with people who feel powerless in the face of globalization and economic inequality, ensuring that the myth of the Illuminati's control over global financial institutions remains a powerful and enduring part of conspiracy culture.

The Role of Billionaires and Modern Financial Moguls

In the modern world, billionaires are often seen as the embodiment of unchecked wealth and influence. Figures such as George Soros, the Koch Brothers, and the Walton family are household names, not just for their immense fortunes, but also for their perceived roles in shaping the political and economic landscape. For conspiracy theorists, however, these billionaires are more than just influential individuals—they are part of a global elite working in secret, often associated with the Illuminati, to steer the world toward a New World Order.

One of the most frequently cited individuals in Illuminati conspiracy theories is George Soros, a Hungarian-American billionaire and philanthropist. Soros has become a central figure in many conspiracy narratives due to his involvement in global political movements, funding of progressive causes, and his vast wealth. His Open Society Foundations, which advocate for human rights, democracy, and economic reform, have been particularly controversial in some circles. To conspiracy theorists, Soros' funding of political causes and social movements is not simply a reflection of his beliefs but part of a grander scheme to destabilize governments and societies to pave the way for a New World Order. They argue that Soros' influence on global politics, through his donations and lobbying efforts, is evidence of his deep ties to the Illuminati, who they claim are using him as a front to manipulate world events.

The narrative surrounding Soros is often built on misinformation and false associations. For instance, during events like the European refugee crisis or various political protests, conspiracy theorists claimed that Soros was orchestrating these movements behind the scenes to further a globalist agenda. His advocacy for open borders, transparency in governance, and his opposition to authoritarianism are interpreted by believers in these conspiracies as attempts to erode national sovereignty and usher in a centralized, global government—hallmarks of the Illuminati's supposed plans. This portrayal of Soros, while popular in conspiracy circles, is not based on factual evidence but rather on a mix of anti-globalist sentiment and often anti-Semitic tropes.

The Koch Brothers, Charles and the late David Koch, have also been implicated in Illuminati conspiracies. Known for their massive wealth derived from Koch Industries and their funding of libertarian and conservative political causes in the United States, the Koch brothers have long been viewed as political power brokers. Their extensive lobbying efforts, combined with their financial support of think tanks, academic institutions, and political candidates, have made them a focal point in discussions about the influence of money in politics. Conspiracy theorists often argue that the Koch brothers' actions are not merely about promoting free-market economics or limited government but are part of a coordinated effort to control political systems from behind the scenes.

In this narrative, the Koch brothers are portrayed as key players in a shadowy network of elites—sometimes referred to as the "deep state"—that is working in concert with the Illuminati. The theory suggests that their influence over American politics, particularly through organizations like Americans for Prosperity and the Cato

Institute, is part of a broader strategy to reshape governments to fit the Illuminati's long-term vision of a global ruling class. As with Soros, this interpretation relies on the assumption that billionaires use their wealth not just for personal or ideological interests but to further an overarching, secretive agenda that seeks to control the world.

The Walton family, heirs to the Walmart fortune, is another modern dynasty often implicated in Illuminati conspiracy theories. As the owners of the world's largest retailer, the Waltons have amassed vast wealth, and their business practices have had significant effects on global trade, labor policies, and local economies. For conspiracy theorists, Walmart's dominance in global retail is not just a reflection of market success but a sign of Illuminati control over consumer behavior and economic systems. The idea is that the Walton family, like other powerful business dynasties, is part of a network that uses corporate power to shape global economic trends in ways that benefit the few while controlling the many.

The focus on billionaires like Soros, the Koch brothers, and the Waltons in Illuminati conspiracy theories is rooted in the public's perception of extreme wealth and influence. In a world where economic inequality is stark and growing, it is easy for people to believe that those at the top are part of a secretive group working to maintain and expand their power. The vast resources at the disposal of these billionaires, combined with their involvement in politics, philanthropy, and business, make them prime targets for conspiracy narratives. These figures are often portrayed not just as wealthy individuals but as key actors in a global plot to centralize power and wealth under the control of the Illuminati.

This view is exacerbated by the fact that many of these billionaires operate in relatively opaque ways. Their donations to political causes, their control over large multinational corporations, and their participation in global forums like the World Economic Forum create an aura of mystery that conspiracy theorists latch onto. When these elites meet behind closed doors or influence policy through lobbying, it is easy for some to believe that there are more sinister motives at play. The secrecy that often surrounds wealth and power creates fertile ground for speculation, and the Illuminati conspiracy provides a framework to explain the influence of billionaires on global events.

While the accusations against these individuals are varied, the underlying narrative is the same: billionaires are not just wealthy and influential, they are part of a secret global elite—often linked to the Illuminati—that is working to establish a New World Order. For those who believe in these theories, the immense wealth of individuals like Soros, the Koch brothers, and the Waltons is not just a byproduct of capitalism, but a tool for manipulating economies, societies, and governments for a hidden, nefarious purpose. The Illuminati, in this context, is not just a mythological secret society, but a stand-in for the very real anxieties many people feel about concentrated wealth and political influence in the hands of a few powerful individuals.

In reality, while billionaires do exert significant influence in many areas of life, there is no credible evidence to suggest that they are part of a secret society orchestrating global events for the purpose of creating a New World Order. The actions of figures like Soros, the Koch brothers, and the Waltons are motivated by a complex mix of personal beliefs, business interests, and political ideologies, rather than by membership in a hidden cabal. However, as long as wealth inequality persists and people feel disenfranchised by the political and economic systems that govern their lives, the myth of the Illuminati and its supposed control over the world's billionaires will continue to thrive.

Banking Dynasties and the Illuminati Connection

Few names resonate within the world of conspiracy theories quite like the Rothschild family. For centuries, this banking dynasty has been central to accusations of global control and manipulation. For those who believe in the Illuminati, the Rothschilds are often depicted as one of its core families, responsible for orchestrating world events from behind the scenes. The idea that this family of bankers wields extraordinary influence over international finance and politics feeds into the larger narrative that a secret elite group controls the world's wealth and, by extension, its power.

The Rothschild family's prominence in the banking world dates back to the 18th century when Mayer Amschel Rothschild, the family patriarch, established a banking business in Frankfurt, Germany. Over time, his sons expanded the family's banking empire across Europe, establishing branches in major cities such as London, Paris, Vienna, and Naples. The family's success in providing loans to governments, particularly during the Napoleonic Wars, cemented their reputation as one of the most powerful financial dynasties in history. However, it also made them a target for conspiracy theories that claimed their wealth and influence extended far beyond legitimate business dealings.

Conspiracy theorists argue that the Rothschild family's financial empire is part of a larger Illuminati plot to control global banking systems. They believe that the Rothschilds, through their connections to central banks and financial institutions, secretly control the flow of money worldwide, dictating the economic fate of nations. According to this theory, the Rothschilds not only control central banks but have also been instrumental in shaping events such as wars, economic crises, and political revolutions—all to maintain and expand their wealth and influence. This portrayal of the Rothschilds as puppet masters pulling the strings of global finance has persisted for centuries, despite a lack of concrete evidence to support such claims.

The Federal Reserve, the central banking system of the United States, is often implicated in these theories as being under Rothschild control, even though no credible link exists between the family and the institution. The myth suggests that the Rothschilds, alongside other powerful banking families like the Rockefellers and Morgans, conspired to create the Federal Reserve in 1913 as a means to manipulate the U.S. economy. According to conspiracy theorists, these families use the Federal Reserve to control interest rates, money supply, and inflation, all to serve their own financial interests and advance the Illuminati's goal of global dominance.

While the Rothschild family is the most frequently cited, other banking dynasties have also been pulled into the Illuminati conspiracy narrative. The Rockefeller family, particularly during the 20th century, became another focal point for accusations of secretive global influence. John D. Rockefeller, the founder of Standard Oil and one of the wealthiest men in history, established a financial empire that extended into banking, philanthropy, and politics. His descendants, through their control of institutions like Chase Bank and their involvement in organizations like the Council on Foreign Relations and the Trilateral Commission, are often seen as key players in the supposed Illuminati agenda.

Conspiracy theorists claim that the Rockefellers, like the Rothschilds, use their wealth and influence to manipulate global events. They are accused of being part of a network of elites who aim to centralize power by controlling governments, corporations, and financial institutions. This narrative often includes claims that the Rockefeller family was instrumental in founding international organizations like the United Nations, which conspiracy theorists argue is a front for the Illuminati's global governance plan. The Rockefellers' philanthropic efforts, such as their funding of educational, medical, and cultural institutions, are also viewed with suspicion, seen not as acts of charity but as part of a broader strategy to shape public opinion and advance their hidden agenda.

The notion of banking dynasties controlling world events is also tied to the broader theme of central banking systems being tools of the Illuminati. The idea that central banks, particularly the Bank of England, the European Central Bank, and the U.S. Federal Reserve, are secretly controlled by an elite few is a common thread in Illuminati conspiracy theories. These theories suggest that central banks, which control national monetary policy, are used to create economic crises that benefit the global elite. For example, conspiracy theorists claim that the Great Depression, the 2008 financial crisis, and other economic downturns were deliberately engineered by the Illuminati to consolidate wealth and power.

The notion that banking families and central banks are part of an Illuminati-controlled financial system is often fueled by the complexity of modern economics. To the average person, the workings of international finance, currency manipulation, and government debt are difficult to understand, which can lead to feelings of mistrust and suspicion. Conspiracy theories about the Rothschilds, Rockefellers, and other banking dynasties provide a simplified explanation for these complexities: a small group of powerful individuals, acting through the Illuminati, are manipulating the system for their own gain.

It is important to note that many of these conspiracy theories, particularly those involving the Rothschild family, have roots in anti-Semitic propaganda that dates back centuries. The idea of Jewish bankers controlling the world's finances was a central theme in numerous anti-Semitic works, most notably *The Protocols of the Elders of Zion*, a fabricated document that purported to reveal a Jewish plan for global domination. Although *The Protocols* was exposed as a hoax long ago, its ideas have persisted and continue to influence modern conspiracy theories about the Illuminati and global finance. The Rothschilds, being a prominent Jewish family in banking, became the target of these false and harmful narratives, and their name has since become synonymous with unfounded accusations of secretive global control.

Despite the prevalence of these conspiracy theories, the reality is far more mundane. The Rothschild and Rockefeller families, while historically influential in the world of finance, do not control the global banking system or manipulate world events for the benefit of a secret society. Their businesses, like those of many other wealthy families, have faced challenges and setbacks, and their influence has waned in the face of modern economic developments. The idea that these families are part of an Illuminati conspiracy reflects a deep mistrust of wealth and power, but it is not supported by factual evidence.

In summary, the portrayal of banking dynasties like the Rothschilds and Rockefellers as key players in an Illuminati-controlled financial system is a central theme in many conspiracy theories. These narratives, often rooted in historical prejudices and misunderstandings of global finance, offer a simplified explanation for the complexities of economic systems and the concentration of wealth. However, the claims of Illuminati control over these families and global banking institutions remain unsubstantiated, driven more by fear and speculation than by reality.

The Financial Crisis and Economic Control—Manipulation or Mismanagement?

One of the most persistent ideas in Illuminati conspiracy theories is the notion that global financial crises are not accidental or due to mismanagement but are intentionally orchestrated by a hidden elite to consolidate power and control. This theory suggests that events like the Great Depression, the 2008 financial crisis, and even ongoing economic instability are part of a deliberate strategy by the Illuminati to manipulate markets, create chaos, and then impose their preferred solutions—solutions that ultimately benefit a select few at the expense of the masses.

The 2008 global financial crisis, in particular, has been a focal point for these conspiracy theories. The crisis, which began with the collapse of the housing market in the United States and quickly spread to financial markets worldwide, led to severe economic downturns, widespread unemployment, and a loss of confidence in the global banking system. For many, the crisis exposed the vulnerabilities and failings of modern capitalism. But for conspiracy theorists, it was seen as a carefully crafted event, engineered by the Illuminati to seize greater control over the world's economies.

According to this narrative, the financial crisis was not merely the result of reckless lending practices or the failure of regulatory systems, but the result of a coordinated effort by global elites, particularly those within the banking and finance industries, to intentionally crash the economy. The purpose, conspiracy theorists argue, was twofold: first, to create widespread fear and instability, making people more amenable to drastic changes in the global financial system; and second, to allow the Illuminati and its allies in government and finance to step in as "saviors" with solutions that would increase their control over economic and political systems.

The idea that crises are manufactured for the benefit of the elite is not new. Similar theories have been applied to historical events like the Great Depression of the 1930s. In that case, conspiracy theorists claimed that the economic collapse was deliberately caused by banking elites, including the Rothschilds, to gain control over national economies and force governments to adopt policies that would benefit international bankers. These theories often revolve around the idea that global financial institutions like the Federal Reserve, the International Monetary Fund (IMF), and the World Bank are tools of the Illuminati, designed to centralize economic control and reduce national sovereignty.

The role of the Federal Reserve is particularly contentious in these conspiracy theories. Established in 1913, the Federal Reserve is responsible for managing the U.S. money supply, interest rates, and overall economic stability. For conspiracy theorists, however, the Federal Reserve is not just a national institution but a key instrument of the Illuminati's global financial control. They argue that the Federal Reserve, through its control over monetary policy, manipulates the economy to create booms and busts that benefit a small, hidden elite. In this view, the 2008 financial crisis, and other economic downturns, were not just unfortunate events but part of a larger, orchestrated plan.

One of the most popular conspiracy theories surrounding the 2008 crisis involves the bailout of major banks and financial institutions. The U.S. government, along with other nations, injected trillions of dollars into the banking system to prevent a total collapse. To many, these actions were seen as necessary to avoid a deeper depression. However, conspiracy theorists saw them as proof that the financial elite had been manipulating the system all along. The bailout, they argued, was not about saving the economy but about ensuring that the wealthiest individuals and institutions, many of whom they believe are part of the Illuminati, would not suffer from the consequences of the crisis they had created.

Another key aspect of this theory is the belief that the financial elite, through the Illuminati, use debt as a tool of control. By encouraging nations to take on massive debt, whether through loans from international institutions like the IMF or by manipulating domestic fiscal policies, the Illuminati allegedly create a system in which countries are perpetually in debt. This debt, in turn, limits the ability of nations to govern independently and forces them to comply with the demands of their creditors—who, in the view of conspiracy theorists, are ultimately part of the Illuminati's plan for global domination.

The austerity measures imposed on countries like Greece and Spain in the aftermath of the 2008 crisis are often cited as examples of how this system of control works. In these cases, countries were required to implement strict economic reforms in exchange for financial assistance from international lenders. These reforms, which included cuts to public services, pension reductions, and tax hikes, were deeply unpopular and caused widespread social unrest. For conspiracy theorists, this was further evidence that the Illuminati were using debt and financial crises to impose their will on sovereign nations, pushing them toward economic policies that benefit the global elite while harming ordinary citizens.

The narrative of the Illuminati controlling financial crises also extends to more recent economic disruptions, including the volatility caused by the COVID-19 pandemic. As the world entered lockdown and economies ground to a halt, conspiracy theorists quickly adapted their views to suggest that the pandemic itself was part of a larger plan by the Illuminati. According to this theory, the economic impact of the pandemic—mass unemployment, increased government debt, and the shift toward a more digital economy—was engineered by the elite to accelerate their control over the global economy.

These theories often revolve around the idea of "order out of chaos," a phrase commonly associated with Illuminati conspiracy lore. The concept suggests that by creating chaos—whether through financial crises, pandemics, or wars—the Illuminati can present themselves as the solution to the problems they caused. By offering stability in the form of new economic policies, global governance structures, or technological solutions like digital currencies, they tighten their grip on power while appearing to act in the public's best interest.

While these ideas are compelling to those who feel disenfranchised or suspicious of global financial systems, they are not grounded in reality. Financial crises are complex events with multiple causes, including poor risk management, regulatory failures, and market fluctuations. While powerful institutions and individuals certainly play a role in shaping economic outcomes, there is no credible evidence to suggest that the Illuminati, or any secret society, is intentionally creating crises to further a global agenda.

Nevertheless, the persistence of these conspiracy theories reflects deep-rooted concerns about inequality, wealth concentration, and the power of global financial institutions. In a world where economic systems often seem opaque and unaccountable, the myth of the Illuminati provides a way for people to make sense of events that feel beyond their control. Whether or not the Illuminati exists, the fear of hidden forces manipulating the economy will likely continue as long as economic inequality and financial instability remain pressing global issues.

8

Chapter 8: Government and Political Leaders

The Role of Political Power in Illuminati Theories

The intertwining of political power with Illuminati conspiracy theories is not a modern phenomenon, but rather a belief system that has evolved over centuries. At its core, the notion that government and political leaders are manipulated or even controlled by a secret elite taps into a long-standing fear of centralized authority and hidden agendas. This belief suggests that political leaders—whether they are elected officials, monarchs, or dictators—are not acting in the interest of the public, but rather as pawns of a covert organization aiming for global dominance. The Illuminati, according to this theory, is the shadowy force behind the world's most powerful political figures.

This idea can be traced back to the very origins of Illuminati lore. In the late 18th century, following the establishment of the Bavarian Illuminati, fears spread that this group was not merely a philosophical society but a dangerous network intent on undermining governments and religious institutions. These suspicions, though based on little more than rumor, took root and have been adapted to fit various political contexts ever since. Over time, conspiracy theorists began to argue that the Illuminati infiltrated governments, embedding its members within the highest ranks of power to advance its agenda of establishing a New World Order.

One of the key arguments made by proponents of the Illuminati conspiracy is that political leaders do not achieve their positions of power independently. Instead, they are groomed, selected, and promoted by the Illuminati to serve its global goals. In this view, democratic elections are not genuine expressions of the people's will but carefully orchestrated events in which the Illuminati ensures its chosen candidates rise to the top. This theory gives rise to the idea that no matter which political party wins an election, the outcome is ultimately the same—the Illuminati maintains control.

This belief has had a profound effect on how certain segments of the public perceive political power. Whenever a leader rises to prominence, particularly in Western democracies, conspiracy theorists are quick to point out any connections—real or imagined—that suggest ties to secretive organizations. For example, involvement in elite academic institutions, membership in exclusive clubs or societies, or even associations with prominent global figures can be enough to spark rumors of Illuminati affiliation. These connections are often presented as evidence that the individual in question is part of a global network that transcends national borders, working not for their constituents, but for a hidden cabal.

The fear of centralized power plays a critical role in these theories. As governments grow more complex and interconnected, especially in the context of globalism and international cooperation, conspiracy theorists see this as further evidence of a move toward a single, unified world government—an essential component of the Illuminati's supposed plan for domination. Global organizations like the United Nations, the International Monetary Fund, and the World Health Organization are often viewed as stepping stones toward this eventual New World Order, with political leaders acting as the enforcers of these international bodies' policies.

In this worldview, political leaders become symbols of a larger, more insidious system. Rather than being seen as independent agents, they are portrayed as part of a coordinated effort to strip nations of their sovereignty, erode individual freedoms, and centralize power under a single global authority. This suspicion of political authority has been exacerbated by historical events, such as wars, economic crises, and government scandals, which conspiracy theorists interpret as carefully orchestrated moves by the Illuminati to consolidate control. For example, decisions related to military intervention, global trade agreements, and immigration policies are often framed as serving the interests of the global elite rather than the citizens they affect.

Furthermore, political leaders who advocate for policies aligned with global cooperation, such as environmental regulations, international trade deals, or multilateral military actions, are frequently cast as agents of the Illuminati. For conspiracy theorists, these policies are not aimed at addressing global challenges, but are instead designed to weaken national governments, undermine borders, and pave the way for a centralized world government. This narrative plays into broader fears about the loss of national identity and autonomy in an increasingly interconnected world.

It is important to recognize that these theories thrive on ambiguity and selective interpretation of facts. In many cases, the mere suggestion of elite connections or involvement in global initiatives is enough to trigger accusations of Illuminati involvement. Conspiracy theorists rarely rely on concrete evidence; instead, they build their arguments by connecting dots that may not actually be related. This approach allows them to interpret any political action or event as part of a broader Illuminati strategy, reinforcing the belief that political leaders are not working for the people, but for a hidden agenda.

In recent years, the rise of populist movements has further fueled the idea that political leaders are puppets of a secret elite. Populist leaders often campaign on the promise of reclaiming power from "the establishment" and returning it to the people, positioning themselves as outsiders who are fighting against the hidden forces that control traditional politics. For those who believe in Illuminati conspiracy theories, these populist leaders are seen as potential disruptors of the global elite's plans—unless, of course, they too are eventually suspected of being part of the conspiracy.

The belief that political leaders are either controlled by or are members of the Illuminati reflects a deep mistrust of power and authority. In an age where transparency is often demanded but rarely delivered, the idea that a secret group could be manipulating world events behind the scenes becomes an attractive explanation for the complexities and challenges of modern politics. Whether it is due to dissatisfaction with government, disillusionment with the political process, or frustration with global elites, the narrative of the Illuminati's influence over political leaders continues to captivate the imagination of conspiracy theorists worldwide.

U.S. Presidents and the Illuminati Allegations

Throughout American history, U.S. presidents have been central figures in Illuminati conspiracy theories. The office of the president is one of the most powerful and visible positions in the world, and as such, it has become a focal point for those who believe in secret societies and covert agendas. For conspiracy theorists, the notion that certain U.S. presidents are not just political leaders but members or agents of the Illuminati adds a new layer to their interpretation of American history and global governance. The belief that these presidents have secretly worked to advance a New World Order has become a persistent theme in these theories, casting suspicion on some of the most famous figures in U.S. political history.

One of the earliest U.S. presidents to be linked to Illuminati speculation is George Washington himself. The first president of the United States and a prominent Freemason, Washington's connection to Freemasonry has often been misconstrued as evidence of Illuminati influence. The Masonic symbols, such as the all-seeing eye and the pyramid, which appear on the Great Seal of the United States and the one-dollar bill, have fueled these conspiracy theories. For those who believe in the Illuminati, the inclusion of these symbols in American iconography is seen as a hidden message indicating that the country's founders, including Washington, were part of a secretive plot to create a new global order under the control of a select few.

However, these symbols, while Masonic in origin, do not prove any link to the Illuminati. Freemasonry and the Illuminati were separate organizations with different goals, and Washington's involvement in Freemasonry was public knowledge, not a secret conspiracy. Yet, the narrative that Washington and other Founding Fathers were part of a grand Illuminati scheme persists in some circles. These theorists argue that the American Revolution and the founding of the United States were not driven by a desire for independence and liberty, but by the Illuminati's plans for a new form of global governance—a theory that has endured despite historical evidence to the contrary.

The association between U.S. presidents and the Illuminati did not stop with the Founding Fathers. In the 20th century, Franklin D. Roosevelt became another president frequently linked to the Illuminati. Like Washington, Roosevelt's connection to Freemasonry sparked rumors that he was advancing the Illuminati's agenda through his political actions. The New Deal, which Roosevelt implemented in response to the Great Depression, was seen by conspiracy theorists as a step toward centralizing power and creating a more controlling government—a key goal of the supposed Illuminati. Moreover, Roosevelt's decision to place the all-seeing eye and the unfinished pyramid on the back of the dollar bill in 1935 further fueled suspicions. To many, these symbols were clear indicators of Illuminati influence over the U.S. government, even though Roosevelt likely saw them as historical emblems rather than secretive messages.

John F. Kennedy, one of the most charismatic and beloved presidents in American history, has also been the subject of Illuminati rumors, particularly surrounding his assassination in 1963. According to some conspiracy theorists, Kennedy was killed because he attempted to expose the Illuminati and disrupt their plans for global domination. His speeches calling for greater transparency in government and his criticism of secret societies have been interpreted as veiled references to the Illuminati. This theory gained traction over the decades as people sought explanations for the murky circumstances surrounding Kennedy's death. While official investigations concluded that Kennedy's assassination was the work of a lone gunman, conspiracy theorists remain convinced that the Illuminati was involved, viewing the event as a pivotal moment in the battle between global elites and the forces of democracy.

Another U.S. president frequently accused of Illuminati ties is Barack Obama. As the first African American president, Obama's historic election in 2008 was met with immense enthusiasm and hope for change. However, almost immediately, conspiracy theories surfaced suggesting that Obama was part of a hidden Illuminati agenda. These theories pointed to his rapid rise in politics, his globalist policies, and even his speeches, which emphasized international cooperation and multilateralism. For those inclined to see the Illuminati's hand in global affairs, Obama's emphasis on global governance, his involvement in international organizations, and his vision for a more interconnected world were all signs that he was working to advance the New World Order.

One of the most widely circulated theories regarding Obama's alleged Illuminati connections revolved around his administration's handling of the global financial crisis and the subsequent bailouts of major banks and corporations. Conspiracy theorists argued that the crisis was a manufactured event designed to transfer wealth to the global elite, with Obama acting as their political agent. This narrative was often linked to the belief that Obama's healthcare reforms, environmental policies, and foreign relations strategies were part of a larger plan to centralize power and weaken the sovereignty of individual nations, pushing the world closer to the Illuminati's vision of global control.

Obama's symbolic use of hand gestures and certain imagery during public appearances also fed into these conspiracy theories. For example, the "devil horns" hand sign, which Obama was occasionally photographed using, was interpreted by theorists as an Illuminati signal, despite the gesture being widely recognized in many cultures as a simple, harmless sign. Similarly, Obama's speeches at international summits, where he spoke of cooperation and global solutions to issues like climate change, were seized upon as proof that he was advancing a hidden agenda dictated by the global elite.

These accusations reached their peak during Obama's presidency, with countless internet forums, YouTube videos, and books speculating about his alleged ties to the Illuminati. Though these theories lacked credible evidence, they persisted in certain fringe communities, reflecting a broader distrust of government and global institutions.

The linking of U.S. presidents to Illuminati conspiracy theories reveals a deep-seated mistrust in political power. For many, the idea that a secret organization like the Illuminati could control the world's most powerful leaders is a way to explain the complexities of modern governance. When presidents make controversial decisions, pass unpopular legislation, or pursue policies that seem to undermine national interests in favor of global ones, these actions are interpreted as evidence of Illuminati influence. Rather than viewing political leaders as individuals making decisions based on their principles or the demands of their office, conspiracy theorists see them as pawns of a shadowy elite working behind the scenes.

This suspicion of political authority has grown in the age of the internet, where information—both credible and false—spreads rapidly. Theories about the Illuminati's influence over U.S. presidents are part of a broader narrative that questions the legitimacy of political power and the transparency of democratic processes. For those who feel disconnected from or disillusioned by politics, the idea that the Illuminati controls the presidency offers an explanation for the inequalities and injustices they perceive in the world. However, these theories often overlook the complexity of governance and the many factors—both internal and external—that influence political decision-making.

Ultimately, while the idea that U.S. presidents are part of an Illuminati plot is a compelling narrative for some, it is not grounded in fact. The reality of political power is far more nuanced, shaped by a combination of public opinion, economic forces, and geopolitical challenges. Nonetheless, as long as there is a mistrust of government and a belief in hidden elites pulling the strings, the specter of the Illuminati will continue to loom over the office of the U.S. presidency.

World Leaders and the Global Elite

Beyond U.S. presidents, the Illuminati conspiracy theory extends to world leaders across the globe. Prominent figures in politics, royalty, and international organizations are often implicated as members or agents of a hidden global elite working in concert to establish a New World Order. The belief is that these leaders, despite representing different nations, ideologies, and political systems, are part of a unified conspiracy to centralize power and manipulate global events. Conspiracy theorists point to global institutions such as the United Nations, the World Bank, and the European Union as platforms where this elite exerts its influence. The implication is clear: world leaders, whether democratic or autocratic, are mere players in a grand Illuminati scheme.

One of the most commonly mentioned figures in this context is the British monarchy, particularly Queen Elizabeth II and other members of the royal family. As one of the world's oldest and most visible monarchies, the British royal family has long been associated with elite circles. Conspiracy theorists argue that their wealth, influence, and connections to international organizations position them at the top of a secret global hierarchy. The Queen's ceremonial role in global affairs, as well as the royal family's perceived aloofness and access to vast resources, feeds into the idea that they are part of an ancient Illuminati bloodline—a group of families supposedly controlling the world through intergenerational power. Royal events, such as weddings, coronations, and public appearances, are sometimes scrutinized for hidden symbols or messages that indicate Illuminati involvement.

In a similar vein, European political figures—particularly those involved in the European Union—are frequently targeted by Illuminati conspiracy theories. The EU, with its mission to unify Europe under a single political and economic system, is often portrayed as a stepping stone toward a broader, global government. Figures like former German Chancellor Angela Merkel, French President Emmanuel Macron, and other EU leaders are accused of advancing policies that weaken national sovereignty and promote a centralized global order. The economic and political integration of Europe, according to conspiracy theorists, is not a means of ensuring peace and stability but rather part of a grand design orchestrated by the Illuminati to consolidate power in the hands of a few elites.

The idea that global leaders are working in tandem to create a New World Order extends beyond Europe. Russian President Vladimir Putin and Chinese President Xi Jinping, despite being seen as adversaries of the West, are also implicated in Illuminati theories. Conspiracy theorists argue that these seemingly opposing powers are, in fact, collaborating behind the scenes, engaging in a staged geopolitical rivalry that distracts the public from the true agenda of global domination. Putin's long reign and Xi's consolidation of power are viewed as signs of authoritarian leadership serving the interests of the Illuminati, with their respective nations acting as counterweights in a carefully managed global balance of power.

Leaders of multinational organizations and international bodies are also frequent targets of Illuminati conspiracies. The United Nations (UN), in particular, is seen as a critical player in the supposed globalist agenda. Conspiracy theorists argue that the UN's mission of promoting international peace and security is a cover for its true goal of establishing a one-world government. Secret meetings and summits of world leaders, such as the annual World Economic Forum in Davos or the Bilderberg Group gatherings, are viewed as venues where global elites meet to coordinate their plans for controlling the world's political and economic systems.

The Bilderberg Group, in particular, has been a focal point for Illuminati-related conspiracies. Founded in 1954, the Bilderberg Group is an annual conference attended by political leaders, business executives, and academics from around the world. While the meetings are private and the discussions are not disclosed to the public, conspiracy theorists interpret this secrecy as evidence of a shadowy global elite dictating world events. The group's exclusivity and the participation of influential figures from various sectors of society lead many to believe that these meetings are where decisions about wars, economies, and political systems are made—decisions that, according to these theories, serve the interests of the Illuminati.

Another frequently mentioned organization is the Trilateral Commission, a group founded in 1973 to foster cooperation between North America, Europe, and Asia. The commission's focus on strengthening international ties is seen by conspiracy theorists as another step toward global governance. Leaders who have been involved with the Trilateral Commission, such as former U.S. President Jimmy Carter or former Canadian Prime Minister Pierre Trudeau, are often accused of furthering the Illuminati's objectives. The commission's influence over trade agreements, economic policies, and global institutions is portrayed as part of a broader agenda to undermine national sovereignty in favor of a global ruling class.

In addition to these organizations, conspiracy theorists frequently claim that wealthy business leaders and financial elites, often referred to as the "global elite," are closely tied to Illuminati plots. Figures like George Soros, Bill Gates, and the Rothschild family are repeatedly named in such theories, accused of using their vast wealth and influence to manipulate governments and advance the Illuminati's goals. The rise of global corporations, the concentration of wealth in the hands of a few, and the increasing influence of tech and finance sectors on global politics are seen as further evidence of a hidden elite pulling the strings behind the scenes.

What makes these theories so compelling to their adherents is the apparent consistency of their narrative. Whether it's a democratic leader in the West, an authoritarian ruler in the East, or a monarch in Europe, conspiracy theorists argue that all these figures are united by a common thread: they are either members of the Illuminati or, at the very least, complicit in its agenda. Global events, such as wars, economic crises, and even pandemics, are interpreted as carefully orchestrated moves by this elite to increase their control over the world's population.

However, while these theories may provide a satisfying explanation for the complexity and uncertainty of global politics, they overlook the significant differences and conflicts that exist between nations and their leaders. The idea that world leaders from vastly different political systems and cultures are secretly collaborating to establish a New World Order is difficult to reconcile with the reality of international relations, which is often characterized by competition, conflict, and differing national interests.

Ultimately, the belief that world leaders are part of an Illuminati conspiracy reflects a broader distrust of power and authority. In an era where political systems can seem distant or unresponsive to the needs of the public, conspiracy theories offer a way to explain the seemingly inexplicable decisions and actions of global leaders. While these theories provide a narrative of hidden control, they often rely on circumstantial evidence and selective interpretation of events, ignoring the complexity of global governance and the competing interests that shape world politics. Nonetheless, as long as there are global leaders with significant influence, the belief in an Illuminati-run world government will persist, feeding into the larger narrative of a global elite working toward a secret agenda.

The Power of the Media and Entertainment Industry

One of the most pervasive aspects of Illuminati conspiracy theories is the belief that the media and entertainment industry are key tools used by the global elite to manipulate public perception and shape the global narrative. According to conspiracy theorists, the Illuminati controls major news outlets, film studios, music companies, and other cultural institutions, using them to subtly promote their agenda and desensitize the public to their ultimate goal: the establishment of a New World Order.

The media is seen as a particularly powerful tool in the hands of the Illuminati. By controlling the flow of information, they are believed to shape how people view world events, political developments, and even personal beliefs. Major news organizations such as CNN, Fox News, The New York Times, and the BBC are frequently accused of being mouthpieces for the global elite, disseminating propaganda that serves the interests of the Illuminati. Conspiracy theorists argue that the media presents a carefully curated version of reality, one that obscures the true nature of global events and reinforces a narrative that keeps people distracted, divided, and unaware of the hidden forces at work.

For instance, the reporting on wars, economic crises, and political conflicts is often cited as evidence of media manipulation. Conspiracy theorists claim that these events are either staged or deliberately misrepresented to promote fear and instability, which in turn justifies the expansion of government control and the erosion of individual freedoms. The constant focus on sensational stories—terrorism, pandemics, natural disasters—distracts people from questioning the broader systems of power and control. This, they argue, is all part of the Illuminati's plan to create a passive and compliant populace, one that will ultimately accept the New World Order without resistance.

Entertainment, particularly Hollywood, also plays a central role in Illuminati conspiracy theories. Popular films, television shows, and music videos are believed to contain subliminal messages that either promote Illuminati values or prepare the public for the changes the global elite are planning. Movies like *The Matrix, The Hunger*

Games, and *V for Vendetta* are often cited as examples of films that subtly reveal the existence of a controlled and manipulated world, while also conditioning audiences to accept dystopian futures where government surveillance, authoritarian control, and mass conformity are normalized.

Moreover, certain celebrities are often singled out as either members of the Illuminati or as puppets being used to promote the elite's agenda. Figures like Beyoncé, Jay-Z, Madonna, and Lady Gaga are frequently targeted by conspiracy theorists who claim that their success is due not to talent or hard work, but to their allegiance to the Illuminati. These celebrities are said to flaunt their connection to the Illuminati through the use of symbolic imagery—such as the all-seeing eye, pyramids, and other occult symbols—in their music videos, performances, and public appearances. The widespread use of these symbols is seen not only as evidence of Illuminati involvement but also as a form of indoctrination, subtly influencing fans to accept Illuminati values of materialism, power, and control.

Music videos, in particular, are often scrutinized for hidden messages. For example, Beyoncé's 2013 Super Bowl performance, which included imagery of pyramids and the all-seeing eye, was interpreted by conspiracy theorists as a public display of her Illuminati ties. Similarly, Jay-Z has been accused of using Illuminati symbolism in his clothing line, Rocawear, and in his music. These interpretations are fueled by a broader belief that the entertainment industry is used as a tool of mass influence, shaping not just tastes and trends, but also political and social views in a way that benefits the global elite.

The concept of predictive programming is another key element of how conspiracy theorists view the entertainment industry's role in promoting the Illuminati's agenda. Predictive programming is the idea that the elite use movies, TV shows, and other forms of entertainment to subtly prepare the public for future events or societal changes. For example, conspiracy theorists point to films like *1984*, *Contagion*, or even episodes of *The Simpsons* as examples of media that "predict" real-world events—such as government surveillance, pandemics, or major political changes—before they happen. In this view, the global elite use entertainment to gradually acclimate people to the idea of a more controlled, authoritarian world, so that when these changes occur in reality, the public is more likely to accept them without question.

Beyond celebrities and films, entire genres of music have also been implicated in Illuminati conspiracies. Hip-hop and pop music, in particular, are often seen as vehicles for spreading the elite's message. The glorification of wealth, power, and excess in many popular songs is viewed as an attempt to promote a materialistic and individualistic culture, one that prioritizes personal gain over community or collective well-being. This, conspiracy theorists argue, serves the interests of the Illuminati by creating a society where people are more focused on consumerism and status than on questioning the systems of power that govern their lives.

Interestingly, conspiracy theorists also claim that those who try to expose the Illuminati within the entertainment industry are often silenced or punished. For example, the deaths of high-profile figures like Michael Jackson, Whitney Houston, and Tupac Shakur have been cited as evidence of the Illuminati eliminating those who posed a threat to their control. These artists, according to the theory, either tried to speak out against the Illuminati or were killed to serve as a warning to others in the industry who might consider doing so. The tragic and sometimes mysterious circumstances surrounding these deaths only add fuel to the conspiracy, reinforcing the belief that the Illuminati wields vast power not only in shaping popular culture but also in determining the fates of those who operate within it.

The power of the media and entertainment industry in the Illuminati conspiracy narrative cannot be understated. For those who subscribe to these beliefs, the pervasive influence of news outlets, movies, music, and celebrities serves as constant proof that a shadowy elite is working to control not only governments and economies but also the very way people think and perceive the world around them. Whether through subtle symbolism, overt messages, or predictive programming, the media is viewed as a tool of indoctrination, conditioning the masses to accept a world ruled by the Illuminati and their vision for a New World Order.

In reality, while the media and entertainment industries undeniably shape public opinion and culture, the idea that they are coordinated by a secret group of elites to control society is unfounded. The complexity and diversity of media organizations, combined with the sheer number of voices and perspectives in the entertainment industry, make it highly unlikely that a single, unified agenda could be enforced. However, the persistent belief in this conspiracy speaks to a broader fear of manipulation and a distrust of powerful institutions that resonates deeply with those who feel alienated or powerless in a rapidly changing world.

Chapter 9: The Role of the Media in Illuminati The

The Media as a Tool of Disinformation

One of the core beliefs of Illuminati conspiracy theorists is that mainstream media is not merely an impartial observer of global events, but an active tool of disinformation used by the elite to shape public opinion and obscure the truth. The idea that media outlets are part of a larger system of control feeds into a deep mistrust of the information being disseminated, with the belief that journalists and news organizations are complicit in promoting the agendas of the powerful. According to these theories, the Illuminati use media to direct attention away from their secret plans for global domination, focusing instead on trivial matters or manipulated narratives designed to keep the masses distracted, divided, and unaware of the true power structures in play.

At the heart of this belief is the idea that the Illuminati—or a similar secret society—holds significant influence over global media conglomerates. Conspiracy theorists often claim that the same small group of elites, who they argue are members of the Illuminati, control the majority of media outlets worldwide. They believe that through ownership of television networks, newspapers, online platforms, and radio stations, these elites are able to control what information is shared with the public, and more importantly, what is kept hidden. The goal, according to these theories, is to manipulate public perception and maintain a sense of normalcy while working toward a larger, more sinister agenda—the establishment of a New World Order.

A common accusation is that the media focuses on divisive or sensationalist stories to create fear, anxiety, or distraction. Instead of addressing systemic issues or questioning the power structures that govern global politics and economics, news organizations are accused of amplifying conflicts, reporting on celebrity scandals, or promoting a constant cycle of fear-driven stories such as terrorism, pandemics, and economic crises. For example, conspiracy theorists often point to the extensive media coverage of terrorist attacks or public health scares, suggesting that these events are either manufactured or exaggerated to keep the public in a state of fear. By doing so, the theory goes, the Illuminati are able to justify greater governmental control, erosion of personal freedoms, and a passive, compliant populace that does not question authority.

A frequently cited example is the 9/11 attacks. Many conspiracy theorists claim that the way these events were reported in the media—particularly the swift identification of the perpetrators and the subsequent justification for military action—was part of a larger Illuminati agenda to manipulate the public into supporting wars that ultimately benefited the elite. In this narrative, the media's role was not simply to report on what had happened, but to shape the public's understanding of the event in a way that served the interests of those in power. By controlling the narrative, the Illuminati were allegedly able to turn a tragic event into an opportunity for expanding global surveillance, increasing military intervention, and furthering their long-term goal of centralized global governance.

Conspiracy theorists also believe that the media plays a critical role in covering up the activities of the Illuminati. Stories that threaten to expose the true nature of global power dynamics are either ignored or discredited, while those that serve the elite's purposes are given extensive coverage. Theories about the Illuminati frequently claim that whistleblowers, investigative journalists, or political figures who attempt to reveal the truth are either silenced or portrayed as unstable. This perception contributes to the overall distrust of the media, as it reinforces the belief that anyone who challenges the official narrative will be ostracized or eliminated. High-profile cases of media manipulation, such as the suppression of certain investigative reports or the discrediting of controversial political figures, are often used as "evidence" to support the idea that the media is complicit in hiding the truth about the Illuminati's influence.

The rise of major media conglomerates is seen as further proof of Illuminati control. Over the last few decades, media ownership has become increasingly concentrated in the hands of a few powerful corporations, which conspiracy theorists claim is part of a deliberate effort to centralize information and limit the diversity of voices in public discourse. Companies like Disney, Comcast, and News Corporation are often named as key players in this scheme, with theorists suggesting that these corporations are either directly controlled by Illuminati members or act as willing collaborators in their agenda. The shrinking number of independent news outlets is viewed as part of a broader effort to control the flow of information and ensure that only content favorable to the elite is widely distributed.

However, these beliefs often overlook the complex nature of media organizations and the variety of factors that influence news coverage. While it is true that media conglomerates hold significant power, attributing their actions to a secret society like the Illuminati is an oversimplification of the challenges facing modern journalism. Corporate interests, political pressure, and the need to attract viewership all play a role in shaping what stories are covered and how they are presented. Yet, for conspiracy theorists, this complexity only serves to reinforce their suspicions—after all, a hidden agenda can be much more easily concealed behind a facade of chaos and competing interests.

In conclusion, the notion that mainstream media is a tool of disinformation used by the Illuminati to manipulate public perception and maintain control is central to many conspiracy theories. From claims of manufactured crises to accusations of media ownership consolidation, theorists believe that the global elite use their influence over news organizations to keep the public distracted and unaware of their true agenda. While these beliefs are largely unsubstantiated, they reflect a deep mistrust of powerful institutions and a widespread sense of alienation in a world where information is increasingly mediated by large, seemingly impersonal corporations.

The Spread of Illuminati Theories through Alternative Media

In recent years, alternative media has become a powerful force for the spread of conspiracy theories, particularly those centered around the Illuminati. As traditional news outlets are increasingly viewed with suspicion by segments of the population, many turn to alternative sources in search of what they believe to be the "real truth" about world events and power structures. These platforms, often decentralized and unregulated, have provided fertile ground for the growth and dissemination of Illuminati-related content, allowing conspiracy theories to reach a global audience in ways that were previously unimaginable.

The rise of the internet, and specifically social media, has democratized the production and sharing of information. No longer is the dissemination of news and ideas limited to large media corporations; anyone with a smartphone or computer can now publish content, create videos, or engage in discussions with like-minded individuals. This has led to an explosion of conspiracy theories in online spaces, where Illuminati-related content is widespread and easily accessible. Platforms like YouTube, Reddit, Twitter, and Facebook have become central hubs for conspiracy theorists, allowing them to connect, collaborate, and share their ideas with millions of people around the world.

YouTube, in particular, has played a pivotal role in spreading Illuminati theories. The platform's vast reach and algorithm-driven content recommendations have made it a hotspot for conspiracy content creators. Videos that claim to expose the Illuminati's influence in politics, entertainment, and finance can garner millions of views, especially when they are sensational or tap into existing fears and anxieties. These videos often present themselves as "documentaries" or "investigations," using a mixture of ominous music, selectively edited footage, and dramatic narration to convince viewers of the Illuminati's existence and influence.

Creators of this content often blend fact with fiction, citing real-world events and weaving them into elaborate conspiracy narratives. For instance, the financial crisis of 2008, the election of controversial political figures, or even natural disasters are framed as orchestrated by the Illuminati to further their global agenda. By mixing credible information with speculative claims, these videos create an aura of plausibility that can be compelling for viewers who are already inclined to distrust mainstream sources. Once a viewer watches one such video, YouTube's recommendation algorithm may suggest similar content, creating a feedback loop that exposes them to even more conspiracy theories.

Reddit has also become a significant platform for the spread of Illuminati theories, with entire subreddits dedicated to discussing the hidden machinations of the global elite. These forums offer a space for users to share theories, links to articles or videos, and personal anecdotes that support the belief in the Illuminati's influence. The anonymity of Reddit allows for free expression of ideas that might be dismissed or ridiculed in mainstream spaces, creating an echo chamber where believers can find validation and reinforcement for their views. Posts that gain popularity through upvotes can quickly reach thousands of users, spreading theories far beyond the original community.

Social media platforms like Twitter and Facebook amplify this effect even further. Conspiracy theorists use hashtags, viral posts, and retweets to reach wider audiences, spreading their ideas across social networks with alarming speed. A single tweet or Facebook post claiming that a political leader, celebrity, or global event is connected to the Illuminati can quickly go viral, being shared and reshared by users across the world. These platforms also allow for the rapid spread of misinformation and rumors, often without any oversight or fact-checking, making them ideal for the propagation of conspiracy theories. Once a claim is out there, it becomes part of the broader narrative, whether or not there is any factual basis for it.

A significant aspect of the appeal of alternative media for Illuminati conspiracy theorists is the perception that it offers "unfiltered" truth. Traditional news organizations are often seen as part of the elite establishment, and as such, many conspiracy theorists believe they cannot be trusted. In contrast, alternative media is viewed as grassroots, authentic, and independent from the corrupting influence of power. This perception of authenticity allows alternative media to thrive, even when the content is sensational or lacks credible evidence. For many, the allure of alternative media lies not in its accuracy but in its ability to challenge the status quo and offer a narrative that feels more empowering, exciting, or even dangerous.

Podcasts have also emerged as a popular medium for spreading Illuminati theories. Shows that focus on paranormal activity, unsolved mysteries, and conspiracies often devote entire episodes to exploring the supposed influence of the Illuminati in various facets of life. These podcasts attract a dedicated listenership, with hosts often positioning themselves as truth-seekers who are bravely exposing hidden realities. The conversational nature of podcasts allows for deeper dives into complex theories, giving believers a space to explore these ideas in greater detail than a tweet or video clip might allow. In many cases, podcast hosts will interview "experts" in conspiracy theory culture, further legitimizing their claims in the minds of their listeners.

Independent news websites also contribute to the spread of Illuminati theories by publishing articles that blend real news with speculative conspiracy narratives. These sites often present themselves as alternatives to mainstream media, claiming to offer stories that "the elites don't want you to know about." Articles on these websites might examine major political events, economic shifts, or celebrity behavior through the lens of Illuminati control. For example, an election might be framed as being manipulated by the Illuminati to ensure that their chosen candidate takes power, or a global summit might be described as a secret meeting of world leaders to plan the next stage of the New World Order.

While traditional media outlets may debunk these claims, the audience for alternative media often views such rebuttals as further evidence of Illuminati control. In this way, alternative media creates a self-reinforcing cycle: the more that mainstream sources attempt to discredit Illuminati theories, the more conspiracy theorists believe they are being lied to and the more they turn to alternative platforms for information.

The success of alternative media in spreading Illuminati theories reflects broader societal trends, including the erosion of trust in traditional institutions and the increasing skepticism toward established sources of authority. As more people seek out alternative narratives to make sense of a rapidly changing world, conspiracy theories about the Illuminati continue to flourish. The democratization of media, while empowering in many ways, has also created new challenges in distinguishing fact from fiction, and the Illuminati conspiracy is a prime example of how alternative media can both reflect and amplify these tensions in society.

Symbolism in Pop Culture and the Media

One of the most pervasive elements of Illuminati conspiracy theories is the belief that the organization hides in plain sight by embedding its symbols in popular culture. From movies and music videos to advertisements and fashion, conspiracy theorists claim that the Illuminati uses various forms of media to desensitize the public to their presence and subtly announce their control. The all-seeing eye, pyramids, and occult imagery—often associated with Freemasonry and other secret societies—are said to be ubiquitous in entertainment and advertising. According to believers, these symbols are not random or artistic choices, but deliberate markers of Illuminati influence.

The all-seeing eye, often depicted as an eye within a triangle, is perhaps the most recognizable symbol linked to the Illuminati. Conspiracy theorists argue that this symbol represents the Illuminati's surveillance and control over the world, a nod to the group's supposed omnipotence. The eye can be found on the U.S. dollar bill as part of the Great Seal of the United States, which conspiracy theorists claim is evidence of the Illuminati's influence in the founding of the country and its continued control over government institutions. The presence of the eye in music videos, fashion, and film is interpreted as a covert way for the Illuminati to flaunt their power and condition the masses to accept their dominance.

Pop stars, particularly those with global influence, are often accused of being part of the Illuminati or at least pawns in their agenda. Artists such as Beyoncé, Jay-Z, Lady Gaga, and Rihanna have been repeatedly linked to the Illuminati, primarily because their work frequently features imagery associated with the conspiracy. Beyoncé and Jay-Z, in particular, have been targeted for their use of the pyramid hand gesture—interpreted by theorists as a reference to the Illuminati's pyramid of power. In reality, Jay-Z's Roc-A-Fella Records symbol, a triangle formed by the hands, represents his record label, but for conspiracy theorists, this is further proof of Illuminati affiliation. Beyoncé's powerful, often mysterious stage presence, and her incorporation of esoteric symbols in music videos like *Run the World (Girls)*, have led many to believe that she is either a member of the Illuminati or is being used to promote their influence.

Lady Gaga's eccentric and theatrical performances are also frequently cited as evidence of Illuminati symbolism. Her music videos, often laden with abstract and surrealist imagery, are analyzed by conspiracy theorists as hidden messages from the Illuminati. For example, the music video for *Bad Romance* has been dissected as an allegory for Gaga's initiation into the Illuminati, with theorists pointing to specific visual elements such as the all-seeing eye, cages, and occult symbols as clues. Rihanna's use of symbols like the all-seeing eye in her videos and live performances has led to similar accusations. In fact, any pop star who uses abstract or symbolic imagery in their work is likely to attract attention from Illuminati watchers, who view these elements as deliberate messaging rather than creative expression.

The use of pyramids, another frequent symbol associated with the Illuminati, is a common visual motif in fashion and entertainment. Pyramids, particularly when topped with the all-seeing eye, are believed to represent the Illuminati's hierarchical structure of power, with the elite at the top controlling the masses below. Conspiracy theorists often point to the prominence of pyramids in high-fashion campaigns, music videos, and films as a form of hidden communication between Illuminati members and a way to remind the public of their control. Major fashion houses and designers, who regularly incorporate pyramid shapes and mystical symbols into their collections, are often accused of being complicit in this alleged manipulation.

Hollywood itself is seen by conspiracy theorists as a major player in the dissemination of Illuminati symbols. Certain films and television shows are believed to be packed with hidden messages or predictive programming, where future events are subtly foreshadowed by the Illuminati through popular media. Movies such as *Eyes Wide Shut*, directed by Stanley Kubrick, have become focal points for these theories. Kubrick's film, which explores the secret lives of the wealthy elite and their involvement in mysterious and occult rituals, is viewed as a thinly veiled exposé of the Illuminati. Similarly, conspiracy theorists argue that films like *The Matrix* or *The Da Vinci Code* carry coded messages that reflect the Illuminati's control over reality or their historical influence on world events. The prevalence of occult themes and secret societies in entertainment, particularly in genres like science fiction and fantasy, is seen as a calculated effort to normalize the idea of hidden rulers and mysterious organizations.

Advertising is also viewed as a key medium for Illuminati symbolism. Major corporations are believed to incorporate these symbols into their logos and marketing materials as a way of signaling their allegiance to the Illuminati. Theories abound about the hidden meanings behind corporate logos, with companies like Apple, Nike, and Starbucks frequently named as complicit in the Illuminati's agenda. For example, Apple's logo—a bitten apple—is interpreted as a reference to the biblical story of Adam and Eve, suggesting a link to secret knowledge and forbidden power. Nike's swoosh is sometimes linked to occult symbolism, while the Starbucks mermaid is seen as a representation of pagan goddesses associated with power and control. Even when these connections are tenuous at best, they feed into the broader narrative of Illuminati influence in everyday life.

What makes this particular aspect of the Illuminati theory so compelling for many is that it seems to provide a way to make sense of the overwhelming presence of symbols and imagery in modern media. In a world saturated with content, where images and icons are everywhere, Illuminati theorists offer a simple yet sinister explanation: these symbols are not random or meaningless, but intentional, planted by a hidden elite to gradually reveal their presence or manipulate the masses. For believers, seeing these symbols in their favorite movies, music videos, or commercials serves as a kind of confirmation that their suspicions about the Illuminati's power are valid.

This fascination with symbols also speaks to a deeper psychological need for order and explanation. In a complex, often chaotic world, the idea that there is a hidden structure behind the media we consume can offer a sense of control and understanding. While most of these interpretations lack any factual basis, they serve as a framework through which conspiracy theorists can explain the influence of the Illuminati and its purported grip on global culture.

In conclusion, symbolism in pop culture and the media is a cornerstone of Illuminati conspiracy theories. From the all-seeing eye and pyramids to occult references in fashion and film, conspiracy theorists believe these symbols are deliberately used by the Illuminati to desensitize the public and display their power. Whether through the music of pop stars, the plots of blockbuster films, or corporate logos, these symbols are seen as markers of a hidden elite working toward global control. For believers, recognizing these symbols is not just a matter of entertainment, but a key to understanding the larger, secretive forces they believe shape the world.

The Role of Music in Illuminati Theories

The music industry, especially the realm of popular music, plays a central role in Illuminati conspiracy theories. For decades, theorists have claimed that the most influential musicians are either members of the Illuminati or are being used as tools to promote its agenda. These theories posit that the Illuminati controls the entertainment industry as a way to manipulate the masses, using music as a medium to spread their ideology, indoctrinate listeners, and distract the public from real-world events and the true power structures behind global affairs.

The belief that musicians are tied to the Illuminati hinges on the idea that fame and fortune come at a cost. In the world of conspiracy theorists, becoming a superstar means making a deal with the Illuminati—selling one's soul in exchange for success, wealth, and influence. This idea is often reinforced by the public personas of certain artists, particularly those who cultivate mysterious, edgy, or controversial images. Artists who push boundaries, challenge societal norms, or present themselves as larger-than-life figures are seen as prime candidates for Illuminati involvement. The notion of a Faustian bargain between artists and the Illuminati feeds into the narrative that nothing in the entertainment industry happens by chance.

One of the most frequently cited examples of Illuminati influence in music is Beyoncé, who has become a focal point for conspiracy theorists. As one of the most successful and powerful figures in the music industry, Beyoncé's fame and influence have sparked endless speculation. Theories about her alleged connection to the Illuminati often focus on her music videos and performances, where conspiracy theorists claim to spot occult symbols, such as the all-seeing eye, triangles, and references to ancient gods. Her performance at the 2013 Super Bowl halftime show, for instance, was scrutinized for supposed Illuminati symbols, with some even suggesting that the entire event was a ritual broadcast to millions of people. Her stage persona, "Sasha Fierce," is often interpreted as an alter ego created by the Illuminati to control and influence her behavior.

Similarly, Jay-Z, Beyoncé's husband and collaborator, is frequently accused of being either a high-ranking member or a puppet of the Illuminati. Theories often cite his Roc-A-Fella hand gesture, which forms a diamond shape, as a secret Illuminati symbol. While Jay-Z has stated that the gesture simply represents his record label, theorists insist that it is a covert reference to the Illuminati's pyramid structure. His wealth, influence in the music industry, and connections to powerful figures in business and politics only add fuel to these claims. For many conspiracy theorists, Jay-Z and Beyoncé represent the perfect Illuminati power couple, using their music and public personas to subtly promote the organization's hidden agenda.

Another artist frequently associated with Illuminati theories is rapper Kanye West. His erratic behavior, outspoken personality, and controversial public statements make him a frequent target of speculation. Some conspiracy theorists believe that West's career is a product of Illuminati manipulation and that his public outbursts are signs of rebellion against his Illuminati handlers. For example, his infamous interruption of Taylor Swift at the 2009 MTV Video Music Awards was interpreted by some as an Illuminati-sanctioned move designed to humiliate Swift, who is also often implicated in conspiracy theories. West's song lyrics, music videos, and fashion choices are dissected for hidden meanings and symbols that suggest his involvement with the secret society. His later embrace of religious themes, particularly in his *Sunday Service* performances, has been interpreted as either a break from or a deepening involvement with Illuminati symbolism, depending on the theorist.

Pop star Madonna has long been a source of fascination for Illuminati theorists as well. Her provocative imagery, religious references, and constant reinvention are seen as hallmarks of an artist under the influence of the Illuminati. Her performances often feature symbolism tied to the occult, and her willingness to incorporate religious and mystical themes into her work has made her a prime target for conspiracy theorists. Madonna's 2015 single *Illuminati* added fuel to the fire, as the lyrics directly reference the conspiracy theories surrounding her and other celebrities. While Madonna has openly mocked these theories, the song itself has only further solidified her position as a key figure in the Illuminati narrative.

Beyond individual artists, entire genres of music have been accused of promoting Illuminati ideals. Hip-hop, in particular, is often singled out by conspiracy theorists who believe that its themes of wealth, power, and rebellion align with the Illuminati's goals. According to these theories, the commercialization of hip-hop and its global reach have been orchestrated by the Illuminati as a way to control youth culture and spread materialistic values. The prevalence of luxury brands, private jets, and lavish lifestyles in hip-hop music videos is seen as evidence that the genre promotes the values of the elite, encouraging listeners to aspire to wealth and status without questioning the power structures that make such success possible.

Other genres, such as rock and heavy metal, are also frequently associated with Illuminati symbolism. The use of occult imagery, dark themes, and rebellious attitudes in rock music has long been a target of conspiracy theories, particularly those tied to Satanic panic in the 1980s. Bands like Led Zeppelin, Black Sabbath, and even more contemporary artists like Marilyn Manson are often accused of promoting Illuminati ideals or being directly involved with secret societies. For conspiracy theorists, these artists' embrace of occult themes is not just a creative choice, but a deliberate attempt to desensitize listeners to the existence of dark forces controlling the world.

Music videos are perhaps the richest source of Illuminati symbolism for conspiracy theorists. Videos by major pop stars are often analyzed frame by frame for hidden messages, with special attention given to symbols like the all-seeing eye, pyramids, and references to ancient mythology. The use of mirrors, duality, and transformation in music videos is also frequently cited as evidence of Illuminati mind control techniques, with theorists claiming that these visual motifs represent the manipulation and transformation of the artist by the secret society. Even when music videos are clearly artistic or abstract in nature, conspiracy theorists interpret them as coded messages meant to signal the Illuminati's presence and influence.

For those who subscribe to these theories, the music industry is not just entertainment, but a tool of mass manipulation. The belief that the Illuminati controls the industry taps into broader fears about corporate control, cultural homogenization, and the influence of powerful elites. Whether through symbolism in music videos, the meteoric rise of certain artists, or the omnipresence of particular genres, conspiracy theorists view the world of music as a carefully orchestrated stage on which the Illuminati reveals itself to the world, one beat at a time.

Hollywood and the Illuminati Agenda

Hollywood, as a global cultural powerhouse, occupies a central position in Illuminati conspiracy theories. Conspiracy theorists believe that the entertainment industry, especially major film studios, is one of the most effective tools the Illuminati uses to manipulate the masses, pushing a covert agenda to subtly prepare people for a New World Order. Movies and television are seen not just as entertainment, but as vehicles for propaganda that condition audiences to accept the Illuminati's dominance and control over world events. Through hidden messages, symbolism, and the promotion of specific worldviews, theorists argue that Hollywood is a willing participant in advancing the Illuminati's ultimate goal of global governance.

One of the most enduring ideas is that Hollywood films contain subliminal messages or predictive programming that reflect the plans of the Illuminati. Predictive programming refers to the notion that certain films and TV shows foreshadow real-world events, conditioning viewers to accept these occurrences when they happen. For example, conspiracy theorists point to films like *The Matrix*, *V for Vendetta*, and *1984*, claiming that these movies reveal aspects of an authoritarian future controlled by an unseen elite, mirroring the Illuminati's supposed endgame. According to this line of thinking, these films desensitize viewers to the loss of freedom, mass surveillance, and the erosion of individual rights, making them more likely to accept such conditions in reality.

The Matrix, in particular, is a favorite among Illuminati conspiracy theorists. The film's central premise—that the world as we know it is an illusion controlled by powerful forces—resonates with those who believe that the Illuminati exerts a similar control over society. The movie's themes of awakening to the truth and fighting back against a hidden system of oppression are interpreted as both a warning and a reflection of the Illuminati's manipulation of the real world. Neo, the protagonist who discovers the truth about the Matrix and rebels against it, is seen as an allegory for those who "wake up" to the existence of the Illuminati and resist its control.

Another film frequently cited by conspiracy theorists is *Stanley Kubrick's Eyes Wide Shut.* The 1999 film, which explores the secret lives of the elite and their participation in mysterious, ritualistic orgies, is considered by some to be a thinly veiled depiction of the Illuminati. The film's portrayal of a wealthy, powerful society engaged in occult practices has led theorists to conclude that Kubrick was attempting to expose the Illuminati's hidden influence. Kubrick's sudden death shortly after the film's completion only fuels the belief that he was silenced for revealing too much. For many theorists, *Eyes Wide Shut* stands as proof that secretive, powerful groups engage in dark rituals behind the scenes, controlling the world from the shadows.

The prominence of occult symbolism in Hollywood movies is another key factor in linking the entertainment industry to the Illuminati. Theorists argue that many blockbuster films are filled with Illuminati symbols, such as the all-seeing eye, pyramids, and references to ancient deities. For instance, movies like *The Lord of the Rings* and *Harry Potter*—both immensely popular franchises—are often accused of promoting occult themes that align with Illuminati beliefs. In these films, symbols like the Eye of Sauron or the recurring use of powerful magical symbols are interpreted as messages meant to normalize the existence of secret knowledge and hidden power. The fact that these films are globally successful only adds to the belief that Hollywood is intentionally spreading these ideas to vast audiences.

Superhero movies, which have become a dominant force in modern cinema, are also viewed through an Illuminati lens. Theorists claim that the narrative of powerful, god-like figures who protect or rule over humanity in films like *The Avengers* or *Justice League* is part of the Illuminati's effort to promote the idea of a powerful elite that is above the masses. In this interpretation, superheroes are stand-ins for the Illuminati themselves—beings with extraordinary abilities who, although they might appear to act for the greater good, ultimately represent a ruling class that controls the fate of humanity. The frequent references to hidden organizations, secret identities, and powerful, shadowy figures in superhero films are seen as further evidence of this agenda.

Television is also viewed as a major player in the dissemination of Illuminati propaganda. Shows that feature political intrigue, secret societies, or dystopian futures are analyzed for hidden messages. Programs like *House of Cards*, *The Man in the High Castle*, and *Mr. Robot* are seen as reflections of the Illuminati's influence on world affairs, depicting a reality where powerful elites manipulate events behind the scenes. Even seemingly innocent shows like *The Simpsons* have been accused of predictive programming, with theorists pointing to specific episodes that appear to have foreshadowed real-world events, such as the election of Donald Trump as president of the United States. For conspiracy theorists, the fact that these shows often blur the line between fiction and reality is a deliberate tactic used by the Illuminati to condition audiences to accept their hidden rule.

Hollywood's influence on global culture extends beyond film and television, with theorists claiming that the industry promotes values aligned with the Illuminati's goals. The rise of materialism, celebrity worship, and the glorification of wealth and power in Hollywood are seen as part of a larger effort to distract people from the true nature of global power dynamics. By encouraging a focus on superficial success, fame, and consumption, Hollywood is believed to play a key role in keeping the masses preoccupied with trivial matters, making it easier for the Illuminati to operate without scrutiny. Celebrities, in this view, are not just entertainers but symbols of the power and control the Illuminati seeks to exert over society. Their wealth, influence, and glamorous lifestyles are presented as something to aspire to, even as they are seen as puppets of a larger, more sinister force.

For those who believe in these theories, Hollywood is not just a cultural engine but a vital component of the Illuminati's strategy for control. Through movies, television, and the cult of celebrity, the Illuminati is thought to shape public perception, promote its values, and prepare the world for the eventual establishment of a New World Order. Whether through hidden symbols, predictive programming, or the manipulation of popular culture, Hollywood is viewed as a willing accomplice in the Illuminati's quest for global dominance.

In conclusion, the belief that Hollywood is a tool of the Illuminati is deeply ingrained in conspiracy culture. From blockbuster films to hit TV shows, theorists argue that the entertainment industry is saturated with symbols, messages, and narratives that serve the Illuminati's agenda. Whether through the promotion of occult themes, the foreshadowing of future events, or the elevation of a powerful elite, Hollywood is seen as a key player in the Illuminati's efforts to shape the world and manipulate the masses. For believers, the glamour and allure of Hollywood mask a darker reality—one in which a secretive organization uses the power of storytelling to influence minds and control society from the shadows.

10

Chapter 10: Illuminati and Technological Surveilla

The Rise of the Surveillance State

The development of surveillance technology has come a long way, evolving from rudimentary wiretapping and basic physical monitoring into the highly sophisticated digital systems we know today. For many conspiracy theorists, this evolution is far from coincidental—it is seen as part of a deliberate, long-term plan orchestrated by the Illuminati to control the masses. The idea of a "surveillance state," where governments and organizations monitor and record every aspect of people's lives, is often linked to the shadowy influence of the Illuminati. According to these theories, surveillance has been incrementally ramped up to a point where nearly every human interaction, both online and offline, can be tracked, analyzed, and used as a tool for domination.

Historically, the foundations of modern surveillance were laid during times of war and geopolitical tension. The Cold War era was a critical turning point, as both the United States and the Soviet Union developed advanced intelligence capabilities to keep tabs on each other's activities. Spying, wiretapping, and the use of satellite technology for reconnaissance became common. Intelligence agencies like the CIA and KGB made surveillance a key weapon in their ideological battles, and the technological breakthroughs of the time set the stage for future innovations. However, what was once limited to monitoring governments and military operations would soon expand into the everyday lives of citizens.

The introduction of closed-circuit television (CCTV) in the mid-20th century marked the beginning of mass visual surveillance. Initially, CCTVs were used for security purposes, installed in public spaces to deter crime and monitor key locations like banks, airports, and government buildings. But over time, their use proliferated, and cameras became a standard feature in cities around the world. Today, it's nearly impossible to walk down a city street without being recorded by some form of surveillance technology. While proponents argue that CCTV cameras help maintain public safety, conspiracy theorists believe they are a tool of the Illuminati to track the movements of ordinary citizens, creating a society where privacy is all but extinct.

The advent of the internet and the rise of digital communication systems in the late 20th century represented a quantum leap in surveillance capabilities. As people began to communicate more frequently via emails, instant messages, and online platforms, it became possible for governments and corporations to monitor digital conversations on a scale that was previously unimaginable. This newfound ability to track digital footprints gave rise to the idea of a "surveillance society," where everyone's personal information, from browsing habits to private conversations, could be collected and stored. To those who believe in Illuminati conspiracies, this was the moment when the secret elite began to establish full control over the flow of information.

The 9/11 attacks in 2001 brought about a significant shift in how surveillance was justified and implemented. In the wake of the attacks, governments around the world introduced sweeping security measures to prevent future terrorist threats, and many of these measures involved increased surveillance of citizens. The USA PA-TRIOT Act, passed in the United States shortly after 9/11, gave law enforcement agencies unprecedented powers to monitor phone calls, emails, and other forms of communication. While these actions were presented as necessary for national security, conspiracy theorists viewed them as a calculated step by the Illuminati to tighten their grip on global societies.

Mass surveillance continued to expand with the rise of smart-phones and social media. By the mid-2000s, people were willingly carrying devices in their pockets that tracked their every movement, recorded their conversations, and stored vast amounts of personal data. Social media platforms encouraged users to share personal de-tails about their lives, from their daily activities to their political beliefs, all of which could be analyzed by both governments and cor-porations. The rise of these technologies created a perfect storm for mass data collection—an opportunity that conspiracy theorists ar-gue the Illuminati has seized upon.

For those who believe in the Illuminati's influence, these tech-nologies are not merely tools for convenience or safety; they are the mechanisms of control. According to their view, the surveillance state is designed to monitor dissent and crush any potential resis-tance to the eventual implementation of a New World Order. Every phone call, every text message, every social media post is seen as part of a vast network of intelligence gathering that feeds into the hands of the elite. The aim is not just to track criminals or terrorists, but to keep the general population under constant watch, eroding the pos-sibility of rebellion or resistance to Illuminati control.

As surveillance technology has become more advanced, the idea that the Illuminati is behind its proliferation has only gained trac-tion. The modern surveillance state, characterized by the near-total absence of privacy, is often viewed as a key element in the Illuminati's plan to maintain global dominance. Whether it's through satellite tracking, facial recognition software, or the data collected by smartphones, the belief is that the Illuminati has created a system in which everyone's actions can be monitored and controlled, ensuring that no one escapes their influence.

In this light, the rise of the surveillance state is not just a byproduct of technological progress or national security concerns, but rather a methodical effort by the Illuminati to eliminate personal privacy and establish total control over society. Through decades of gradual advancements in surveillance technology, they have built a world where everyone is watched, and nothing goes unseen.

Big Data and the Influence of Tech Giants

In the modern world, the collection and analysis of data—often referred to as "big data"—has become one of the most powerful tools at the disposal of corporations and governments alike. From our browsing habits to our online purchases, the data we generate on a daily basis is meticulously tracked, stored, and analyzed by tech giants like Google, Facebook, and Amazon. While these companies present their data-gathering practices as necessary for improving user experience and personalizing services, conspiracy theorists see a much darker motive behind the scenes. They argue that the Illuminati, operating through these vast corporations, is using big data as part of a global effort to monitor and control individuals, pushing humanity closer to a dystopian future.

The business model of these tech giants relies heavily on their ability to collect and process enormous amounts of user data. Each search query typed into Google, each post made on Facebook, and each product purchased on Amazon adds to a growing database of personal information. This data, which includes everything from our interests and opinions to our physical locations, forms detailed profiles of each user. By analyzing these profiles, companies can not only tailor ads to individual users but also predict their behavior with increasing accuracy. While this can be seen as a breakthrough in the fields of marketing and personalization, conspiracy theorists argue that this capability extends far beyond simple commercial purposes.

For those who believe in Illuminati influence, the world's largest tech companies are not simply businesses; they are extensions of the secretive organization's power. According to these theories, the Illuminati has infiltrated or even outright controls these corporations, turning them into tools for mass surveillance. Every time a user logs into Facebook, posts a photo on Instagram, or sends a message via WhatsApp, they are voluntarily handing over personal information to a system that is, in the eyes of conspiracy theorists, part of a broader mechanism of control. The collection of such vast amounts of personal data enables what they perceive as a level of surveillance far beyond anything previously possible, laying the groundwork for the Illuminati's envisioned New World Order.

One of the most critical moments for these theories came in 2013, when former NSA contractor Edward Snowden leaked classified information revealing the extent of government surveillance. Among the revelations was the fact that tech companies, including giants like Google, Microsoft, and Facebook, had been cooperating with the U.S. government's PRISM program, allowing agencies such as the NSA to access users' private data. While the companies in question denied any wrongdoing, the leaks confirmed for many conspiracy theorists what they had long suspected: that governments and corporations were working hand in hand to create a global surveillance apparatus.

In the minds of those who subscribe to Illuminati conspiracy theories, Snowden's revelations were just the tip of the iceberg. They believe that the Illuminati, through their influence over both governments and tech companies, have engineered a system where every aspect of human life is tracked and monitored. The rationale behind this, according to these theorists, is not just about gathering information for the sake of national security or profit but about using that information to shape the behavior of entire populations. By understanding the habits, preferences, and desires of individuals, those in power can more easily manipulate society, nudging people toward certain beliefs or actions that align with the goals of the Illuminati.

Another facet of this conspiracy involves the way in which big data is used to influence political outcomes. In recent years, there has been growing concern over how tech companies and data analysis firms can sway elections by manipulating the information seen by voters. One of the most infamous examples of this was the Cambridge Analytica scandal, where it was revealed that the personal data of millions of Facebook users had been harvested and used to target political ads during the 2016 U.S. presidential election. Conspiracy theorists argue that this kind of manipulation is part of a broader Illuminati agenda, where elections are no longer decided by the will of the people but by carefully orchestrated data-driven campaigns designed to install leaders who align with the Illuminati's interests.

The manipulation of information extends beyond politics and into nearly every aspect of modern life. Algorithms that curate content on social media platforms like Facebook and YouTube are seen as tools for shaping public perception. What news stories are promoted, what opinions are given visibility, and even which products are advertised are all believed to be influenced by an agenda set by the Illuminati. By controlling the flow of information, these tech companies—acting under Illuminati guidance, according to conspiracy theorists—can guide public opinion in subtle but powerful ways.

Ultimately, for those who believe in these conspiracies, big data represents not just a technological innovation but a key instrument in the Illuminati's arsenal of control. The vast quantities of data collected by tech giants allow for unprecedented insight into the lives of individuals, insight that can be used not only to influence behavior but to monitor potential dissent. The Illuminati's goal, as posited by conspiracy theorists, is to create a system in which no action, no thought, and no belief can escape their observation. Through their influence over the world's largest tech companies, the Illuminati are believed to be inching ever closer to this reality, where the surveillance state and corporate interests combine to serve a single, shadowy power.

In this view, the internet, once hailed as a space of freedom and expression, has instead become a tool for totalitarian control. While tech companies argue that their data collection practices are intended to improve services, those who subscribe to Illuminati theories see a much more sinister purpose at work. For them, big data is not just about convenience or marketing—it's about control on a global scale.

The Internet of Things and Digital Monitoring

The rapid expansion of the "Internet of Things" (IoT) has added a new dimension to the debate over surveillance and control. The IoT refers to the network of physical objects embedded with sensors, software, and other technologies that connect and exchange data with other devices over the internet. These "smart" devices—ranging from thermostats and refrigerators to wearable fitness trackers and home security systems—are designed to make life more convenient. However, for conspiracy theorists who believe in the influence of the Illuminati, the IoT is seen as a new frontier for mass surveillance, allowing for unprecedented levels of intrusion into private lives.

The idea behind IoT technology is that everyday devices can be interconnected, creating a seamless environment where data flows freely between appliances, smartphones, and cloud-based systems. This can enhance efficiency, save energy, and improve personal convenience. For example, a smart refrigerator might track your food consumption and automatically order groceries when you're running low, while a fitness tracker records your daily activities and syncs them with health apps to monitor your well-being. However, each of these devices collects vast amounts of data, much of which can reveal intimate details about your personal habits, preferences, and routines.

Conspiracy theorists argue that these devices, which are often marketed as tools of convenience, are actually part of a far-reaching surveillance network designed to keep tabs on every aspect of daily life. According to this belief, the IoT is not just about improving user experiences but is instead a carefully orchestrated system of monitoring and control overseen by the Illuminati. The more connected devices we use, the more data we generate, and the easier it becomes for those in power to track our movements, predict our behavior, and influence our decisions.

One of the key concerns raised by conspiracy theorists is the sheer volume of data these devices collect. Smart home assistants like Amazon's Alexa, Google Home, or Apple's Siri can listen to conversations, respond to commands, and record interactions with the device. Even when users aren't actively engaging with these assistants, they often remain "always on," ready to capture any command that might be spoken. This constant state of readiness has led to fears that these devices are secretly recording conversations and sending the data to tech companies—or worse, to shadowy organizations like the Illuminati. While companies insist that the devices only record when activated by a user, the idea that smart assistants could be used for surveillance has fed into widespread fears of a global monitoring system.

Beyond smart assistants, many IoT devices in the home are connected to external servers via the internet, meaning that data is frequently being uploaded, processed, and stored in the cloud. From security cameras to smart thermostats, these devices collect real-time information about who is in the house, what they are doing, and even how they interact with their environment. Conspiracy theorists view this constant data collection as a means for the Illuminati to build comprehensive profiles on individuals, tracking every aspect of their daily routines in real-time. By knowing when you leave the house, what you eat, how much you sleep, and what media you consume, those in power—allegedly the Illuminati—can exert influence over your life in ways that might not be immediately apparent.

A key feature of the IoT is its integration with wearable technology, such as smartwatches, fitness trackers, and even medical devices that monitor health conditions. While these devices can provide valuable health data and insights, they also raise concerns about privacy. Fitness trackers, for instance, monitor heart rate, steps taken, sleep patterns, and other personal health metrics. This data is often synced to cloud-based servers for analysis, which can then be accessed by health apps or sold to third parties for targeted advertising. For conspiracy theorists, the very idea that a device can continuously monitor an individual's body and behavior is chilling. They argue that this technology could be weaponized by the Illuminati to not only monitor personal health but to control or manipulate behavior through the use of subtle, data-driven nudges.

Another area of concern is the rise of "smart cities," where IoT technology is used to create interconnected urban environments. In smart cities, sensors embedded in public infrastructure can monitor everything from traffic flow to air quality, while surveillance cameras and facial recognition technology can track individuals as they move through the city. While proponents argue that smart cities improve efficiency and enhance public safety, conspiracy theorists believe that these initiatives are part of a grander Illuminati plan to create a global surveillance grid. In their view, smart cities offer a perfect cover for mass surveillance, where governments, under the influence of the Illuminati, can track citizens' every movement without their consent or knowledge.

The convergence of IoT devices with artificial intelligence (AI) only heightens these concerns. As AI systems become more sophisticated, they are increasingly capable of analyzing the vast amounts of data generated by IoT devices and using that data to make decisions or predictions about human behavior. For conspiracy theorists, this is a terrifying prospect. They believe that AI systems, under the control of the Illuminati, will be used to predict and influence people's actions in ways that are both subtle and pervasive. From determining what ads to show you based on your browsing history to predicting your next move based on your daily routine, AI is seen as the ultimate tool for behavioral manipulation.

In this context, the Internet of Things represents a major step toward the kind of total control envisioned by the Illuminati in conspiracy theory circles. Every smart device, every wearable tracker, and every connected appliance is perceived as part of a larger puzzle that leads to the erosion of privacy and the establishment of a global surveillance network. While the convenience of IoT devices is undeniable, conspiracy theorists argue that the real cost is far greater: the surrender of personal freedom and autonomy to an all-seeing, all-knowing system of control. Through the IoT, they believe the Illuminati is moving closer to its ultimate goal—total domination over every aspect of human life, facilitated by the very technologies we invite into our homes.

Biometric Surveillance and the Rise of Digital Identification

As technology continues to advance, the use of biometric data—such as fingerprints, facial recognition, and retinal scans—has become increasingly common in daily life. From unlocking smartphones with a fingerprint to passing through airport security using facial recognition software, biometric surveillance has been marketed as a secure and convenient solution. However, for those who believe in the Illuminati's influence, this rise in biometric data collection represents yet another tool in a broader scheme of global control, part of a larger effort to track and monitor every individual in the world.

Biometric surveillance is the process of identifying individuals based on unique physical or behavioral traits. Unlike passwords or ID cards, which can be lost or stolen, biometric data is inherently tied to the individual, making it a highly reliable form of identification. Governments and corporations have adopted this technology for everything from national ID programs to workplace security systems. Yet, as this technology becomes more widespread, concerns about privacy and the potential for misuse have grown, particularly among those who see biometric systems as part of a more sinister plan.

For conspiracy theorists, the collection of biometric data is not simply about improving security or streamlining identification processes. Instead, they argue that this technology is being used to build a vast global database of personal information that can be exploited for surveillance and control. According to these beliefs, the Illuminati—working through governments and multinational corporations—are using biometric systems to create a world where every individual can be tracked and monitored, no matter where they are or what they do.

One of the key concerns is the way biometric data is collected and stored. Unlike passwords, which can be changed, biometric data is permanent. Once your fingerprint or facial scan is stored in a database, it becomes a lasting identifier that can be used to track your movements and activities. In many countries, governments are implementing biometric identification systems as part of national ID programs, requiring citizens to submit fingerprints, facial scans, or other biometric data for access to essential services. While these systems are often presented as a way to improve security and reduce fraud, conspiracy theorists argue that they are part of a broader effort to build a global surveillance network under the control of the Illuminati.

Facial recognition technology is one of the most controversial aspects of biometric surveillance. In recent years, it has been adopted by law enforcement agencies, airports, and even private companies to identify individuals in real-time. With the ability to scan crowds and match faces to databases of known individuals, this technology offers unprecedented tracking capabilities. Conspiracy theorists argue that facial recognition systems are a key tool for the Illuminati to keep tabs on the global population. By deploying these systems in public spaces, they believe the Illuminati can track individuals' movements, monitor their associations, and even identify potential dissenters.

China, in particular, has become a focal point for discussions about the dangers of biometric surveillance. The Chinese government has implemented a massive surveillance network that includes facial recognition cameras in public spaces and a national ID system that links biometric data with personal information. This system is part of China's broader "social credit" program, which tracks citizens' behavior and assigns them scores based on their actions. Those with low scores may face restrictions on travel, employment, or access to services. For conspiracy theorists, China's social credit system is a harbinger of things to come: a real-world example of how biometric surveillance can be used to control and manipulate entire populations, allegedly under the influence of the Illuminati.

In the West, biometric systems are being integrated into everyday life through the use of smartphones and other personal devices. Apple's Face ID and Touch ID systems, which allow users to unlock their phones and authorize payments using facial recognition or fingerprint scans, have normalized the collection of biometric data in daily activities. While these systems are promoted as secure and user-friendly, conspiracy theorists argue that they are part of a larger plan to acclimate people to constant biometric surveillance. By embedding this technology into personal devices, they believe the Illuminati is conditioning society to accept a future where biometric identification is required for all transactions, movements, and interactions.

The concept of digital identification has also raised alarms among those who believe in Illuminati control. Many governments and tech companies are working on digital ID programs that would link biometric data to online identities, allowing for seamless integration between physical and digital worlds. These digital IDs could be used for everything from accessing government services to verifying identity in online transactions. While proponents argue that digital IDs would simplify processes and enhance security, conspiracy theorists see them as a tool for totalitarian control. They fear that once biometric data is tied to digital identities, individuals could be tracked not only in the physical world but also across their online activities, leaving no aspect of life beyond the reach of surveillance.

One of the most frequently cited concerns is the potential for biometric data to be used in conjunction with artificial intelligence (AI) to predict and control behavior. AI systems that analyze biometric data could, in theory, be used to identify not just who a person is but what they are likely to do. For conspiracy theorists, this represents the ultimate threat: a world where individuals' every move is predicted and controlled by an all-powerful, unseen force—the Illuminati. In this vision of the future, biometric surveillance, combined with AI, would allow for the creation of a society in which personal autonomy is severely limited, and every action is monitored and guided by those in power.

The potential for abuse in biometric systems has already been demonstrated in cases of surveillance overreach. In many countries, law enforcement agencies have used facial recognition technology to track protestors, monitor public gatherings, and identify individuals participating in political demonstrations. For those who believe in Illuminati theories, this is clear evidence of how biometric data can be weaponized to suppress dissent and control populations. They argue that as biometric technology becomes more advanced and more widespread, it will become increasingly difficult to escape the watchful eye of the Illuminati-controlled surveillance state.

In conclusion, biometric surveillance, once a futuristic concept, is now a reality in many parts of the world. While it offers undeniable benefits in terms of security and convenience, it also raises serious concerns about privacy, autonomy, and the potential for abuse. For conspiracy theorists, the rise of biometric identification systems is not just a technological advancement but a key component of the Illuminati's plan to monitor and control humanity. Through the widespread adoption of biometric surveillance, they believe that the Illuminati is building the infrastructure for a world where every individual can be tracked, monitored, and ultimately controlled, bringing us one step closer to the realization of the New World Order.

The Future of Digital Currencies and Cashless Societies

As we move deeper into the digital age, the idea of a cashless society is no longer a distant fantasy but an emerging reality. The transition from physical currency to digital payment systems is accelerating, with mobile payments, cryptocurrencies, and digital wallets becoming increasingly prevalent. For most people, these technologies offer convenience, speed, and security in financial transactions. However, for those who believe in the Illuminati conspiracy, the rise of digital currencies and the move toward a cashless society represent another step toward a system of total control, where all financial activity can be tracked, monitored, and potentially manipulated by a shadowy elite.

In a cashless society, all financial transactions—whether buying groceries, paying bills, or even giving to charity—are conducted digitally. This means that every transaction leaves a traceable record, stored in databases that can be accessed by financial institutions, governments, and tech companies. For conspiracy theorists, this level of transparency is not just a feature of modern finance but a tool of control. They argue that by eliminating physical currency, those in power—allegedly the Illuminati—can ensure that every individual's financial activities are fully visible, leaving no room for privacy or autonomy.

One of the key concerns surrounding digital currencies is the centralization of control over financial systems. In a world where all transactions are digital, governments or central banks could, in theory, have the power to monitor, regulate, or even freeze the accounts of individuals. This level of control over personal finances is viewed by conspiracy theorists as a critical component of the New World Order, where an elite group controls not just political and social structures but the very flow of money itself. According to this belief, the Illuminati's ultimate goal is to create a global financial system where all money is digital, and individuals can be easily controlled by cutting off their access to funds if they do not comply with the established order.

Cryptocurrencies, which were initially hailed as a decentralized alternative to traditional banking systems, have become a major focus of both fascination and fear in Illuminati conspiracy theories. Bitcoin, Ethereum, and other digital currencies operate on blockchain technology, which is decentralized by design, meaning that no single institution controls the currency. However, conspiracy theorists argue that even cryptocurrencies could eventually be co-opted by the Illuminati, or at least serve as a stepping stone toward a fully cashless society. They point to the growing interest from governments and major corporations in blockchain technology as evidence that what started as a rebellious, decentralized movement could be integrated into a more centralized system of control.

One of the most significant developments in this realm is the rise of Central Bank Digital Currencies (CBDCs). Several countries, including China, Sweden, and the European Union, are exploring or have already begun piloting their own digital currencies. Unlike cryptocurrencies, which operate independently of government control, CBDCs are state-issued and fully regulated by central banks. This means that governments would have complete oversight of all transactions conducted with these digital currencies. Conspiracy theorists argue that CBDCs are the Illuminati's ultimate financial weapon, allowing governments to track every purchase, control how money is spent, and impose restrictions on financial activity as they see fit. For those who believe in the Illuminati, the adoption of CBDCs is seen as the final nail in the coffin for financial freedom, giving an unseen elite the ability to control the global economy and, by extension, the behavior of every individual.

Another area of concern is the increasing use of biometric authentication in financial transactions. Digital wallets like Apple Pay,

Google Pay, and other mobile payment systems often require fingerprint scans or facial recognition to authorize payments. While these systems are designed to enhance security, conspiracy theorists argue that they further entrench the link between personal identity, biometric data, and financial control. In a cashless society, where all transactions require biometric verification, the fear is that individuals could be denied access to their own funds if they do not comply with the systems in place. This, in turn, feeds into a broader fear of social control, where dissenters or those who refuse to conform to the demands of the Illuminati could find themselves financially cut off and powerless.

For those who subscribe to Illuminati conspiracy theories, the rise of digital currencies is not just about convenience or technological progress—it is about the gradual erosion of personal freedom. In their view, the move toward a cashless society is part of a larger agenda to create a world where all aspects of life are monitored and controlled by a centralized authority. This is often tied to the concept of the "Mark of the Beast" from Christian eschatology, where individuals are required to accept a form of identification or currency in order to participate in the global economy. Many conspiracy theorists believe that digital currencies, especially when linked to biometric data, represent a modern manifestation of this prophecy, with the Illuminati playing the role of the global enforcer.

The fear of financial control also extends to the possibility of social credit systems, similar to those implemented in China, being adopted on a global scale. In a cashless world, where all transactions are digital and traceable, it would be relatively easy for governments or corporations to monitor spending patterns and assign individuals scores based on their behavior. Conspiracy theorists argue that such systems could be used to punish those who do not conform to societal norms or who express dissenting opinions. For example, someone who participates in anti-government protests or speaks out against the establishment might find their social credit score lowered, resulting in restricted access to services, employment, or even their own financial resources. This is seen as yet another tool in the Illuminati's alleged plan to create a world where compliance is mandatory and resistance is futile.

In this context, the push toward digital currencies and a cashless society represents a profound shift in the balance of power between individuals and institutions. While the proponents of these technologies argue that they offer greater efficiency, security, and accessibility, conspiracy theorists believe that they are part of a much darker agenda. For those who subscribe to Illuminati theories, the transition to a cashless world is not just about the convenience of digital payments—it is about control, surveillance, and the loss of personal freedom on a global scale.

In conclusion, the rise of digital currencies, combined with the increasing integration of biometric data and surveillance technologies, is seen by conspiracy theorists as a key component of the Illuminati's plan to establish a New World Order. The elimination of cash and the move toward fully digital transactions are viewed as steps toward a world where financial autonomy is a thing of the past, and every individual's economic activity is subject to scrutiny and control. Whether or not these fears are justified, they highlight the deep unease that many feel about the future of finance in an increasingly digital world—and the potential for that future to be shaped by forces beyond our control.

Chapter 11: Debunking Illuminati Myths

The Origins of Modern Illuminati Conspiracy Theories
The modern conception of the Illuminati as a powerful, secret organization controlling world events is vastly different from the historical reality of the Bavarian Illuminati. To understand how this myth evolved, it's essential to start with the real Illuminati—a short-lived Enlightenment-era society that was neither as powerful nor as sinister as the conspiracy theories suggest.

The Illuminati was founded on May 1, 1776, by Adam Weishaupt, a professor of canon law at the University of Ingolstadt in Bavaria (modern-day Germany). Weishaupt's vision for the group was to promote Enlightenment ideals such as reason, secularism, and freedom of thought. The group sought to influence political and social reforms, pushing back against the traditional authority of the monarchy and the Catholic Church. At its peak, the Bavarian Illuminati had around 2,000 members, including intellectuals and political figures. However, it was far from the all-powerful organization depicted in modern conspiracy lore.

The downfall of the Bavarian Illuminati came swiftly. In the late 1780s, the group was outlawed by the Bavarian government, which feared the influence of secret societies. By 1785, the organization had been officially disbanded, with many of its members fleeing or going into hiding. Within a decade of its founding, the Illuminati had ceased to exist as an organized group. There was no secret cabal pulling the strings behind the scenes of world events; it was simply another failed attempt at social reform.

Yet, despite the Illuminati's dissolution, the myth of a secret society lurking in the shadows endured and evolved. This transformation began in the late 18th century when conspiracy theories about secret societies gained traction, fueled by the political turbulence of the time. The French Revolution, in particular, played a significant role in shaping the narrative. As France descended into chaos, people looked for hidden causes behind the revolution's violence and upheaval. Some found their answer in the Illuminati, despite the group's formal disbandment years earlier.

In 1797, a French Jesuit priest named Augustin Barruel published *Memoirs Illustrating the History of Jacobinism*, in which he claimed that the French Revolution was the result of a conspiracy orchestrated by the Illuminati, Freemasons, and other secret societies. Barruel's work gained popularity, despite a lack of credible evidence, because it provided a simple explanation for the complex political and social changes happening in France. A year later, John Robison, a Scottish physicist and philosopher, published *Proofs of a Conspiracy*, which echoed Barruel's claims and further cemented the Illuminati as a shadowy force behind global events.

These works marked the beginning of a new chapter in the Illuminati myth. No longer just a group of Enlightenment thinkers, the Illuminati was now viewed as an insidious secret society bent on world domination. As these conspiracy theories spread across Europe, they gained momentum, linking the Illuminati to a variety of events, from revolutions to assassinations.

Throughout the 19th and 20th centuries, the Illuminati myth continued to evolve. Anti-Masonic movements, particularly in the United States, played a significant role in this evolution. The anti-Masonic sentiment was rooted in suspicion of Freemasonry and other secret societies, and the Illuminati was often lumped into these broader conspiracies. The Illuminati became a catch-all term for any secret group supposedly influencing political or economic systems behind the scenes.

By the time the 20th century rolled around, the Illuminati conspiracy had expanded far beyond its historical origins. The group was now blamed for everything from world wars to the rise of communism, with some theorists even claiming that the Illuminati was working toward the establishment of a "New World Order"—a single, totalitarian government that would control every aspect of human life. This idea of the Illuminati manipulating world events to bring about global domination has become a cornerstone of modern conspiracy theories.

The Illuminati's transformation from a small group of Enlightenment intellectuals to an omnipotent secret society highlights the power of myth and fear. In the absence of facts, the story of the Illuminati has been reshaped and exaggerated over centuries, feeding on political unrest, social upheaval, and human psychology's tendency to seek simple answers for complex problems. The historical Illuminati may have disappeared, but the myth they inspired continues to thrive, deeply rooted in the fabric of modern conspiracy thinking.

Understanding Psychological Factors Behind Conspiracy Beliefs

The enduring appeal of Illuminati conspiracy theories cannot be fully explained by history alone. To understand why people continue to believe in these myths, we must explore the psychological mechanisms that make conspiracy theories so alluring. Human psychology, particularly in times of uncertainty and fear, plays a crucial role in shaping beliefs in secret societies like the Illuminati.

At the heart of many conspiracy theories is a basic human cognitive trait: pattern recognition. Humans are naturally wired to seek patterns in the world around them. This ability, which evolved for survival purposes, helps us navigate complex environments and make quick decisions. For our ancestors, being able to recognize the patterns of predator behavior or seasonal changes was essential. However, this same instinct can lead us to find connections where none exist—especially when faced with random or chaotic events. This phenomenon, known as *apophenia*, is a key driver behind conspiracy beliefs.

In the context of the Illuminati, apophenia leads people to connect unrelated events—political upheaval, celebrity scandals, global crises—and attribute them to a hidden force pulling the strings behind the scenes. From a cognitive standpoint, it feels comforting to impose order on chaos, even if that order is imaginary. When the world seems too complex or unpredictable, the idea that a secret society like the Illuminati is orchestrating events from the shadows provides a sense of structure. The randomness of reality is replaced with a narrative that makes sense of the confusion.

Another cognitive bias that fuels belief in Illuminati conspiracies is *confirmation bias*. This is the tendency to seek out, interpret, and remember information that confirms one's existing beliefs, while ignoring or dismissing evidence that contradicts them. Once someone starts to believe in the Illuminati or similar conspiracy theories, they begin to filter the information they encounter through this lens. Any event that seems suspicious—whether it's a celebrity making a certain hand gesture or a political leader using specific language—is seen as evidence of Illuminati influence. This creates a self-reinforcing loop, where the believer constantly finds more "proof" to validate their theory, no matter how tenuous the connections may be.

This selective thinking is particularly powerful in the age of social media, where algorithms often show users content that aligns with their interests and existing views. Someone who begins to dabble in Illuminati conspiracy theories will quickly be presented with more and more content that supports their beliefs, deepening their conviction. The internet has made it easier than ever to fall into an echo chamber, where opposing viewpoints are minimized, and only evidence supporting the conspiracy is amplified.

The emotional appeal of Illuminati conspiracy theories also cannot be underestimated. People are more likely to believe in conspiracies during times of fear, anxiety, and uncertainty. Political upheaval, economic crises, natural disasters, and global pandemics create an environment ripe for conspiracy thinking. The world feels out of control, and people look for explanations that can provide a sense of clarity. The Illuminati myth offers a simple, albeit fictional, answer: the chaos we see is not random or incomprehensible; it is the result of deliberate actions by a secret, powerful group. This narrative gives people a way to make sense of their fear and anxiety, even if it's based on misinformation.

Moreover, Illuminati conspiracy theories provide an emotional outlet for people who feel powerless. In a world where many feel disconnected from the political and economic systems that govern their lives, the belief in an all-powerful group controlling everything can explain personal frustrations and societal injustices. If the world is controlled by a secret elite, it explains why the average person struggles to make an impact. This belief offers both an explanation for perceived helplessness and a target for anger—often elites, politicians, or celebrities.

Projection is another psychological mechanism that fuels Illuminati theories. Often, conspiracy theories reflect our own fears and desires projected onto an external "other." Those who believe in the Illuminati might be projecting their own concerns about inequality, government overreach, or societal corruption onto this fictional group. The Illuminati becomes a stand-in for all the power and influence they feel is being unfairly wielded in the world. By focusing on this imagined enemy, they can channel their frustrations and fears in a way that feels tangible, even if it's not grounded in reality.

Finally, the concept of *agency detection*—the tendency to assume that events are caused by intentional agents rather than random forces—further strengthens belief in the Illuminati. Humans have a deep-seated inclination to assign intentionality to events. When something happens, especially something negative, we naturally ask, "Who did this?" Conspiracy theories thrive on this question by providing a clear answer. The Illuminati, in this case, becomes the agent responsible for everything from political revolutions to economic downturns. Even when evidence points to more mundane or complex causes, the conspiracy believer sees the hand of the Illuminati behind it all.

In sum, the psychology behind Illuminati conspiracy theories is driven by a combination of cognitive biases, emotional needs, and innate tendencies to assign patterns and agency where none exist. While the myth itself is historically unfounded, the reasons for its persistence are deeply rooted in human nature. By understanding these psychological factors, we can better grasp why conspiracy theories like the Illuminati remain so popular and why, in times of crisis, they are likely to gain even more traction.

The Role of Media and Entertainment in Perpetuating the Illuminati Myth

In the modern world, few things have kept the Illuminati myth alive as much as media and entertainment. From blockbuster films and chart-topping songs to viral videos and online communities, the media has played a central role in transforming what was once a niche conspiracy theory into a cultural phenomenon. The image of the Illuminati—a shadowy, powerful organization manipulating world events—has been popularized through fiction, music videos, social media platforms, and even news coverage. This constant exposure has helped the myth seep into mainstream consciousness, making it seem plausible to many despite its baselessness.

One of the most significant ways in which the Illuminati myth has been perpetuated is through popular music. Over the last two decades, some of the world's biggest celebrities, particularly in the music industry, have been repeatedly linked to the Illuminati in conspiracy theories. Artists like Beyoncé, Jay-Z, Rihanna, and Kanye West have all been accused of being members of the secret society. Their performances, music videos, and public personas are often dissected by conspiracy theorists searching for hidden Illuminati symbols—whether it's a triangle, the "all-seeing eye," or hand gestures resembling the pyramid sign.

Take Beyoncé and Jay-Z, for example. The couple, who are among the most successful and influential figures in the music industry, have long been associated with Illuminati theories. Conspiracy theorists often cite Jay-Z's use of a triangle symbol, which he refers to as the "Roc Sign," during his performances as evidence of his membership in the secret society. Similarly, Beyoncé's imagery in her music videos and performances—whether intentional or coincidental—is frequently linked to Illuminati symbolism. This connection between celebrity culture and Illuminati theories has created a powerful feedback loop, where any success or prominence achieved by these artists is seen as further proof of their involvement in a secret, all-powerful organization.

What drives these accusations is not only the symbolism itself but also the broader narrative of control and influence. In the eyes of conspiracy theorists, celebrities are viewed as "puppets" of the Illuminati, used to influence the masses and distract them from what's really happening in the world. This notion is particularly compelling because of the immense visibility and cultural sway that celebrities wield. The global reach of music, particularly pop and hip-hop, ensures that images and symbols spread rapidly and become ingrained in the public imagination. For conspiracy believers, it's not a coincidence that the most famous people in the world would be connected to a secret group bent on controlling society.

Beyond the music industry, films and TV shows have also played a role in keeping the Illuminati myth alive. Hollywood's penchant for stories about secret societies, hidden conspiracies, and shadow governments has indirectly fueled the belief in the Illuminati. Movies like *Eyes Wide Shut*, *National Treasure*, and *The Da Vinci Code*—all featuring secretive, powerful organizations—have shaped how many people think about groups like the Illuminati. While these films are clearly fictional, they tap into the allure of secret knowledge and hidden power, blurring the lines between entertainment and belief.

Additionally, Hollywood's fascination with the concept of the New World Order has further stoked the flames of conspiracy theories. Films that depict dystopian futures where governments or shadow organizations control every aspect of society feed into the narratives pushed by Illuminati believers. These movies, while designed to entertain, have helped to reinforce the notion that such scenarios are not only possible but already in motion. For viewers already inclined to believe in Illuminati conspiracies, these depictions offer validation for their fears about global control and secret elites.

Social media has arguably had the most significant impact on the proliferation of Illuminati theories in recent years. Platforms like YouTube, TikTok, and Instagram are rife with videos and posts dedicated to "exposing" the Illuminati's influence in everything from politics to pop culture. YouTube, in particular, is home to a vast network of conspiracy channels that analyze music videos, film scenes, and news clips for supposed Illuminati symbols. These videos, often filled with ominous music and dramatic narration, break down imagery and gestures to support their claims, drawing millions of views in the process.

The viral nature of social media has allowed Illuminati theories to spread like wildfire. Memes, hashtags, and short video clips make the conspiracy accessible to a wider audience, often reaching younger generations who may not have been exposed to these ideas through traditional media. A single post suggesting that a major event—such as a celebrity's death or a political scandal—was orchestrated by the Illuminati can be shared thousands of times in a matter of minutes, planting the seed of conspiracy in the minds of countless viewers. Social media algorithms, designed to keep users engaged, often exacerbate this by recommending similar content, creating an echo chamber where users are continuously fed conspiracy material.

The news media has also played an inadvertent role in perpetuating the Illuminati myth. While most mainstream outlets do not endorse conspiracy theories, the sheer act of reporting on the phenomenon gives it more visibility. Articles debunking Illuminati claims, or even covering celebrity accusations, bring the myth to the forefront of public attention. In a media landscape that thrives on sensationalism, the Illuminati narrative—no matter how baseless—often makes for compelling headlines and click-worthy content. As a result, even skeptics can become more familiar with the conspiracy simply by seeing it repeatedly in the media.

In summary, the media and entertainment industries have been instrumental in maintaining the Illuminati myth. Whether through pop music, films, viral videos, or news reports, the image of a powerful secret society manipulating world events has become ingrained in popular culture. This constant exposure, combined with the psychological need for simple explanations to complex problems, ensures that the myth continues to thrive in the collective imagination.

Illuminati Symbolism in Popular Culture

One of the most enduring elements of the Illuminati myth is its association with a set of recognizable symbols that appear throughout popular culture. These symbols, which are often interpreted as visual cues of the Illuminati's supposed influence, have become integral to the myth's staying power. They range from the infamous "all-seeing eye" and the pyramid to more abstract symbols like the number 666 and the pentagram. The prominence of these symbols in music videos, films, advertisements, and even architecture has led conspiracy theorists to believe that the Illuminati are signaling their presence and control through coded messages in plain sight.

The most famous of these symbols is undoubtedly the "all-seeing eye," often depicted as an eye within a triangle or pyramid. Its origin can be traced back to ancient Egyptian mythology, where the Eye of Horus was a symbol of protection and royal power. However, its modern association with the Illuminati comes from its use on the U.S. dollar bill, where it appears atop a pyramid as part of the Great Seal of the United States. This image has long been a focal point for conspiracy theorists, who argue that its placement on the currency is proof of the Illuminati's influence in the highest levels of government and finance. To them, the all-seeing eye represents the Illuminati's surveillance over society, a metaphor for their ability to watch and control every aspect of the world.

This symbol has found its way into various forms of entertainment, particularly music videos and films. Artists like Jay-Z, Kanye West, and Lady Gaga have been accused of incorporating the all-seeing eye into their work, whether through gestures, hand signs, or visual elements in their performances. In Jay-Z's case, his use of a triangle-shaped hand gesture, often referred to as the "Roc Sign," has been widely interpreted as a representation of the pyramid and eye, even though he has publicly explained it as a symbol of his record label, Roc-A-Fella Records. Nevertheless, conspiracy theorists see these uses as deliberate nods to Illuminati affiliation.

Another prevalent symbol linked to the Illuminati is the pyramid itself. The pyramid, especially when topped with the all-seeing eye, is seen as a representation of hierarchical power structures, with the Illuminati at the top, controlling the masses below. This idea of a pyramid-shaped power structure fits neatly with the conspiracy's narrative of a small, elite group secretly governing the world. As with the all-seeing eye, pyramids are often spotted in music videos, concert stages, and movie sets, further fueling the theory that these symbols are intentionally used to signal Illuminati membership.

In addition to the all-seeing eye and pyramid, other symbols like the number 666 and the pentagram have been co-opted into the Illuminati narrative. The number 666 is traditionally associated with the devil in Christian theology, referred to as the "number of the beast" in the Book of Revelation. Conspiracy theorists argue that the Illuminati, which they often link to satanic rituals and occult practices, use this number as a hidden code. Any appearance of 666 in popular culture—whether in logos, artwork, or even the configuration of a product's price—is seen as a deliberate reference to the Illuminati's supposed dark influence.

The pentagram, a five-pointed star often associated with occult and magical practices, is another symbol that appears in Illuminati lore. While the pentagram has been used for centuries in various cultures and spiritual practices, conspiracy theorists believe that its presence in entertainment or corporate branding is a sign of the Illuminati's hidden agenda. For instance, the appearance of pentagrams in music videos, fashion designs, or even in the layout of certain city streets is interpreted as evidence of the Illuminati's occult power and their desire to influence society through symbolism.

One of the reasons why these symbols are so effective in perpetuating the Illuminati myth is their ubiquity. Many of these symbols, particularly the pyramid and all-seeing eye, are common visual motifs that have been used across cultures and throughout history. This makes it easy for conspiracy theorists to find them everywhere, even in places where their presence is purely coincidental or the result of artistic design choices. The very nature of these symbols—abstract, open to interpretation, and deeply rooted in history—makes them perfect fodder for conspiracy theorists who are constantly looking for hidden meaning in the world around them.

Moreover, the deliberate use of these symbols by artists and creators, whether for aesthetic purposes or to provoke controversy, only adds fuel to the fire. In some cases, celebrities and filmmakers may even play into the Illuminati narrative for attention or to generate buzz around their work. By incorporating Illuminati symbols into their music videos or performances, they know that it will spark discussion, drive engagement, and ultimately increase their visibility. This self-reinforcing cycle keeps the Illuminati myth alive in popular culture, as every new instance of a pyramid or eye symbol in the media becomes further "evidence" for conspiracy believers.

Additionally, the rise of internet meme culture has played a significant role in popularizing Illuminati symbols. The phrase "Illuminati confirmed" has become a common joke online, often used sarcastically when a triangle or eye symbol is spotted in random or unrelated contexts. While these memes are often created and shared with humor in mind, they also serve to keep the concept of the Illuminati alive in the collective consciousness. The line between genuine belief and ironic joking becomes blurred, making it difficult to discern whether people are sincerely buying into the conspiracy or simply playing along for the sake of the meme.

In conclusion, the use of Illuminati symbols in popular culture has been one of the driving forces behind the conspiracy theory's continued relevance. The prevalence of the all-seeing eye, pyramid, 666, and pentagram in entertainment and media provides constant visual reinforcement for believers, while the viral nature of social media ensures that these symbols are seen by millions. Whether through deliberate artistic choices or coincidental appearances, these symbols have become ingrained in the public imagination, ensuring that the Illuminati myth endures in the modern world.

The Self-Sustaining Nature of the Illuminati in Popular Culture

One of the most fascinating aspects of the Illuminati conspiracy theory is its self-sustaining nature, particularly within the context of popular culture. As the theory has evolved over time, it has developed a momentum of its own, becoming a sort of cultural feedback loop. Each new reference to the Illuminati, whether in jest or as part of a larger conspiracy narrative, adds another layer to the myth. This phenomenon has allowed the Illuminati conspiracy to not only survive but thrive in the modern world, gaining new followers and evolving with every generation.

The self-perpetuating nature of the Illuminati myth is largely due to the way it adapts to new cultural contexts and technologies. Unlike other conspiracy theories that are bound to specific events or time periods, the Illuminati narrative is flexible and can be molded to fit almost any situation. This adaptability ensures that the theory remains relevant, no matter how much the world changes. Whether it's a political upheaval, a major celebrity scandal, or the rise of new technologies, the Illuminati is consistently invoked as the hidden hand pulling the strings. As long as there are people who feel disempowered or distrustful of authority, the Illuminati theory will find fertile ground.

The rise of the internet has played a pivotal role in this self-sustaining cycle. Before the digital age, conspiracy theories were often confined to fringe publications, niche groups, or whispered conversations. But with the advent of the internet and social media, the Illuminati myth exploded into the mainstream. Websites, forums, and social platforms dedicated to conspiracy theories have flourished, allowing people from all over the world to connect, share ideas, and build upon each other's beliefs. In these online communities, the Illuminati narrative grows, becoming more elaborate with each passing day.

Social media, in particular, has had a profound impact on how the Illuminati myth is consumed and propagated. Platforms like Twitter, Facebook, Instagram, and YouTube are rife with content about the Illuminati—whether in the form of conspiracy videos, memes, or serious discussions. The viral nature of these platforms means that once an idea takes hold, it can spread like wildfire. A single tweet or video suggesting that a major event, such as a natural disaster or political decision, was orchestrated by the Illuminati can quickly reach millions of people. Even those who don't believe in the conspiracy are exposed to it repeatedly, keeping the myth alive in public consciousness.

What makes the Illuminati myth particularly resilient is the way it incorporates new elements over time. Whenever a significant global event occurs, conspiracy theorists are quick to link it to the Illuminati. From the 9/11 attacks to the COVID-19 pandemic, major historical moments are often framed as part of the Illuminati's grand plan for world domination. This ability to evolve and stay current gives the myth a timeless quality, ensuring its continued relevance.

Popular culture plays a crucial role in this cycle. When celebrities, films, or music videos are accused of being connected to the Illuminati, it often sparks widespread discussion, which in turn keeps the theory alive. For example, when a major artist like Beyoncé or Jay-Z is accused of being part of the Illuminati, their fans and detractors alike take notice. The mere mention of the Illuminati, whether serious or ironic, ensures that the myth remains part of the cultural conversation. In this way, pop culture becomes both a catalyst and a vehicle for the conspiracy's survival.

This feedback loop is further reinforced by the way the Illuminati myth interacts with other conspiracy theories. The Illuminati is often linked to other popular conspiracies, such as the New World Order, Freemasonry, or government cover-ups. These connections create a web of beliefs that reinforce one another. For example, someone who believes in the existence of a secret government program may also be inclined to believe that the Illuminati is involved in it. The more these ideas intersect, the stronger the overall narrative becomes, creating a conspiracy ecosystem that is difficult to disprove or dismantle.

The entertainment industry has also played into the self-sustaining nature of the Illuminati myth. Films, television shows, and even video games have incorporated Illuminati themes or symbols, either as a plot device or as part of the visual aesthetic. For instance, the 1999 film *The Matrix* features a dystopian world controlled by hidden forces, which many conspiracy theorists interpret as a metaphor for the Illuminati's influence. Other films like *Eyes Wide Shut* and

Angels & Demons explicitly explore secret societies, further cementing the idea of powerful, unseen forces controlling global events.

These cultural representations, while fictional, have a real-world impact on how people perceive the Illuminati myth. The more the conspiracy is depicted in mainstream media, the more it feels plausible to those who are already predisposed to believe in such ideas. Even for those who view these films and shows as mere entertainment, the constant presence of Illuminati themes reinforces the notion that secret societies and global control are not entirely far-fetched.

Moreover, the myth's persistence in popular culture is sustained by the human tendency to look for patterns and hidden meanings in complex, chaotic events. The Illuminati conspiracy offers a simple explanation for an increasingly complicated world. It provides a narrative where everything makes sense: there is a reason for every war, every economic downturn, every political scandal. For believers, the Illuminati is a convenient scapegoat for a world that often feels out of control. And because the myth offers this sense of order and clarity, it continues to appeal to new generations of conspiracy theorists.

In conclusion, the self-sustaining nature of the Illuminati myth is one of its most powerful attributes. By adapting to new cultural trends, leveraging the viral nature of social media, and incorporating itself into the fabric of popular culture, the Illuminati conspiracy has ensured its survival. As long as there are symbols to interpret, events to question, and authority figures to distrust, the myth will continue to thrive, feeding off its own momentum in an endless cycle.

Chapter 12: Psychological Aspects of Illuminati Be

The Human Need for Control in a Chaotic World

The human mind has a natural tendency to seek control, especially in a world filled with uncertainty and complexity. When faced with overwhelming events—economic crises, political up-heavals, or sudden societal shifts—many people experience feelings of helplessness. It is during these moments of chaos that the allure of conspiracy theories, like the belief in the Illuminati, becomes most powerful. Conspiracy theories offer a sense of order and explanation where none seems readily available, providing the believer with a framework to understand the seemingly incomprehensible.

One of the key psychological reasons behind the belief in the Illu-minati is the human desire for *cognitive closure*—a need for answers and certainty. This need intensifies during times of crisis or rapid change, when individuals are more likely to feel a lack of control over their own lives or the world around them. Belief in a hidden, omnipotent force like the Illuminati offers a straightforward narra-tive: the world is not random or chaotic, but is instead being ma-nipulated by a powerful, secretive group with a clear agenda. This explanation, while frightening, can paradoxically be comforting. It provides a structure for understanding events that would otherwise seem unpredictable or senseless.

Moreover, the brain's natural inclination for *pattern recognition* plays a crucial role in sustaining Illuminati beliefs. Humans are wired to look for patterns in their environment, an evolutionary trait that once helped our ancestors avoid predators and find resources. However, in the context of modern society, this instinct can lead individuals to draw connections where none exist. For example, the repeated appearance of certain symbols—such as pyramids, the Eye of Providence, or even specific hand gestures—across various media is often interpreted by conspiracy theorists as evidence of the Illuminati's influence. What might be mere coincidence or artistic choices are seen instead as deliberate markers left by a secret cabal. This form of *apophenia*—the tendency to perceive meaningful connections between unrelated things—fuels the belief that a hidden group controls world events.

The desire for control also stems from existential anxieties, particularly in a world where random events can have devastating consequences. Natural disasters, economic recessions, terrorist attacks—these are frightening because they are often unpredictable and beyond the control of any individual. In such an environment, it is far easier to believe that these events are orchestrated by an all-powerful group like the Illuminati than to accept that they are simply the result of chance or systemic failures. By attributing these occurrences to a malevolent force, believers gain a sense of psychological closure, as though the mystery of the world has been solved.

Furthermore, belief in the Illuminati can serve as a coping mechanism in the face of personal powerlessness. Those who feel marginalized or disenfranchised by society—whether due to economic struggles, political disillusionment, or social alienation—may be drawn to conspiracy theories as a way to explain their predicament.

The narrative of the Illuminati provides a clear villain: a shadowy elite manipulating the masses, responsible for societal inequality and injustice. For those who feel powerless, this explanation is appealing because it shifts the blame for their struggles onto an external force, rather than requiring them to confront more complex or abstract societal issues.

In this way, the Illuminati myth offers a sense of order in a world that often feels chaotic. It simplifies the complexities of modern life, providing believers with a narrative that makes sense of the incomprehensible. For many, the idea that a secret group controls everything, while frightening, is preferable to the discomforting reality that much of life is shaped by randomness, chance, and systemic forces beyond individual understanding. By believing in the Illuminati, individuals can regain a sense of control, even if that control is ultimately illusory.

This human need for control, combined with the brain's natural tendency to seek patterns and answers, makes conspiracy theories like the Illuminati particularly resilient. In times of societal upheaval or personal crisis, these beliefs offer a form of psychological security, shielding believers from the full weight of uncertainty in the modern world. While this sense of control may be comforting, it also traps individuals in a worldview that distorts reality, preventing them from engaging with more nuanced or evidence-based explanations for the world around them.

Cognitive Biases and the Appeal of Conspiratorial Thinking

At the heart of the belief in the Illuminati lies a series of cognitive biases that distort our understanding of reality. These psychological mechanisms shape how individuals interpret information and influence their willingness to accept the convoluted narratives presented by conspiracy theories. By examining these biases, we can gain insight into why the idea of a powerful, hidden group manipulating world events resonates so deeply with many people.

One of the most prominent cognitive biases at play is *confirmation bias*. This bias refers to the tendency of individuals to seek out, interpret, and remember information in a way that confirms their existing beliefs. For those who already have a predisposition to distrust authority or are drawn to conspiracy theories, confirmation bias reinforces the belief in the Illuminati by filtering out any evidence that contradicts it. When presented with ambiguous or complex information—such as political maneuvers, corporate actions, or global events—believers may selectively focus on details that align with their suspicions. This creates a feedback loop where their beliefs are continuously validated, making it difficult to challenge or dismantle their worldview.

The *availability heuristic* also plays a crucial role in the spread of Illuminati beliefs. This cognitive shortcut leads individuals to judge the likelihood of an event based on how easily they can recall similar instances. In the age of social media, where information spreads rapidly and sensational stories gain traction, those who encounter multiple claims of Illuminati involvement in various events may come to believe that such involvement is commonplace. For example, if a celebrity's unexpected behavior is linked to the Illuminati, it becomes easier for individuals to accept future allegations without critical examination. The more frequently they hear these connections, the more credible they appear, reinforcing the notion that the Illuminati is omnipresent and manipulative.

Another significant factor is the *proportionality bias*, which posits that people often believe significant events must have equally significant causes. This bias leads individuals to assume that extraordinary occurrences—like natural disasters, political upheavals, or economic collapses—cannot simply happen by chance. Instead, they must be the result of deliberate actions taken by powerful entities, such as the Illuminati. This belief offers a simplistic explanation for complex issues, allowing individuals to attribute blame and identify a clear enemy. In doing so, they gain a sense of understanding and empowerment in the face of bewildering global dynamics.

Additionally, the emotional appeal of conspiratorial thinking cannot be overlooked. Conspiracy theories often evoke strong emotions, such as fear, anger, and indignation, which can create a sense of urgency and compel individuals to dig deeper into the narrative. The notion that the Illuminati is orchestrating events from the shadows taps into primal fears of manipulation and loss of control, driving believers to seek out further evidence of the conspiracy. This emotional engagement can heighten their commitment to the belief, making it even more resistant to rational scrutiny.

The cognitive biases that underpin belief in the Illuminati also interact with social dynamics. When individuals engage with like-minded communities—whether online or in person—they find themselves in environments that validate their beliefs and reinforce these biases. Echo chambers amplify confirmation bias, as group members share and promote information that aligns with their views while dismissing or discrediting opposing perspectives. In such settings, the allure of the Illuminati becomes even stronger, as believers rally around shared convictions and engage in collective sense-making.

Moreover, the narrative structure of Illuminati conspiracies appeals to the human penchant for storytelling. Conspiracy theories often frame complex events as part of an epic struggle between good and evil, casting believers as heroes in a fight against a nefarious elite. This dramatic framing captures the imagination, providing a compelling narrative that draws individuals in and keeps them engaged.

The need for coherence in an increasingly fragmented world makes such stories particularly attractive.

In summary, cognitive biases like confirmation bias, availability heuristic, and proportionality bias contribute significantly to the appeal of the Illuminati belief. These psychological tendencies simplify the complexity of global events, allowing individuals to create a narrative that fits their worldview. In a time when uncertainty and chaos often reign, the belief in a hidden force like the Illuminati provides not just a scapegoat, but also a framework for understanding a bewildering reality. By acknowledging these biases, we can better understand why conspiracy theories endure and why they continue to attract followers across generations.

The Role of Distrust in Authority and Institutions

Distrust in authority is a powerful driver behind belief in conspiracy theories, particularly those surrounding the Illuminati. As individuals grapple with feelings of powerlessness and disenfranchisement, the notion that a secretive group is orchestrating global events offers an appealing explanation for the complexities of modern life. This chapter delves into how societal distrust, fueled by historical events and a perceived disconnect from political processes, contributes to the allure of Illuminati beliefs.

Historically, trust in institutions such as government, media, and large corporations has been eroded by scandals, corruption, and failures. Events like the Watergate scandal in the 1970s and the more recent financial crisis of 2008 have created a pervasive sense of skepticism. When people witness those in power acting against the public's interest, it fosters a belief that elite groups manipulate society for their own gain. The belief in the Illuminati thrives in this environment, where disillusionment with traditional institutions leads individuals to seek alternative explanations for their experiences. The idea that a hidden elite is pulling the strings becomes a narrative that resonates with those who feel let down by the very structures meant to protect and serve them.

Furthermore, the modern political landscape often exacerbates feelings of alienation. Many individuals feel that their voices are not heard in the political arena, leading to an "us vs. them" mentality. This disconnect encourages conspiracy thinking as people search for explanations that affirm their suspicions about the motives of those in power. The Illuminati serves as a convenient scapegoat, embodying the fears and frustrations of a populace that feels marginalized. The belief that a small group controls global affairs offers a straightforward way to interpret the complexities of political maneuvering, making the chaos of modern governance more digestible.

The rise of social media has further complicated this dynamic. Platforms like Twitter and Facebook allow for the rapid spread of information, but they also create environments where misinformation can flourish. Conspiracy theories can gain traction quickly, as users share sensational claims about the Illuminati without verifying their sources. This digital landscape amplifies distrust in established institutions, as people turn to alternative sources for information that align with their beliefs. In this context, the Illuminati is often portrayed as the ultimate puppet master, manipulating events from behind the scenes. As individuals gravitate toward narratives that reinforce their distrust, they may become increasingly convinced of the existence of a global conspiracy.

In addition to distrust in institutions, cultural narratives also shape how individuals perceive authority. Movies, television shows, and literature often depict powerful elites as corrupt or manipulative. This pervasive portrayal influences public perception, leading many to internalize the belief that those in positions of authority cannot be trusted. The repeated suggestion that the elite are engaged in nefarious activities primes audiences to accept conspiracy theories as plausible explanations for societal issues. When popular culture continually reinforces the idea of a shadowy elite, it becomes easier for individuals to believe in the existence of groups like the Illuminati.

Moreover, the emotional impact of distrust cannot be understated. Feeling powerless against a system that appears rigged creates anxiety and frustration. For some, believing in the Illuminati provides a sense of agency in a world that often feels overwhelming. By attributing their struggles to a malevolent force, individuals can direct their anger and frustrations toward a concrete target. This allows them to engage with their circumstances in a way that feels proactive, even if that engagement is based on unfounded beliefs.

The allure of conspiracy theories like the Illuminati also lies in their ability to foster a sense of community among believers. Those who distrust the mainstream narrative often seek out others who share their concerns, forming groups that reinforce their views. Within these communities, the narrative of the Illuminati is not only accepted but celebrated, creating a powerful sense of belonging. This social reinforcement makes it even more challenging to break free from the grip of conspiracy thinking, as individuals become invested in a collective identity centered around skepticism and distrust.

In conclusion, the belief in the Illuminati is deeply intertwined with widespread distrust in authority and institutions. Historical events, cultural narratives, and the emotional impact of feeling powerless all contribute to the allure of this conspiracy theory. In a world where many feel disconnected from the systems that govern their lives, the Illuminati serves as both a scapegoat and a framework for understanding the complexities of modern existence. As long as distrust persists, so too will the appeal of the Illuminati, perpetuating a cycle of skepticism and belief that is difficult to break.

The Social Reinforcement of Illuminati Beliefs

Belief in the Illuminati does not exist in a vacuum; it thrives within social contexts that validate and reinforce these conspiratorial ideas. The phenomenon of social reinforcement plays a critical role in the propagation of Illuminati theories, as individuals seek out communities that echo their beliefs and provide a sense of belonging. This chapter examines how group dynamics, social media, and collective behaviors contribute to the persistence of these theories, creating an environment where conspiratorial thinking can flourish.

One of the most significant factors contributing to the reinforcement of Illuminati beliefs is the phenomenon known as *groupthink*. In environments where dissent is discouraged and conformity is valued, individuals often feel pressure to align their opinions with the prevailing view of the group. This can lead to the amplification of beliefs that might otherwise be challenged. Within communities that discuss or promote conspiracy theories, groupthink creates a feedback loop: as members share information and validate each other's beliefs, the narrative surrounding the Illuminati becomes increasingly entrenched. Dissenters may be ridiculed or ostracized, which further solidifies the beliefs of those who remain, as they rally around a common cause.

Social media platforms are particularly effective in fostering this environment. In today's digital age, individuals can easily find and join groups dedicated to discussing the Illuminati and other conspiracy theories. These online communities often create echo chambers where ideas are circulated and reinforced without critical examination. Algorithms designed to maximize engagement frequently serve to amplify sensational content, pushing conspiracy-related material to the forefront. As users engage with this content, they receive positive reinforcement in the form of likes, shares, and comments, solidifying their beliefs. This process not only perpetuates existing ideas but also encourages the creation of even more elaborate conspiracy narratives.

The concept of the *bandwagon effect* also plays a vital role in social reinforcement. When individuals observe others subscribing to a particular belief—such as the existence of the Illuminati—they are more likely to adopt that belief themselves. The bandwagon effect operates on the principle that individuals often look to others to gauge what is considered acceptable or true, especially in ambiguous situations. As more people express belief in the Illuminati, this narrative gains legitimacy in the eyes of potential followers, making it easier for individuals to jump on board without critically examining the evidence. This dynamic creates a snowball effect, where belief in the conspiracy grows exponentially as more individuals join the movement.

Furthermore, charismatic leaders and influencers within these communities can significantly impact the reinforcement of Illuminati beliefs. Figures who advocate for conspiracy theories often possess persuasive skills that enable them to draw in followers. They may present complex information in a digestible format, appealing to the emotions of their audience and establishing a sense of urgency around their claims. As these leaders gain influence, their narratives take on an air of authority, making it even more difficult for members to question the information being presented. The allure of having a trusted figure guide them through the complexities of the world can be immensely powerful, further entrenching their beliefs in the Illuminati.

Additionally, the social satisfaction derived from belonging to a community of "truth-seekers" cannot be overlooked. For many individuals, being part of a group that shares a common goal—uncovering the supposed hidden truths of the world—provides a sense of purpose and identity. This collective engagement reinforces their beliefs, as members bond over shared experiences and stories of supposed Illuminati encounters. The thrill of being part of an exclusive group that perceives itself as enlightened fosters a sense of camaraderie, making it difficult for individuals to abandon these beliefs even when faced with contradicting evidence.

Moreover, the emotional dimension of social reinforcement should not be underestimated. Individuals often turn to conspiracy theories as a means of coping with feelings of uncertainty and anxiety in their lives. Within supportive communities, they find validation for their fears and frustrations, leading to a deepened commitment to the belief in the Illuminati. This emotional support can be particularly potent in times of crisis, where individuals may feel vulnerable and seek refuge in a shared narrative that explains their circumstances and offers a sense of agency.

In conclusion, the social reinforcement of Illuminati beliefs is a multifaceted process driven by group dynamics, social media, and the influence of charismatic leaders. These elements create a powerful environment where conspiratorial thinking can thrive, allowing individuals to find validation and belonging within a community of like-minded believers. As long as social structures continue to support and amplify these narratives, the belief in the Illuminati will likely endure, perpetuating a cycle of reinforcement that challenges critical engagement and rational discourse. The interplay of social dynamics and psychological needs ensures that the allure of the Illuminati remains a compelling and resilient part of contemporary culture.

The Impact of Fear and Anxiety on Belief in the Illuminati

The psychological landscape of fear and anxiety plays a pivotal role in shaping belief in conspiracy theories, including the notion of the Illuminati. In a world increasingly characterized by uncertainty—whether through political instability, economic turmoil, or social unrest—individuals often turn to conspiratorial narratives as a means of making sense of their fears. This chapter explores how fear and anxiety feed into the belief in the Illuminati, creating a compelling psychological feedback loop that reinforces these conspiratorial ideas.

At its core, fear is a powerful motivator. It triggers a fight-or-flight response, compelling individuals to seek out explanations that provide clarity and reassurance. When faced with unsettling global events—such as pandemics, terrorist attacks, or natural disasters—people often experience heightened anxiety. This emotional state can lead them to search for meaning and understanding in the chaos around them. Conspiracy theories like those surrounding the Illuminati offer a structured narrative that explains these complex phenomena, transforming random events into orchestrated actions by a malevolent group. The belief that there is an identifiable enemy—one that can be fought against or blamed—can provide a sense of comfort amidst uncertainty.

Furthermore, the human brain is naturally inclined to perceive threats. Evolutionarily, this instinct has been beneficial, helping individuals recognize and avoid danger. However, in a modern context, this tendency can distort perceptions of reality. When people become overly fixated on potential threats—whether real or perceived—they may become more susceptible to conspiracy theories. The idea that the Illuminati is controlling world events plays into this fear, as it paints a picture of a shadowy group that influences outcomes in ways that threaten the safety and well-being of the average person. This constant undercurrent of anxiety makes the narrative of the Illuminati particularly appealing, as it provides an explanation for why the world feels increasingly precarious.

Moreover, the concept of "us versus them" is a common theme in times of crisis. Individuals may feel a growing divide between themselves and the perceived elite, which fuels feelings of resentment and fear. In this context, the Illuminati is often portrayed as the ultimate embodiment of this divide—a powerful group operating outside of the democratic process, manipulating events for their own benefit. This framing creates a clear antagonist in the minds of believers, allowing them to channel their anxiety and frustration toward a specific target. The belief that they are part of a larger struggle against an oppressive elite can be empowering, even as it fosters further paranoia and division.

The emotional response to fear is often compounded by the phenomenon of "doomscrolling"—the habit of continuously consuming negative news on social media and other platforms. In this digital age, individuals are bombarded with alarming headlines and narratives that can exacerbate feelings of anxiety. The continuous exposure to distressing information can create a sense of helplessness, prompting individuals to seek out alternative explanations for the chaos they perceive. In this environment, conspiracy theories can flourish, as they provide a narrative that seems to make sense of the overwhelming flood of negativity. The belief in the Illuminati emerges as a way to regain a sense of agency in an uncontrollable world.

Additionally, the impact of fear is not only psychological but also social. Individuals who express fears about the Illuminati often find validation within like-minded communities. These groups can create an echo chamber where fears are amplified and reinforced, further entrenching members in their beliefs. The social reinforcement of shared anxieties creates a feedback loop, where individuals rally around their fears, strengthening their commitment to the idea that a secretive group is responsible for the world's problems. This communal aspect of fear can make it even more challenging for individuals to confront or question their beliefs.

In conclusion, fear and anxiety are central to understanding the belief in the Illuminati. As individuals navigate a world filled with uncertainty and distress, they seek explanations that provide clarity and reassurance. The narrative of a powerful, manipulative elite serves to alleviate some of this anxiety by creating a structured framework for interpreting complex events. However, this belief also perpetuates a cycle of fear, leading individuals further into the rabbit hole of conspiracy thinking. As long as societal fears persist and the world remains unpredictable, the allure of the Illuminati will likely continue to captivate those searching for answers in an increasingly chaotic landscape.

Chapter 13: The Real Impact of Illuminati Conspira

Societal Distrust and Polarization

One of the most significant impacts of Illuminati conspiracy theories is their ability to breed distrust and polarization in society. At the core of these theories is the belief that a powerful, secretive elite is manipulating world events, pulling the strings behind governments, financial institutions, and the media. This narrative not only fosters a sense of suspicion toward those in positions of power but also erodes trust in the very systems that are meant to govern and protect society. As individuals increasingly question the motives of politicians, corporations, and even scientists, a dangerous divide forms between those who believe in these conspiracies and those who do not.

The spread of distrust is not limited to governments or large institutions. It seeps into everyday interactions, fracturing relationships between individuals who hold differing beliefs. Illuminati conspiracy theories, like other forms of conspiratorial thinking, encourage an "us versus them" mentality. Believers often view skeptics as either naïve or complicit in the grand scheme they perceive, while skeptics may see believers as irrational or paranoid. This dynamic fosters deep polarization, not just in political discourse but also within families, social groups, and communities. Over time, this division weakens the fabric of society, making it more difficult to find common ground on important issues.

The role of social media in amplifying this distrust cannot be overstated. Platforms like Facebook, Twitter, and YouTube have become breeding grounds for conspiracy theories, with algorithms that prioritize sensational content often pushing Illuminati-related videos, articles, and posts to the forefront. These platforms create echo chambers where individuals are exposed primarily to information that reinforces their pre-existing beliefs, further entrenching their suspicion toward mainstream narratives. In these spaces, Illuminati conspiracy theories can flourish unchecked, as believers find validation and community, while opposing viewpoints are often dismissed or ignored.

Moreover, Illuminati conspiracy theories contribute to the broader crisis of information overload. In a world where people are constantly bombarded with conflicting news and viewpoints, distinguishing between credible sources and misinformation becomes increasingly challenging. For some, turning to conspiracy theories offers a way to make sense of the chaos. The Illuminati narrative provides a simple, all-encompassing explanation for the world's complexities, absolving believers of the need to sift through the nuances of political, economic, or social issues. In this way, conspiracy theories offer a form of cognitive relief, but they also encourage a wholesale rejection of legitimate information sources, further deepening societal distrust.

As this distrust grows, so too does polarization. The belief in an Illuminati-led agenda often aligns with other divisive ideologies, including anti-establishment movements and populist rhetoric. These movements feed off one another, creating a feedback loop where distrust in one area—such as politics—spills over into other domains, like science or public health. This can lead to extreme polarization on a wide range of issues, from climate change to vaccine safety, as individuals come to view any form of expertise or authority with suspicion. The result is a fragmented society, where consensus is nearly impossible to achieve and collaboration across ideological lines becomes increasingly rare.

The erosion of trust in institutions also has significant political consequences. When large segments of the population believe that the government is controlled by a secret cabal, faith in democratic processes falters. Voter apathy can increase as individuals feel powerless to influence a system they perceive as rigged. On the other hand, some may become radicalized, convinced that only extreme measures—whether through protest, rebellion, or even violence—can dismantle the so-called Illuminati-controlled establishment. This creates fertile ground for anti-democratic movements and authoritarian tendencies, as individuals seek out leaders who promise to fight against the shadowy forces they believe are controlling the world.

In conclusion, the societal distrust and polarization fueled by Illuminati conspiracy theories pose a serious threat to social cohesion. By encouraging suspicion of institutions, experts, and even fellow citizens, these theories drive wedges between individuals and groups, making it harder to address collective challenges. As distrust spreads, the possibility for constructive dialogue diminishes, leaving societies more divided and less capable of tackling the complex issues they face. The legacy of Illuminati conspiracy theories is not just one of paranoia, but one of fractured communities and a weakened public trust in the very systems that sustain democratic life.

Influence on Political Behavior

Illuminati conspiracy theories have a profound impact on political behavior, shaping how individuals perceive the political system, engage with elections, and relate to political leaders. The central claim of these theories—that a hidden elite is manipulating global events—can lead to widespread disillusionment with traditional politics. For believers, the notion that elections, policies, and even entire governments are controlled by a secret cabal renders democratic participation seem futile. This cynicism can manifest in voter apathy, radicalization, or, in some cases, a misguided sense of activism aimed at exposing or toppling the supposed Illuminati.

At the root of this influence is the erosion of trust in political institutions. When people believe that world leaders are mere puppets controlled by a shadowy group, the very concept of representative democracy becomes suspect. For these individuals, casting a vote in an election may feel like participating in a rigged game—no matter the outcome, the hidden rulers remain in control. This belief can result in voter apathy, where disillusioned citizens disengage from the political process altogether. Why bother voting, they might reason, if the result has already been predetermined by forces beyond the ballot box?

Voter disengagement, however, is just one possible outcome. For others, Illuminati conspiracy theories can lead to political radicalization. The conviction that a nefarious elite is pulling the strings can fuel anger and frustration, driving some believers to embrace extreme ideologies or support populist movements that promise to "drain the swamp" or "expose the truth." These movements often position themselves as the antidote to the corrupt establishment, and for those who believe in the Illuminati narrative, they may appear to be the only viable option for reclaiming power from the hidden rulers.

Populist leaders, in turn, may exploit these conspiracy beliefs for political gain. By framing themselves as outsiders fighting against a corrupt elite, they tap into the distrust and anger felt by Illuminati believers. Whether or not these leaders personally endorse conspiracy theories, they can benefit from the sentiments they stir, using coded language and vague allusions to "globalists" or "elites" to rally support. This rhetoric can be particularly effective during times of crisis or uncertainty, as individuals are more likely to seek out simple explanations for complex problems. For believers, these leaders may seem like the only figures willing to challenge the invisible forces they perceive as controlling the world.

Illuminati conspiracy theories can also influence political behavior in more insidious ways. In some cases, these beliefs foster a sense of paranoia and suspicion that can lead to violence or acts of extremism. High-profile political events, such as elections or the passage of controversial laws, are often interpreted through the lens of conspiracy, with believers seeing them as part of the Illuminati's plan for world domination. This can lead to a sense of urgency and desperation among some followers, prompting them to take matters into their own hands. From armed protests to violent plots, history has shown that conspiracy theories can radicalize individuals to the point of taking extreme action in the name of fighting a perceived evil.

On a broader scale, the spread of Illuminati conspiracy theories can also affect political discourse. The prevalence of these ideas in the public sphere shifts the tone of debates, making it harder to engage in fact-based discussions about policy and governance. Politicians who lean into conspiracy rhetoric may focus on attacking the supposed hidden elite rather than addressing concrete issues like healthcare, education, or the economy. As a result, political discourse becomes more about defending or debunking conspiracy theories than about solving real-world problems. This undermines the quality of democratic debate, leaving citizens ill-informed and political leaders less accountable for their policies.

Furthermore, Illuminati conspiracy theories often intersect with other forms of political misinformation, amplifying their influence. For example, during elections, conspiracy theories about vote manipulation or political corruption may merge with broader Illuminati narratives, creating a potent mix of distrust and fear. Believers may claim that the Illuminati is rigging elections to ensure their chosen candidates win, further fueling skepticism about electoral integrity. This can have real consequences, such as the refusal to accept election results, widespread distrust in the democratic process, and even calls for political violence.

In addition to influencing individual behavior, the belief in Illuminati conspiracies can shape broader political movements. These movements often coalesce around the idea that they are fighting against a hidden enemy, with conspiracy theories serving as the ideological glue that holds them together. For instance, political factions that promote anti-globalist or anti-establishment agendas may find common cause with Illuminati believers, who view globalization as part of the Illuminati's plan for world domination. This convergence can lead to the formation of coalitions that mix populism, nationalism, and conspiracy theories, creating a potent political force that can disrupt traditional party systems.

In conclusion, Illuminati conspiracy theories exert a significant influence on political behavior, from fostering voter apathy and disengagement to fueling radicalization and extremism. These beliefs can distort political discourse, undermine trust in democratic institutions, and provide fertile ground for populist movements and authoritarian leaders. By creating an environment of suspicion and paranoia, Illuminati conspiracy theories weaken the democratic process, making it more difficult for societies to engage in constructive political dialogue and address the real issues they face. As these theories continue to circulate, their impact on political behavior—and the health of democratic institutions—remains a critical concern for modern societies.

Public Health Implications

Illuminati conspiracy theories not only affect political behavior but also have severe implications for public health, particularly in times of global crises such as pandemics. The belief that a shadowy elite controls major institutions, including the medical and scientific communities, has contributed to widespread skepticism of public health measures. This distrust can lead to resistance against life-saving interventions, as believers question the motives behind policies and recommendations aimed at controlling disease outbreaks, promoting vaccines, or even advising basic hygiene practices. The consequences of this resistance can be devastating, as communities struggle to contain preventable illnesses due to misinformation fueled by conspiracy theories.

A prime example of the intersection between Illuminati beliefs and public health is the spread of misinformation during the COVID-19 pandemic. Early in the outbreak, conspiracy theories suggesting that the virus was part of a deliberate plot by the Illuminati to depopulate the world or control the global population gained significant traction. These theories circulated widely on social media, reinforcing the idea that government-imposed lockdowns, mask mandates, and vaccination campaigns were not about protecting public health, but rather about consolidating power and control under the guise of a public health crisis. Such narratives were often paired with other anti-government and anti-science rhetoric, further eroding trust in medical professionals and health authorities.

The impact of these conspiracy theories was most visible in the realm of vaccine hesitancy. Many individuals who subscribed to Illuminati beliefs were especially resistant to vaccination, convinced that vaccines were part of a larger plot to implant microchips, alter DNA, or even enforce global compliance to a New World Order agenda. Despite overwhelming scientific evidence supporting the safety and efficacy of vaccines, these conspiracy-driven narratives caused many to refuse vaccination, not only putting their own health at risk but also threatening the broader goal of achieving herd immunity. In the process, these individuals unintentionally contributed to prolonging the pandemic, as waves of infections continued to spread through unvaccinated populations.

This resistance to public health measures is not limited to vaccines. During the pandemic, public health authorities issued guidelines recommending the use of face masks, physical distancing, and hand hygiene to reduce the spread of the virus. However, conspiracy theories framed these measures as tools of control rather than public health strategies. Some claimed that mask mandates were a way to muzzle the population, conditioning people to accept future restrictions on their freedom. Others suggested that physical distancing was designed to prevent individuals from coming together to resist the Illuminati's supposed plans. These ideas eroded compliance with public health guidelines, undermining efforts to contain the virus and exacerbating the health crisis.

The influence of conspiracy theories also extended to the perception of scientific research and institutions. Illuminati believers often view scientists and health experts as part of the global elite, casting doubt on their findings and recommendations. This mistrust can lead to the rejection of scientific consensus on critical issues such as disease prevention, environmental health, and mental well-being. For example, conspiracy-driven skepticism toward the World Health Organization (WHO) and the Centers for Disease Control and Prevention (CDC) undermined public confidence in their guidance during the pandemic, leading some to seek alternative, often unproven, treatments. This resulted in dangerous behaviors, such as the use of unapproved drugs or the refusal to follow quarantine measures, which further compounded public health challenges.

The long-term public health implications of these conspiracy theories are substantial. Beyond the immediate danger of disease outbreaks, the erosion of trust in health authorities can have lasting effects on the ability to manage future public health emergencies. If large portions of the population continue to question the legitimacy of scientific expertise and reject evidence-based interventions, it will become increasingly difficult to mount effective responses to emerging health threats. The legacy of Illuminati conspiracy theories, therefore, is not just the damage done during the current crisis but the potential for ongoing harm in the face of future health challenges.

Another dimension of the public health impact is the strain these conspiracy theories place on healthcare systems. Hospitals and clinics have faced additional burdens as they deal not only with the direct consequences of illness but also with the influx of patients who refuse standard treatments, demand unproven therapies, or actively resist medical advice. In some cases, healthcare workers have been subjected to harassment and threats from conspiracy believers who accuse them of being part of the Illuminati's alleged plan. This adds psychological stress to already overworked healthcare professionals, further stretching resources and compromising the overall effectiveness of public health systems.

The role of social media in spreading Illuminati conspiracy theories is also a critical factor in their public health implications. Misinformation spreads rapidly on platforms like Facebook, YouTube, and Twitter, where algorithms prioritize sensational content that often includes conspiracy theories. These platforms have enabled the rapid dissemination of anti-vaccine and anti-mask propaganda, making it difficult for public health officials to counteract false claims with factual information. As a result, the public health response to crises becomes a battle not just against disease but also against the spread of harmful, conspiratorial misinformation that can endanger lives.

In conclusion, Illuminati conspiracy theories pose a significant threat to public health by undermining trust in medical expertise, promoting resistance to proven interventions, and spreading misinformation. The impact of these theories extends beyond individual health decisions, affecting entire communities and healthcare systems. In times of crisis, when swift and coordinated public health efforts are crucial, the proliferation of conspiracy beliefs can delay or derail these efforts, leading to unnecessary suffering and loss of life. As public health challenges continue to arise, addressing the root causes of conspiracy-driven mistrust will be essential to protecting the health and well-being of society at large.

Social Fragmentation and Polarization

Illuminati conspiracy theories do more than just influence individual behavior; they also contribute to social fragmentation and the deepening of polarization within communities. At their core, these theories promote a worldview in which society is sharply divided between an oppressed populace and a powerful, malevolent elite. This binary thinking fosters an "us versus them" mentality, pitting believers against those they view as either complicit in or naive about the supposed conspiracy. As these divisions grow, trust between different social groups erodes, and the capacity for constructive dialogue diminishes, further entrenching divisions in both personal relationships and the broader society.

One of the key ways Illuminati conspiracy theories fuel social fragmentation is by creating an alternate reality for those who believe in them. Believers often operate within closed information loops, consuming content from like-minded individuals and sources that reinforce their views. Whether on social media, in online forums, or even in certain alternative media outlets, conspiracy theorists find validation for their beliefs, often rejecting or ignoring any information that contradicts the narrative of a hidden, controlling elite. This echo chamber effect can isolate them from friends, family members, and colleagues who do not share their views, leading to strained relationships and social alienation.

The impact on family and personal relationships can be particularly pronounced. Many families have experienced significant tension or estrangement due to one or more members adopting Illuminati-related conspiracy beliefs. In the case of major global events, such as elections or health crises, these tensions are magnified. One person's refusal to comply with public health guidelines, such as getting vaccinated or wearing a mask, based on their belief in a grand Illuminati plot, can cause rifts within families and communities. These disagreements may begin as simple differences of opinion but can quickly escalate into deeper conflicts about trust, authority, and reality itself.

Social fragmentation extends beyond the personal level and into the political sphere. Illuminati conspiracy theories have the potential to polarize public discourse by turning political debates into ideological battles between those who believe in the existence of the Illuminati and those who do not. Conspiracy believers may view anyone who denies the Illuminati's influence as part of the problem—either willfully ignorant or, worse, complicit in the conspiracy. This mindset makes it difficult for people to engage in meaningful discussions about real-world issues, as the focus shifts away from facts and policies toward suspicion, paranoia, and accusations of hidden agendas.

This polarization has real consequences for democratic societies. In environments where conspiracy theories are widespread, public trust in institutions such as the government, the judiciary, and the media deteriorates. Instead of seeing these entities as working for the public good, conspiracy believers view them as tools of control wielded by the Illuminati or other shadowy elites. This mistrust can manifest in various ways, from refusal to follow government regulations to outright hostility toward public officials and law enforcement. In extreme cases, this suspicion can lead to civil unrest, protests, or even violence, as individuals act out of a belief that they are defending themselves or society from an oppressive regime.

Moreover, Illuminati conspiracy theories often intersect with other divisive ideologies, such as nationalism, populism, and anti-globalism. These intersections further exacerbate polarization by aligning conspiracy beliefs with broader political movements. For example, Illuminati narratives that focus on the control of global financial systems or multinational corporations often dovetail with nationalist or populist rhetoric, which criticizes globalism and elite influence. This fusion creates a potent and polarizing mix, drawing together groups with different grievances but a shared belief in a corrupt global elite. As a result, these movements can become more radicalized, and the gap between them and more moderate political factions grows wider.

The internet and social media play a significant role in amplifying this polarization. Platforms like YouTube, Facebook, and Twitter provide a fertile ground for the rapid spread of Illuminati-related content, allowing conspiracy theories to reach wider audiences than ever before. Algorithms designed to keep users engaged often promote sensational or emotionally charged content, which includes conspiracy theories. As a result, individuals who may have had only a passing interest in Illuminati ideas can quickly find themselves drawn deeper into the conspiracy subculture. The more they engage with this content, the more they are exposed to extremist views, further entrenching their beliefs and deepening the divisions between them and those who reject conspiracy theories.

This cycle of polarization is difficult to break. Once someone is entrenched in Illuminati conspiracy thinking, it becomes challenging to persuade them to reconsider their views. Efforts to present factual information or debunk conspiracy claims are often met with skepticism or hostility, as believers may view these attempts as further proof that the conspiracy is real. This rejection of alternative viewpoints only deepens the divide between believers and non-believers, making it harder to foster dialogue and mutual understanding.

Additionally, Illuminati conspiracy theories can fragment broader social movements by introducing divisive narratives into otherwise cohesive groups. For instance, in movements focused on legitimate issues like government transparency, environmental protection, or financial reform, conspiracy theories can create splinter factions that focus on the hidden hand of the Illuminati rather than the actual goals of the movement. This can weaken the movement's effectiveness by diverting attention from tangible policy objectives to nebulous and unverifiable claims about secret elites. In some cases, conspiracy-driven factions may alienate potential allies or discredit the movement in the eyes of the broader public, further undermining social cohesion.

In conclusion, Illuminati conspiracy theories have a profound impact on social fragmentation and polarization. By fostering distrust, suspicion, and binary thinking, these theories create divisions between individuals, within families, and across entire societies. As believers become more isolated in their echo chambers, dialogue becomes more difficult, and the ability to engage constructively with opposing viewpoints diminishes. In a world increasingly shaped by misinformation and ideological extremism, the social consequences of conspiracy theories like those surrounding the Illuminati are both significant and far-reaching. Their influence threatens to further divide an already polarized society, making the pursuit of unity, understanding, and collective problem-solving even more challenging.

Undermining Democratic Institutions

One of the most insidious impacts of Illuminati conspiracy theories is the way they undermine trust in democratic institutions. In a functioning democracy, public trust in systems of governance, the rule of law, and the transparency of leadership is essential. Citizens need to believe that their votes matter, that laws are made with their best interests in mind, and that public officials are accountable. However, Illuminati conspiracy theories work to erode these pillars of democracy by suggesting that all of these structures are mere facades controlled by a secret elite.

At the heart of Illuminati-related conspiracies is the idea that governments, no matter how democratic they appear, are actually tools of the Illuminati or some other hidden cabal. This belief undermines the very foundation of democratic participation. If voters believe that elections are rigged or that political leaders are merely puppets of an unseen force, their faith in the democratic process evaporates. This can lead to widespread apathy and disengagement from the political process, as individuals feel that no matter what they do, the outcomes are preordained by powerful, unelected figures.

The idea that democracy is a sham controlled by the Illuminati has been a common theme in conspiracy circles for decades. These theories suggest that no matter which political party is in power, the real decisions are made behind closed doors by shadowy elites who dictate global policy. This can create a sense of hopelessness among citizens, who begin to see political participation as futile. Why vote, advocate, or campaign if the outcome is always controlled by forces beyond the visible government? This cynicism is corrosive to democracy, as it disengages people from civic life, reducing accountability and allowing genuine corruption or incompetence to go unchecked.

A particularly dangerous aspect of this belief is its potential to fuel movements that actively seek to dismantle democratic institutions. When individuals believe that the government is not only corrupt but controlled by an evil force, they may see violent or extreme actions as justified. This has led to real-world consequences, as conspiracy theorists, emboldened by their beliefs, have targeted government buildings, disrupted political processes, and even plotted violent attacks. Such actions are often framed by conspiracists as necessary to "wake up" the public or reclaim freedom from the Illuminati's supposed grip on power.

The January 6th, 2021 storming of the U.S. Capitol provides a stark example of how conspiracy theories can directly undermine democratic institutions. Many of those involved believed in a variety of conspiracy narratives, including the idea that a shadowy elite was manipulating the election results to install their chosen leaders. While not all participants specifically believed in the Illuminati, the overarching framework of elite control and manipulation was a key element driving their actions. This event demonstrated how conspiracy beliefs, when taken to their logical extremes, can lead to an outright assault on the institutions designed to uphold democracy.

In addition to eroding faith in elections, Illuminati conspiracy theories also target the legislative process. Believers often claim that laws are not written or passed by elected representatives, but rather are dictated by secret societies aiming to impose global control. This idea leads to a general mistrust of legislation, especially laws that deal with issues of international trade, climate agreements, or financial regulation, which are often portrayed as attempts by the Illuminati to further their global agenda. As a result, any law or policy that aligns with global cooperation or centralized regulation is viewed with extreme suspicion, and its opponents may invoke conspiracy theories to rally public dissent.

This mistrust extends to the judiciary, another crucial pillar of democracy. Illuminati theories often suggest that the courts, especially in high-profile cases involving the government or wealthy individuals, are rigged. The judiciary, in this view, is part of the larger system of control, with judges and legal authorities beholden to the will of the Illuminati rather than the rule of law. This belief further undermines the public's faith in justice, leading to the dangerous idea that legal outcomes are predetermined or that the legal system exists solely to serve the elite. Such beliefs can encourage people to disregard the law, seeing it as illegitimate, or to take justice into their own hands, bypassing the democratic process entirely.

Conspiracy theories about the Illuminati also damage international institutions that are vital to global cooperation. Organizations like the United Nations, the World Health Organization, and the International Monetary Fund are frequent targets of Illuminati theories, which portray them as tools of global domination. This narrative not only sows distrust but also hampers the ability of these organizations to function effectively. For example, efforts to combat global health crises or address climate change are often met with resistance from individuals and groups who believe these initiatives are part of the Illuminati's alleged agenda to control the world population.

The influence of these conspiracy theories on democratic governance is particularly troubling when it reaches policymakers themselves. In recent years, there have been instances of elected officials subscribing to or endorsing Illuminati-related conspiracies. When lawmakers promote such ideas, it gives them a veneer of legitimacy, spreading them further and making it more difficult to maintain public trust in government. Additionally, politicians who exploit conspiracy theories for political gain undermine the very institutions they are supposed to uphold, weakening the fabric of democracy from within.

Furthermore, Illuminati conspiracy theories often coalesce with anti-establishment movements, contributing to the rise of populist leaders who claim to be fighting against the hidden elite. These leaders may invoke Illuminati-like narratives to galvanize support, framing themselves as the only ones who can stand up to the global cabal that supposedly controls politics and finance. While populism can be a legitimate political movement, when it is fueled by conspiracy theories, it risks leading to authoritarianism, as leaders may justify dismantling democratic institutions under the guise of protecting citizens from a shadowy elite.

In conclusion, Illuminati conspiracy theories profoundly damage democratic institutions by eroding public trust, fostering disengagement, and fueling extremism. By promoting the idea that all political processes are controlled by a hidden elite, these theories discourage civic participation, weaken accountability, and create fertile ground for anti-democratic movements. The impact is not just on individual behavior but on the broader health of democratic societies, which rely on trust, transparency, and the active engagement of citizens. As conspiracy theories continue to proliferate, safeguarding democratic institutions and rebuilding public trust will be an increasingly urgent task for leaders and citizens alike.

Chapter 14: The Future of the Illuminati Myth

The Persistence of Conspiracy Theories in the Digital Age
In the 21st century, the Illuminati myth has found fertile ground in the rapidly evolving landscape of digital media. Unlike previous eras, where information was controlled by traditional gatekeepers like newspapers, television, and books, the rise of the internet and social media has shattered those boundaries. Today, anyone with access to the web can create and share content, and conspiracy theories, including those about the Illuminati, have proliferated in this decentralized environment. The ability to connect across borders, to share ideas instantly, and to form communities around shared beliefs has allowed the Illuminati myth to not only persist but to thrive.

One of the most significant factors contributing to the resilience of Illuminati conspiracy theories is the way social media platforms have democratized the spread of information. On sites like YouTube, Facebook, Twitter, and Reddit, conspiratorial content can quickly gain traction, regardless of its factual accuracy. The more sensational or emotionally charged the content, the more likely it is to be shared and discussed, feeding into a cycle where conspiracy theories, like those involving the Illuminati, continue to grow and mutate. Algorithms designed to keep users engaged often amplify content that provokes strong reactions, leading to a natural bias toward conspiracy-laden material.

This digital age has given rise to what some scholars call the "post-truth" era, in which objective facts are often overshadowed by narratives that appeal to emotions and personal beliefs. The Illuminati myth, with its mysterious undertones and suggestions of hidden power, fits perfectly into this post-truth landscape. As traditional sources of authority, such as governments, academic institutions, and mainstream media outlets, are increasingly distrusted, conspiracy theories fill the vacuum. The Illuminati narrative capitalizes on this environment, providing a simple explanation for complex global events, one that resonates with people who feel disillusioned or powerless in the face of rapidly changing societal structures.

The advent of digital media has also introduced new ways to create and share content that reinforces the Illuminati myth. Podcasts, video documentaries, blogs, and social media posts offer accessible platforms for conspiracy theorists to disseminate their ideas. For example, YouTube has become a hotbed of conspiracy theories, with countless videos dissecting supposed Illuminati symbols in popular culture, analyzing global events through the lens of secret societies, and connecting unrelated incidents as part of an overarching plan for world domination. These videos often present their arguments in a way that seems plausible, using real-world events, historical facts, and visual cues to build a case that, for many viewers, appears compelling.

Another factor that has enabled the Illuminati myth to flourish online is the creation of virtual echo chambers. Social media algorithms are designed to show users content that aligns with their existing beliefs, which can result in users being continually exposed to information that reinforces their conspiratorial views. Over time, these individuals may become further entrenched in their beliefs, as they are less likely to encounter content that challenges their perceptions. Additionally, these online communities provide validation and support to those who believe in the Illuminati, fostering a sense of camaraderie among conspiracy theorists who might feel marginalized or ridiculed in the offline world.

One cannot overlook the role that memes and digital humor have played in the continued relevance of the Illuminati myth. Memes featuring Illuminati symbols, such as the all-seeing eye or pyramid, have become ubiquitous online. While many of these memes are created and shared in jest, their prevalence keeps the myth alive in the public consciousness. What was once an obscure conspiracy theory discussed in dark corners of the internet is now part of mainstream digital culture, as jokes and references to the Illuminati have become common online, especially among younger generations. Ironically, even as these memes mock the idea of a secret global cabal, they also serve to reinforce the association between power, wealth, and hidden control in the minds of those who are already inclined to believe.

The digital age has also blurred the lines between reality and fiction, making it easier for conspiracy theories like the Illuminati to persist. In the past, fringe ideas were often dismissed outright, but today they can spread virally, appearing alongside legitimate news and information in social media feeds. The sheer volume of information available online makes it difficult for the average person to discern fact from fiction, and conspiracy theorists have become adept at exploiting this confusion. They present their claims with the same visual polish and rhetorical style as credible sources, further eroding trust in traditional information outlets and contributing to the persistence of the Illuminati myth.

In conclusion, the digital age has given the Illuminati conspiracy theory new life, allowing it to persist and evolve in ways unimaginable in previous eras. The vast reach of the internet, combined with the algorithms of social media, has created an environment where conspiracies thrive. The decentralization of information, the rise of echo chambers, and the blending of humor with conspiracy have ensured that the Illuminati myth remains firmly embedded in contemporary culture. In this new landscape, where facts and myths can coexist seamlessly, the Illuminati conspiracy theory shows no sign of fading away. Instead, it has become a permanent fixture of digital discourse, constantly mutating and adapting to the changing world around it.

The Role of Emerging Technologies in Shaping Future Narratives

As we move deeper into the 21st century, emerging technologies like artificial intelligence (AI), virtual reality (VR), and deepfake technology are poised to play a significant role in shaping the future of conspiracy theories, including the ever-evolving Illuminati myth. These technologies, while advancing society in many positive ways, also have the potential to blur the lines between reality and fiction in unprecedented ways. The ability to create convincing digital fabrications, simulate immersive alternative realities, and manipulate information on a grand scale will make it increasingly difficult for people to distinguish between legitimate information and conspiracy-fueled fantasies.

Artificial intelligence, in particular, is already transforming the way information is produced and consumed. AI algorithms are responsible for personalizing content on social media platforms, deciding which videos, articles, or posts appear in someone's feed. These algorithms are designed to keep users engaged by showing them content they are more likely to interact with, which often includes sensational or emotionally charged material. In the case of the Illuminati, AI-driven algorithms may unintentionally promote conspiracy theories by continuously recommending videos, articles, and posts that suggest the existence of secret societies or global plots. As users consume more of this content, they may become trapped in a feedback loop where the algorithm pushes increasingly extreme or conspiratorial ideas, reinforcing the belief in the Illuminati's control over world events.

Beyond content recommendation, AI has also paved the way for the creation of deepfake technology, which allows for the generation of hyper-realistic but completely fabricated images, videos, and audio recordings. Deepfakes can convincingly depict individuals saying or doing things they never actually did. While this technology can be used for entertainment or artistic purposes, it also opens the door to a darker use—manipulating public perception by spreading fabricated evidence of world leaders, celebrities, or powerful figures supposedly linked to the Illuminati. Imagine a deepfake video showing a politician discussing secret plans for world domination, or a prominent CEO pledging loyalty to an Illuminati cabal. Even if these videos are quickly debunked, their existence may still sow seeds of doubt in viewers, making it harder to dismiss Illuminati theories as mere fantasy.

The rise of virtual reality technology presents another frontier for the evolution of Illuminati conspiracies. Virtual reality allows users to enter immersive, simulated worlds that feel incredibly real. This technology is still in its early stages, but it is quickly becoming more sophisticated and accessible to the general public. In the future, it's not hard to imagine conspiracy theorists creating virtual environments that "prove" the existence of the Illuminati. These virtual experiences could take users on guided tours through simulated secret meetings of Illuminati members or let them explore a virtual history where the Illuminati are behind key global events. For conspiracy believers, such immersive experiences may further validate their beliefs, even if the entire scenario is fabricated.

Technological advancements in data surveillance and the growing ubiquity of digital footprints also feed into the narrative of an all-powerful, all-seeing elite. Governments and corporations have access to vast amounts of personal data, collected from smartphones, smart devices, and online activity. This surveillance culture, though often intended for commercial purposes or national security, can easily be twisted to fit the Illuminati myth. Conspiracy theorists may claim that the constant collection of data is evidence of a hidden, sinister agenda—a method of control used by the Illuminati to monitor and manipulate the population. In the minds of believers, every targeted advertisement, every smart home device, and every algorithmically curated news feed becomes part of a larger surveillance network operated by secret powers.

Blockchain and cryptocurrency technologies, hailed for their potential to decentralize financial systems and empower individuals, may also play a role in shaping future Illuminati narratives. These technologies, which operate outside traditional financial institutions, are often seen as liberating tools for those who distrust banks and governments. However, conspiracy theorists may suggest that cryptocurrencies are part of an Illuminati scheme—tools designed to track and control individuals through their financial transactions under the guise of decentralization. Alternatively, blockchain's transparency and inability to be easily manipulated might lead some to believe that it is the only tool that can expose the Illuminati's secrets, creating a paradox where the same technology is seen both as a weapon of control and a tool of liberation.

As we look to the future, the convergence of AI, deepfake technology, VR, and surveillance systems creates a perfect storm for conspiracy theorists. These technologies will likely fuel new forms of paranoia, providing more tools for the creation of convincing narratives that blur the line between fact and fiction. The Illuminati myth, which has already adapted so fluidly to previous societal changes, will no doubt find ways to incorporate these technologies into its ever-expanding narrative. Whether these advancements are framed as tools used by the Illuminati to control and manipulate, or as evidence that proves the conspiracy exists, emerging technologies will play a central role in the evolution of the myth.

In conclusion, the future of the Illuminati myth will be shaped in large part by emerging technologies that challenge our ability to discern truth from fiction. AI, deepfakes, virtual reality, and surveillance systems are not inherently malevolent, but their misuse by conspiracy theorists could significantly amplify the spread of false narratives. As these technologies become more sophisticated, the Illuminati myth may become harder to debunk, with increasingly convincing evidence being produced by those who seek to perpetuate the conspiracy. As society navigates the complexities of the digital age, it will become more crucial than ever to develop critical thinking skills and media literacy to counter the growing influence of conspiracy theories rooted in technological manipulation.

The Influence of Global Events on Illuminati Beliefs

Global events have always played a pivotal role in shaping and sustaining conspiracy theories, and the Illuminati myth is no exception. Major political, social, and economic upheavals often give rise to a sense of uncertainty, fear, and powerlessness among the public. In such environments, the Illuminati narrative offers a simplified explanation: a secret, elite group is behind the chaos, manipulating events to further their goal of global domination. The interconnectedness of our modern world—where a crisis in one region can quickly reverberate across the globe—has only intensified the belief in a hidden hand guiding these events. For many believers, global events are not random occurrences but pieces of a larger puzzle that reveal the Illuminati's ultimate agenda.

One of the most significant events that revitalized the Illuminati conspiracy in recent years was the 2008 global financial crisis. The sudden collapse of major financial institutions, coupled with the resulting economic downturn, led to widespread disillusionment with the banking system, governments, and global financial structures. For conspiracy theorists, the financial crisis was not the result of reckless lending or regulatory failures, but rather the deliberate actions of a shadowy elite seeking to tighten their control over the world economy. This interpretation dovetailed neatly with pre-existing ideas about the Illuminati's supposed influence over global finance, reinforcing the belief that a small group of powerful individuals orchestrated the collapse to consolidate their wealth and power.

Similarly, the rise of populism and the polarization of politics in recent years have provided fertile ground for Illuminati theories to flourish. From Brexit to the 2016 U.S. presidential election, these seismic political events have been interpreted by conspiracy theorists as either the work of the Illuminati or a rebellion against their influence. For instance, Donald Trump's election victory was hailed by some conspiracy believers as a sign that the people were rising up against the elite establishment—often framed as being controlled by the Illuminati. On the other hand, Trump's detractors, particularly within the conspiracy community, saw his rise as a continuation of the Illuminati's covert agenda, with Trump portrayed as a puppet controlled by hidden forces.

The COVID-19 pandemic, too, has been a significant driver of new Illuminati theories. In times of crisis, people naturally seek answers, and when those answers are not easily available, conspiracy theories can fill the void. From the outset of the pandemic, conspiracy theorists began speculating about the virus's origin, with many suggesting that it was a planned event by the Illuminati to create a global health emergency that would allow them to impose draconian control measures. The rapid spread of the virus, the implementation of lockdowns, and the development of vaccines were all viewed through the lens of an Illuminati plan to restrict personal freedoms, usher in a "New World Order," and exercise greater control over the global population.

The pandemic also brought new focus to the role of organizations like the World Health Organization (WHO) and the World Economic Forum (WEF), which conspiracy theorists often claim are fronts for Illuminati activity. The "Great Reset," a term used by the WEF to describe a proposal for rebuilding economies after the pandemic, became a focal point for Illuminati theorists. Despite its stated goals of addressing global inequality and promoting sustainability, conspiracy believers interpreted the Great Reset as evidence of the Illuminati's long-standing goal to create a one-world government. For them, this global crisis was the perfect opportunity for the elite to implement sweeping changes that would strip individuals of their autonomy and place power squarely in the hands of a select few.

The interconnectedness of modern global events means that the Illuminati myth is no longer confined to Western-centric narratives. Conspiracy theorists have adapted the myth to include other regions and cultures, tying it to conflicts, revolutions, and power struggles around the world. For instance, the Arab Spring, which saw widespread protests and regime changes across the Middle East, has been interpreted by some conspiracy theorists as part of the Illuminati's plan to destabilize the region. Similarly, the ongoing tensions between the U.S. and China are framed as a battle for global supremacy orchestrated by the Illuminati, with both superpowers seen as pawns in the larger game of global control.

Natural disasters and climate change have also become entwined with Illuminati theories. For believers, the increasing frequency of extreme weather events is not solely the result of climate change, but rather a deliberate manipulation of the environment by the Illuminati. Technologies like weather modification, which are speculative at best, are frequently cited as tools the Illuminati use to create chaos and fear, pushing the global population toward a state of dependency on government intervention. This, in turn, is seen as part of a broader strategy to centralize power and erode personal freedoms under the guise of protecting people from environmental catastrophes.

In essence, the Illuminati myth thrives on the instability of the modern world. Global events—whether political, economic, or environmental—are seldom viewed as isolated occurrences by conspiracy theorists. Instead, they are interpreted as part of a grand design, a carefully orchestrated plan by a powerful few to control the many. This interpretation provides a sense of order and explanation in a chaotic world, offering believers the comfort of certainty in the face of uncertainty. It allows them to see patterns where none may exist and to place blame on an identifiable enemy, making the complexity of global events easier to understand through the lens of a long-standing conspiracy.

In conclusion, the impact of global events on the Illuminati myth cannot be overstated. From financial crises to pandemics, from political upheaval to climate change, conspiracy theorists continually reframe these events as evidence of the Illuminati's hidden hand. As long as the world remains unpredictable and complex, the Illuminati myth will continue to provide a simple, albeit false, explanation for those seeking answers. Global events will remain fertile ground for conspiracy theorists to sow their narratives, ensuring that the Illuminati myth evolves alongside the ever-changing landscape of world affairs.

The Role of Social Media in Propagating Illuminati Theories

In the digital age, the role of social media in shaping and propagating conspiracy theories cannot be overstated, and the Illuminati myth is no exception. Platforms like Facebook, Twitter, Instagram, and YouTube have transformed how information is disseminated, allowing conspiracy theorists to reach a global audience with unprecedented speed and ease. Social media has created an environment where narratives can go viral, echoing through vast networks of users, often without any fact-checking or critical analysis. In this landscape, the Illuminati conspiracy theories thrive, morphing and adapting as they spread from one user to another, fueled by emotional appeals and sensational claims.

One of the primary ways social media promotes Illuminati theories is through the algorithm-driven nature of these platforms. Algorithms are designed to keep users engaged by recommending content that aligns with their interests, often leading them down a rabbit hole of increasingly extreme and conspiratorial ideas. A user who expresses interest in one conspiracy theory, whether it be about the Illuminati or another topic, is likely to be exposed to more related content, creating an echo chamber that reinforces and amplifies their beliefs. This phenomenon can escalate quickly, as users may find themselves encountering increasingly fringe theories that align with their growing skepticism of established narratives.

Moreover, the anonymity provided by social media allows users to share conspiracy theories without fear of repercussion. This anonymity can embolden individuals to spread misinformation, knowing that they are unlikely to face consequences for their statements. As a result, outrageous claims about the Illuminati can be shared freely and widely, often with little regard for truth or accuracy. This environment encourages sensationalism over factual reporting, leading to a distorted portrayal of reality. The emotional weight of conspiracy theories can make them more compelling than dry, fact-based narratives, driving users to share content that resonates with their fears and suspicions.

The impact of social media on the spread of Illuminati theories is further amplified by the visual nature of many platforms. Memes, infographics, and short video clips are often used to communicate complex ideas in easily digestible formats. This has led to the creation of a vast array of shareable content that distills the essence of Illuminati beliefs into catchy, attention-grabbing snippets. Visual content can be particularly effective in conveying emotional messages, making it easier for users to connect with and share conspiratorial narratives. In this way, the Illuminati myth is not just communicated through words but also through images and videos that evoke strong emotional reactions.

Additionally, social media serves as a breeding ground for communities of like-minded individuals who share a belief in the Illuminati and other conspiracy theories. Online forums and groups dedicated to these topics allow users to connect, share information, and validate each other's beliefs. This sense of community can reinforce existing ideas and foster an "us versus them" mentality, where believers view outsiders—particularly those who question or debunk their theories—as part of a broader conspiracy to silence the truth. This tribalism strengthens adherence to the Illuminati narrative, making it increasingly difficult for believers to accept alternative viewpoints.

Prominent figures and influencers on social media have also played a significant role in propagating Illuminati theories. Celebrities, public figures, and self-proclaimed "truth seekers" can wield substantial influence over their followers, often using their platforms to endorse or spread conspiratorial ideas. Their reach can amplify the spread of Illuminati theories, as followers may take their endorsements as validation of these beliefs. This has led to a situation where conspiracy theories are not just the domain of fringe groups but have entered mainstream discourse, often promoted by individuals with large followings who may lack expertise or understanding of the subjects they discuss.

Moreover, social media's fast-paced nature creates a sense of urgency, where users feel compelled to share information quickly, often without verifying its accuracy. This urgency can lead to the rapid spread of false information regarding the Illuminati, with sensational claims being shared widely before they can be debunked. The fear of missing out—coupled with the desire to be the first to share "the truth"—encourages users to prioritize speed over accuracy, further fueling the proliferation of conspiracy theories.

The psychological aspect of social media cannot be overlooked in understanding the appeal of Illuminati beliefs. Many users are drawn to conspiracy theories because they provide a sense of control and understanding in an increasingly complex world. The Illuminati narrative offers a framework through which individuals can make sense of their fears and anxieties about the state of the world, presenting an identifiable enemy responsible for societal issues. Social media fosters this need for connection and understanding, allowing users to find communities that validate their beliefs and reinforce their worldview.

In conclusion, social media plays a crucial role in the propagation and evolution of Illuminati theories. The algorithmic nature of these platforms, combined with the anonymity they provide, creates an environment ripe for the spread of misinformation. The visual culture of social media, along with the influence of public figures, amplifies these narratives, reaching vast audiences in record time. Furthermore, the formation of online communities provides a sense of belonging for believers, reinforcing their ideas and perpetuating the myth of the Illuminati. As long as social media remains a dominant form of communication, the potential for conspiracy theories, including those surrounding the Illuminati, will continue to thrive in the digital landscape, shaping perceptions and influencing beliefs on a global scale.

Mainstream Media's Response to Illuminati Theories

While social media plays a central role in the spread of Illuminati conspiracy theories, mainstream media has also had to navigate the delicate challenge of addressing these beliefs. From news outlets to television shows and documentaries, the mainstream media has been both a platform for debunking these theories and, at times, a contributor to their continued allure. The media's approach to Illuminati beliefs ranges from critical investigations to sensationalized portrayals, influencing how the general public perceives the myth.

One of the primary ways in which mainstream media engages with Illuminati theories is through investigative journalism. Many reputable news outlets have taken it upon themselves to debunk these theories, exposing the lack of evidence behind the claims and highlighting the psychological and social factors that drive conspiracy thinking. These articles often include interviews with experts in psychology, sociology, and history, who provide nuanced explanations for why people believe in the Illuminati despite its debunked origins. Fact-checking organizations, such as Snopes and PolitiFact, have also played a key role in addressing viral conspiracy theories linked to the Illuminati, providing detailed analyses of the falsehoods circulating online.

However, despite these efforts, the debunking process can often be less effective than intended. For true believers, any attempt to discredit Illuminati theories is seen as evidence of the media's complicity in the conspiracy. Mainstream outlets are frequently accused of being "puppets" of the very elite forces the Illuminati is said to represent. This perception creates a cycle of mistrust, where media debunking efforts are dismissed as propaganda, further entrenching believers in their views. In this way, even when the media attempts to clarify or correct the record, it can inadvertently strengthen the appeal of the conspiracy theory among those already convinced of its truth.

Another factor to consider is the way mainstream media has occasionally sensationalized Illuminati theories. In a competitive media landscape, where attention-grabbing stories are key to maintaining viewership, certain programs and publications have been tempted to play up the intrigue and mystery surrounding the Illuminati. Television documentaries, for example, often present the Illuminati as a shadowy, secretive group, leaning heavily into the dramatic and speculative elements of the conspiracy. While such programs typically conclude by questioning or debunking the theory, the build-up of suspense and mystery can leave an impression that the Illuminati might be more than mere fiction.

The entertainment industry also plays a role in shaping perceptions of the Illuminati through its portrayal in film, music, and television. Popular culture frequently references Illuminati symbols—whether in jest or as a plot device—giving the theory a visibility it might not otherwise have. Celebrities who joke about being members of the Illuminati, or music videos that incorporate occult imagery, contribute to the mainstreaming of the myth. While these depictions are often intended to be playful or ironic, they can blur the lines between reality and fiction for some viewers, reinforcing the perception that the Illuminati could be real, or at least worth considering as a possibility.

In recent years, major news events have also fueled media coverage of Illuminati-related conspiracies, further entangling the myth with the narratives of real-world events. When public figures or global organizations are accused of being part of the Illuminati, it can become a media sensation. These claims, no matter how unfounded, may receive disproportionate coverage due to their sensational nature. Media outlets, often driven by the need to report on viral content, may give attention to these conspiracy theories even if only to dismiss them. Yet, by amplifying the discussion, they risk giving credibility to the very ideas they are attempting to debunk.

At the same time, certain segments of the media have openly criticized and ridiculed Illuminati theories, portraying them as fringe ideas with no basis in fact. Satirical programs like *Saturday Night Live* or late-night talk shows have poked fun at conspiracy theorists, using humor to highlight the absurdity of many claims. These portrayals, while entertaining for the general public, can also deepen the divide between mainstream audiences and conspiracy believers. For those entrenched in the Illuminati narrative, mockery from mainstream media only solidifies their belief that they are privy to hidden knowledge the rest of the world is either too blind or too indoctrinated to see.

Interestingly, the rise of alternative media—such as independent podcasts, YouTube channels, and blogs—has also influenced how the Illuminati is discussed in the public sphere. Many of these platforms cater to niche audiences and may offer sympathetic or outright supportive coverage of conspiracy theories, often criticizing mainstream media's handling of these topics. By positioning themselves as alternative sources of "truth," these outlets attract those who are skeptical of mainstream narratives and seek out information that aligns with their beliefs. This decentralized media landscape makes it harder for traditional outlets to control or counter the spread of Illuminati theories effectively.

In addition, social and political movements have further complicated the media's relationship with Illuminati theories. For example, during periods of social unrest or political upheaval, the media may find itself reporting on how conspiracy theories influence real-world events. From protests to elections, belief in the Illuminati and similar theories can shape public discourse in ways that the media cannot ignore. As a result, news organizations may feel compelled to cover these theories, even if doing so gives them unintended legitimacy.

In conclusion, the mainstream media plays a multifaceted role in the life of Illuminati conspiracy theories. While many outlets strive to debunk these myths and provide rational explanations, their efforts are often met with skepticism from believers. Sensationalized portrayals of the Illuminati, both in news coverage and entertainment, can further perpetuate the myth, even when the intention is to critique or dismiss it. As alternative media continues to grow, the mainstream media's influence over conspiracy theories may diminish, leading to an even more fragmented information landscape where the Illuminati narrative can evolve and spread in unpredictable ways. Ultimately, the relationship between the media and the Illuminati myth is a complex interplay of debunking, sensationalism, and the continual challenge of combating misinformation in an increasingly divided world.

Recapitulation of the Illuminati's Origins and Evolution
The Illuminati began as a modest Enlightenment-era secret society, founded in 1776 in Bavaria by Adam Weishaupt. Its
original purpose was to promote reason, secularism, and moral reform in a time dominated by monarchy and the Church. Despite its
relatively short existence, the group's reputation quickly became intertwined with the idea of a hidden power pulling the strings behind
the world's most influential events. By the time it disbanded a few
years after its formation, the myth of the Illuminati had already out-
grown the reality of the historical society.

As the centuries passed, the Illuminati evolved from a tangible
group of intellectuals into a symbol of hidden control, conspiracy,
and shadow governance. The myth found fertile ground in a world
that constantly searched for simple answers to complex issues, especially in times of societal upheaval. Wars, revolutions, and rapid technological advancements heightened public fears, and the Illuminati
became a convenient scapegoat—a figurehead for unseen elites allegedly shaping the world according to their mysterious, self-serving
agendas.

One of the most critical moments in the evolution of the Illuminati myth was its association with Freemasonry. The Freemasons,
already known for their secrecy and influence in European society,
were a natural link for those looking to explain the workings of
hidden powers. The two organizations, while historically distinct,
became fused in the imagination of conspiracy theorists, a fusion solidified by influential documents like the *Protocols of the Elders of
Zion*, which claimed to reveal a global conspiracy led by Jews and
Masons.

This section in the conclusion revisits how the Illuminati's symbolic power transformed it into an adaptable narrative—one that has been reshaped for each new generation, mutating in response to contemporary fears. As different global events unfolded, from the French Revolution to the Cold War, the Illuminati myth grew. It wasn't simply confined to whispered conspiracies, but also became entrenched in culture and politics, influencing how people viewed authority, wealth, and power.

Today, the Illuminati stands as a pillar of conspiracy culture, encompassing far more than its founders could have imagined. From a small Enlightenment-era society aimed at rational reform, it has become the enduring idea of an omnipresent, shadowy force controlling world events from behind the curtain. The myth has outlived its origins, evolving into a universal symbol for paranoia and the mistrust of institutions. Its persistence reveals the power of a narrative that appeals to humanity's deepest fears about control and manipulation. While the original Illuminati faded into history, its legend continues to thrive in modern-day imaginations.

This myth, then, is not static—it changes as society changes. What was once a story rooted in anti-monarchical sentiment has morphed into a global phenomenon tied to concerns about multinational corporations, technology, and media influence. Understanding how the myth originated and evolved provides key insight into why it continues to resonate, even centuries later. The Illuminati's power lies not in its truth, but in its ability to adapt to any time or situation, providing a catch-all explanation for the world's uncertainties.

The Role of Conspiracy Theories in Society

Conspiracy theories have always occupied a unique place in society, serving as a lens through which people interpret complex or threatening events. The Illuminati myth is a prime example of this. When individuals or communities feel powerless, conspiracy theories offer an alluring alternative to chaos—they present a hidden order behind the disorder, a secret force manipulating world events for its own ends. In the case of the Illuminati, this hidden order has been a constant, evolving narrative that positions shadowy elites as the true puppeteers behind politics, finance, and global crises.

At the heart of conspiracy thinking is a psychological need for control. The world is full of events that feel unpredictable, from economic recessions to political upheavals, pandemics, and natural disasters. Conspiracy theories like the Illuminati provide a structure in which these seemingly chaotic events can be explained as part of a larger, intentional plan. It gives individuals a sense of meaning in a world that might otherwise feel random or overwhelming. By blaming a secret, powerful group for their troubles, believers can avoid confronting the more difficult, unsettling reality that sometimes things happen without rhyme or reason.

The rise of conspiracy theories often corresponds with moments of crisis. In times of war, economic uncertainty, or rapid technological change, people are more likely to question the official narratives presented by governments, media, or other trusted institutions. The Illuminati myth, with its narrative of secret manipulation by elites, is tailor-made for such environments. It offers a convenient way to rationalize why the world seems increasingly unstable—shifting blame from the complexity of modern life to an easily identifiable, malevolent force.

This tendency to turn to conspiracy theories during periods of instability has been particularly evident in the 21st century. From the 9/11 attacks to the global financial crisis of 2008 and the COVID-19 pandemic, each major event has spawned a wave of new or revitalized conspiracies. The Illuminati has been linked to these crises in various ways, often being framed as the ultimate orchestrators behind the scenes, pulling strings to engineer global catastrophes for their own gain. Whether it's financial collapse or the spread of disease, the Illuminati is positioned as the shadowy benefactor of disaster.

The appeal of conspiracy theories also stems from a deep-seated distrust in authority. When people lose faith in their leaders, institutions, or the media, they begin to search for alternative explanations. The Illuminati myth feeds into this distrust by suggesting that the real power is not in the hands of elected officials or public institutions, but rather in the clutches of an unseen elite who answer to no one. This fuels suspicion, cynicism, and even anger toward those in positions of authority, leading to a widespread rejection of official narratives, scientific facts, and democratic processes.

In this way, the Illuminati myth becomes more than just a fringe belief—it becomes a reflection of societal fears about power and control. It offers an alternative worldview where nothing is as it seems, and everything is orchestrated by a hidden few. This worldview can be comforting to those who feel alienated or disempowered, giving them a sense of understanding in a confusing world. However, it also comes with dangers, as it can erode trust in institutions and foster an environment where misinformation and paranoia thrive.

In short, conspiracy theories like the Illuminati fill a vital psychological and social role. They offer an explanation for why things go wrong, why the world feels unjust, and why ordinary people seem powerless in the face of large-scale forces. The Illuminati myth, in particular, taps into deep-seated anxieties about control, power, and transparency, providing a narrative that has proven resilient and adaptable in an age of growing uncertainty.

The Enduring Power of Symbols and Imagery

One of the key reasons the Illuminati myth has endured for so long is the symbolic power it wields. Symbols have a unique way of resonating with people on a subconscious level, and the Illuminati narrative is rife with potent imagery that feeds into its allure. Whether it's the pyramid with the all-seeing eye, the pentagram, or other occult signs, these symbols have taken on a life of their own, becoming shorthand for hidden power and control.

The all-seeing eye, also known as the "Eye of Providence," is perhaps the most recognizable Illuminati symbol. Originally a Christian symbol representing God's omniscience, it was later co-opted by Freemasons and eventually became synonymous with the Illuminati. Its placement on the reverse of the U.S. dollar bill in 1935 added fuel to conspiracy theories, suggesting that the nation's financial system was under the control of secretive forces. Over time, the eye has become an emblem of surveillance, manipulation, and omnipresent authority, symbolizing the belief that someone—somewhere—is always watching and controlling the world.

The pyramid, often depicted with the eye at its apex, carries a similar weight. Pyramids are ancient structures, associated with power, mystery, and the ancient Egyptian civilization—a society long linked with esoteric knowledge. For conspiracy theorists, the pyramid represents the hierarchical structure of global power, with the elite few at the top controlling the masses below. This visual metaphor reinforces the idea that a small, secret group rules over the many, perpetuating the belief in a world shaped by unseen elites. In popular culture and conspiracy circles, the pyramid has come to represent the control and manipulation of the global population by those at the very top.

Symbols have a powerful way of reinforcing ideas, particularly when they are open to interpretation. The ambiguity of Illuminati imagery allows believers to project their fears and suspicions onto these symbols, turning them into universal markers of corruption, secrecy, and control. This is particularly effective in the digital age, where such symbols can be endlessly replicated and circulated, taking on new meanings with each iteration. From pop culture to politics, the symbols associated with the Illuminati have become embedded in public consciousness, transcending their original meanings and reinforcing the myth.

Pop culture has played a significant role in spreading and sustaining these symbols. Music videos, films, and art are often dissected by conspiracy theorists who believe they contain coded Illuminati messages. When a pop star covers one eye in a music video or flashes a triangle with their hands, conspiracy theorists often interpret these actions as signs of their allegiance to the Illuminati. While these gestures are usually artistic choices or marketing gimmicks, they further cement the myth in the minds of those already inclined to believe.

This phenomenon also speaks to the power of imagery in reinforcing belief systems. In a world where images and symbols are omnipresent, from advertisements to social media, the recurrence of certain motifs can be compelling. For those who subscribe to the Illuminati conspiracy, spotting these symbols becomes a kind of confirmation bias. Every eye, triangle, or pyramid seen in public spaces or media is interpreted as evidence of the Illuminati's presence and influence, perpetuating the myth through visual repetition.

In sum, the Illuminati's enduring power lies not only in the story it tells but also in the symbols it employs. These images tap into deep-seated fears and suspicions, offering visual proof of an invisible power. The more these symbols are repeated, both in media and popular culture, the more ingrained they become in the collective consciousness. It is this blend of mystery, visual resonance, and symbolic power that keeps the Illuminati myth alive, ensuring its place in both conspiracy lore and mainstream awareness.

The Impact of the Illuminati Myth on Public Trust and Institutions

The persistence of the Illuminati myth has had profound effects on public trust in institutions, eroding confidence in everything from governments to media and even science. In a world where conspiracy theories are becoming increasingly mainstream, the Illuminati myth serves as a stark example of how such narratives can alter the fabric of societal trust. At its core, the myth fosters a sense of skepticism toward official narratives, suggesting that those in positions of power—whether political leaders, corporate executives, or media moguls—are merely puppets serving a hidden elite. This skepticism can have serious consequences, particularly when it comes to undermining faith in democratic institutions and the rule of law.

One of the most dangerous outcomes of the Illuminati myth is its ability to cast doubt on the legitimacy of governments. For believers, elected officials are often seen as either complicit in the global conspiracy or powerless pawns manipulated by those behind the scenes. This worldview can lead to disillusionment with democratic processes, as the idea of secret control nullifies the perceived value of elections, civic participation, and the principles of transparency and accountability. Why vote, engage, or trust in a system that is, in their eyes, rigged by the hidden hand of the Illuminati? This cynicism can discourage engagement with democratic practices and feed political apathy.

Beyond politics, the Illuminati myth also undermines trust in the media, an institution that plays a critical role in informing the public. Conspiracy theories often claim that the media is controlled by the same elite forces that manipulate global events, rendering the news nothing more than propaganda designed to distract or mislead. This deep suspicion fosters a climate where misinformation thrives and people turn to alternative, unverified sources of information. In this environment, social media platforms and fringe websites—where conspiracy theories spread easily—gain influence over more reliable, fact-based journalism. The result is an increasingly fragmented media landscape, where conspiracy theories compete with credible reporting for the public's attention.

This erosion of trust extends to scientific institutions and experts as well. In the context of the Illuminati myth, advances in technology, healthcare, or climate science can be framed as part of a broader conspiracy to control humanity. Whether it's vaccines, surveillance technology, or environmental policies, these advancements are often viewed with suspicion by those who believe in secret global manipulation. The distrust of science can have dire public health consequences, as seen in the anti-vaccine movement or climate change denial, both of which are often linked to larger conspiracy narratives, including those involving the Illuminati. This widespread doubt in expert opinion weakens society's ability to respond effectively to real-world challenges.

The impact of the Illuminati myth on public trust is also evident in the way it influences perceptions of wealth and inequality. Economic disparity is fertile ground for conspiracy theories, particularly those involving secretive elites who control financial institutions and markets. For many, the global financial system seems opaque and unjust, and the Illuminati myth provides a convenient explanation for the wealth gap. It suggests that a cabal of wealthy individuals is manipulating the economy to serve their own interests, deepening inequality and keeping the masses in a perpetual state of struggle. This perception fuels resentment toward the rich and powerful, creating an "us versus them" mentality that exacerbates social divisions.

The danger of this worldview lies in its ability to polarize society. Rather than addressing complex social, economic, or political issues through dialogue and reform, conspiracy theories like the Illuminati encourage the belief that these problems are the result of intentional malice by a select few. This belief not only oversimplifies the challenges facing modern society but also stokes fear, anger, and mistrust among the general public. As more people subscribe to such theories, the rift between those who believe in the legitimacy of institutions and those who see them as corrupt deepens, making it harder to find common ground or engage in constructive civic action.

In conclusion, the Illuminati myth has had a far-reaching and corrosive impact on public trust. By sowing seeds of doubt about the motives of governments, media, science, and the wealthy, it feeds into a culture of suspicion that erodes confidence in the very institutions meant to uphold democracy, justice, and progress. As the myth continues to spread, it not only distorts public perception but also weakens the societal bonds that rely on a shared belief in transparency and accountability. The result is a world where paranoia and mistrust thrive, challenging the foundations of social cohesion.

The Broader Implications of the Illuminati Myth for Society and Culture

The Illuminati myth, while often dismissed as fringe or fantastical, has broader implications for society and culture that extend beyond conspiracy circles. Its reach into everyday conversations, media, and political discourse speaks to a deeper cultural phenomenon—the human need to find meaning and order in a chaotic world. This myth is a reflection of our collective anxieties about power, control, and the uncertainties of modern life. While the Illuminati itself is almost certainly a fabrication, its enduring presence reveals much about how we, as a society, grapple with complex global challenges and the desire for simple explanations to explain them.

At its core, the Illuminati myth functions as a narrative framework that helps people make sense of overwhelming societal forces. Globalization, technological advancements, and rapid social change can feel disorienting, especially when they appear to be driven by faceless institutions or powerful corporations. The idea that a secret group is pulling the strings provides a lens through which individuals can understand these forces. Rather than acknowledging the often random and multifaceted nature of world events, the Illuminati myth offers a straightforward—and ultimately comforting—explanation: that someone, somewhere, is in control, even if their intentions are sinister.

This myth also taps into long-standing cultural themes around the corrupting influence of power. Throughout history, literature and folklore have warned against the dangers of unchecked authority and the hidden machinations of elites. The Illuminati myth is a modern extension of these narratives, rooted in a distrust of those who wield significant influence, whether in politics, finance, or entertainment. It channels age-old fears about tyranny and deception, recasting historical concerns into a contemporary framework. The myth's ability to adapt to different contexts, from the halls of government to the stages of pop culture, ensures its continued relevance in an ever-changing world.

Moreover, the Illuminati myth feeds into a broader trend of anti-establishment sentiment that has gained traction in recent years. As trust in traditional institutions declines, the appeal of alternative narratives—however improbable—grows stronger. In this climate, the Illuminati myth serves as a focal point for resistance against perceived systems of control. It allows individuals to express their frustrations with the status quo and reject the authority of governments, corporations, and media outlets. For some, subscribing to the Illuminati conspiracy is not merely an intellectual exercise but a form of protest against a world they feel is rigged against them.

Yet, while the Illuminati myth may offer a sense of clarity or empowerment to its believers, it also carries significant risks. As conspiracy theories proliferate, they create environments where truth and fiction become increasingly difficult to distinguish. The normalization of conspiratorial thinking undermines the pursuit of knowledge and reason, replacing critical inquiry with suspicion and speculation. This erosion of truth has far-reaching consequences, particularly in areas like public health, climate policy, and social justice, where misinformation can hinder progress and exacerbate existing problems. The Illuminati myth, in this context, is part of a larger cultural shift toward relativism, where facts are treated as subjective and reality is shaped by belief rather than evidence.

The social and cultural implications of the Illuminati myth are not limited to conspiracy theorists alone. Its imagery and themes have seeped into mainstream culture, influencing everything from fashion and art to film and music. The omnipresent triangle or the all-seeing eye has become a symbol of rebellion, mystery, and intrigue, often used without direct reference to the Illuminati itself. This phenomenon illustrates the way in which conspiracy theories can escape their original boundaries and become part of the broader cultural lexicon. The Illuminati myth, in this sense, is not just a fringe belief but a narrative thread woven into the fabric of modern culture, shaping how we view power, authority, and secrecy.

In conclusion, the Illuminati myth is far more than a conspiracy theory relegated to the shadows. It has embedded itself into the psyche of contemporary society, influencing public discourse, cultural production, and even political movements. Its enduring appeal lies in its ability to offer simple answers to complex problems, fulfilling a deep-seated desire for understanding in an increasingly uncertain world. While the myth may seem harmless on the surface, its broader implications raise important questions about the role of conspiracy thinking in shaping societal attitudes, trust, and the search for truth. As long as the need for clarity and control persists, so too will the myths we create to satisfy them.